Oy!
The Great
Jewish
Joke Book

Oy!
The Great
Jewish
Joke Book

David Minkoff

BOOKS

For my beloved children Suzy and Paul, my gorgeous grandchildren Emma, Melissa, Sam and Oliver, and last – but certainly not least – to Andrea, my wife and soul mate.

First published in 2008 by JR Books,
10 Greenland Street, London NW1 0ND
www.jrbooks.com

A catalogue record for this book is available from the British Library.

ISBN 978 1 906217 62 4

1 3 5 7 9 10 8 6 4 2

Typeset by SX Composing DTP, Rayleigh, Essex

Printed in the UK by CPI Bookmarque, Croydon CR0 4TD

CONTENTS

Introduction

My first book of Jewish jokes was published in the UK in March 2005 by Robson Books (an imprint of Anova Books). Later, an Americanised version of this book was published in New York in September 2006 by Thomas Dunne Books (an imprint of St Martin's Press). This first book has turned out to be a great success, although not by J.K. Rowling's standards. I'm thrilled to be able to report that not only have 30,000 copies of the book so far been sold throughout the world, but also the US version was one of the five books nominated for an award in the Humour category of The Quill Book Awards 2007.

You are now holding my second book of Jewish Jokes. This contains around 800 new Jewish jokes, none of which is in my first book. I do hope you like them. If you do, why not tell me about it? You can always contact me by email via a link on my website's home page, as many of my readers have already done. If you want to read what they have been saying about my books and website, there's another link on my website's home page.

My readers also ask me questions about Jewish jokes in general, so I thought I would include some of their questions here along with the responses I tend to give to them. I hope you find this of interest.

Where do you get your jokes from?

All the 800 jokes in my new book have been taken from my website of Jewish jokes: www.awordinyoureye.com. There are now over 2,000 jokes on this website and I spend a lot of time updating it on a monthly basis, something I've been doing since early 2000.

The jokes I choose for my website come from many different sources. They can come from family, friends, TV, radio, books, newspapers, magazines, emails from all over the world, friends at my Israeli dance class and even a number of rabbis! They come from women as well as men, and non-Jews as well as Jews. Jewish humour is definitely enjoyed by people from all religions and denominations. And those that send me jokes always hope that the jokes are ones that I haven't seen before (which is getting harder to achieve).

My ongoing process for adding jokes follows the '3 Rs' principle:

I REVIEW all the jokes that I've heard, received, read, found etc in the period.

I RETAIN only jokes that are new to me, funny and meet my selection criteria.

I REWRITE 10 of the retained jokes each month and add them to my website.

What do you think makes a funny Jewish joke?

I like this question better than the more common one: 'What do you think makes a Jewish joke?' The extra word 'funny' is important to me – it's the ethos of my editorial efforts.

Some people would say a joke about a Jew outsmarting Hitler is a Jewish joke. But I don't regard it at all as a funny Jewish joke. My idea of what makes a funny Jewish joke is different and is central to my joke collection. I choose my jokes carefully and I'm fussy over what I include. First, I have to like a joke and then I have to ensure it fits in with 'my rules'. For example, I nearly always exclude jokes that have been 'doing the rounds' for years, such as jokes about life in the old days, life in Germany/Russia etc, World War II, pogroms and immigrants who can't speak English or don't understand the local customs. I don't enjoy political or racist jokes, or jokes about the Middle East, or Israel versus its neighbours, or jokes about terrorists. I don't find these jokes funny and I exclude them. I filter out obscene jokes, jokes that are cruel and jokes that might offend or embarrass – though I have included a few that might be regarded as more risqué here. On the other hand, I include jokes that not only Jews but also non-Jews – whatever their nationality, race or religion – should be able to understand (I've added a glossary of Yiddish and Hebrew words to help).

I try to 'tick off' as many of the above characteristics as I can. But even excluding all the above types of 'undesirable' joke, there are still over 2,000 jokes on view on my website, spread over my two books.

What happens once you have chosen a joke?

Once I have chosen some jokes to add, I rewrite them in my own style. I work to a kind of unofficial joke template for rewriting them, trying at the same time to be grammatically correct. This is certainly not a 'cut-and-paste' process! In addition, jokes told against wives, or women in general, are balanced where possible against those told against husbands, or men in general (my women friends wouldn't speak to me if I didn't try to be fair to all). I then add the rewritten jokes to my website. I have managed to add between 10 and 20 new jokes to my website every month for the last seven years. I maintain the website entirely on my own.

How do you know whether the jokes you've chosen are indeed funny?

Laughing at a joke is very subjective – I realise that jokes I find funny are not necessarily those that you find funny, and vice versa. I'd obviously like to know how every one of my jokes is received so that I can make adjustments to my joke inventory. But there lies the problem. If a stand-up comedian tells a joke, he can tell right away whether it's a good or bad one by the laughs, smiles or silence of his audience. But I can't tell which jokes bring the loudest laughs from my readers – my audience's laughter (or silence) is done 'out of my sight'. I have therefore no way of telling whether at this very moment there are people somewhere out there in the world reading one of my jokes and laughing out loud. And even if I could hear their laughter, I couldn't tell exactly which joke it was that they found funny. All I have to go by are the unsolicited emails that my readers send me – all of which, good or bad, are posted on my website.

Emails are very important to me personally and, thank God, I do get a quite a number of them. They inform me what readers think of my jokes and/or my website and/or my books. Some emails have even informed me that the jokes helped them recover from illness! Knowing my efforts are making people laugh, or recover from illness, is unbelievably rewarding to me.

Through these emails, I get to converse with a great bunch of people, Jews and non-Jews alike, male and female, of all ages. I have received emails from the UK, USA, Netherlands, Canada, Australia, Israel, Italy, New Zealand, Hungary, South Africa, Germany, Denmark, Austria, France and Venezuela. I'd like to single out some of these contacts: Allan Dolgow, Anna Read, April Brenner, April Black, Bob Kelley, Brian Cain, Charles Kohnfelder, Dan Dyckman, Daniel Stein, Frank Reuben, Hanoch Bernath, Herb Greene, Hilary Ash, John Barkett (The IrRev), Judy Segor, Norman Klegman, Richard G. Klein (*shmuck extraordinaire*), Ron Lane, Shlomo Shahoah, Stan Cohen (Stan The Man) and Uriah Yaniv. There are also others too numerous to list here. So hearty thanks to all of you for your wonderful support.

What if we have already heard one of your chosen jokes?

Joke-telling is a Jewish social activity. In fact, joke-telling might even be the one and only truly Jewish sport. We love to interrupt the telling of a joke to say 'We've heard it,' or 'You're not telling it right,' or 'It was in New York, not London', or 'It was a butcher, not a delivery boy,' or 'It was a rabbi, not a *chazan*.' I know that there must be jokes in my collection that readers will have heard before, although not necessarily in the way that I've rewritten them. But there will be many other jokes that will be new to most readers. And anyway, so what if you've heard a joke before? Do you stop a pianist who is playing Chopin just because you've heard that piece before?

Do you have a favourite joke?

When I'm asked this question, I always reply it's like asking a grandparent which grandchild he likes best. I like jokes about husbands/wives, marital strife, in-laws, matchmakers, growing old, business, *mohels*, health – even Viagra. I really do have many favourites.

So, reading the emails, how are your jokes used?

The emails show that: there are at least five rabbis as well as a Presbyterian minister from Kansas who use my jokes in their sermons; my jokes have been included in speeches for a best man, a 60th birthday and *Bar mitzvahs*; they have played a role in healing; and some of my readers have asked me to help them look for jokes on particular themes – anything from ballet dancers, businessmen, weddings and school reunions to plumbers.

Do you agree that laughter is the best medicine?

A Yiddish expression is, 'Does your heart ache? Then laugh it off.' I believe laughter to be the greatest of medicines. It's been proven to help many of us recover quickly from illness. I've been heartened in my labours by the responses I've been getting from around the world, particularly from those who have been using the jokes for 'medicinal' purposes! That's why you will also find a 'laughter is the best medicine' serious section on my website.

Tell me something about yourself.

My father's family came to the UK from Russia at the beginning of the 1900s. My mother's family were always in the UK. My wife Andrea's family came to the UK from both Russia and Poland at beginning of the 1900s. I grew up in northwest London. My father, grandfather and uncle were all kosher butchers and poulterers. And how's this for something spooky? Andrea's mother, pushing Andrea in her pram, used to go to my *zaydeh's* shop to buy meat. Little did anyone know what was to happen many years later between that little girl in the pram and me.

I currently live on the outskirts of London with Andrea. Not only is she my lovely wife, but she's a qualified counsellor – very caring and a great listener, not like me. We have two wonderful children (Suzy and Paul) and four gorgeous grandchildren (Emma, Melissa, Sam and Oliver).

I love keeping myself fit. I used to captain football and cricket teams at Maccabi, but that was a long time ago. Now I jog around the streets (which I've been doing for 28 years) and go Israeli dancing (which I've been doing for 16 years). Andrea and I like walking a lot, playing bridge, going to the theatre and visiting art galleries.

In my 40-year working life, I held a number of jobs in IT, financial information services and law. But did you know that it doesn't matter how often a Jewish husband changes his job, he still ends up with the same boss anyway?

I'm proud to be a Freeman of the City of London (30 years of my working life were spent in the City). I'm in good company. The Queen, Maggie Thatcher, Winston Churchill, Lord Nelson, Nelson Mandela, Florence Nightingale, Eisenhower and Bill Gates are (or were) all Honorary Freemen of the City of London. Incidentally, it's not true that Freemen can drive sheep over London Bridge, or be hanged by a silken rope, or be married at St Paul's Cathedral; or be drunk and disorderly without fear of arrest, or relieve themselves in public without fear, or go about the City with a drawn sword.

Since I retired, a lot of tension has gone from me. I'm much more relaxed. And I now know why we call someone who enjoys work and who refuses to retire *meshugganah*! But retirement isn't all feet up! Apart from jogging and dancing,

I spend much time on my PC maintaining my Jewish jokes website, I've become an established eBay seller and I help Andrea around the house. It's just like Confucius said: 'Man who sinks into woman's arms soon have arms in woman's sink.' Confucius must have been Jewish to have written that!

David Minkoff

You don't stop laughing because you grow old – you grow old because you stop laughing.

Always remember the two rules of life:
RULE #1: Never forget how to laugh.
RULE #2: Never forget Rule #1.

Give us a sense of humour, Lord,
Give us the grace to see a joke,
To get some humour out of life.
And pass it on to other folk.

Romance
(From First Love To Last Words)

Courtship

You're a...Jewish boy?

Naomi is in love with Peter and takes him home to meet her parents, Moshe and Hetty. 'Dad,' she says, 'I'd like you to meet Peter. We're in love and we would like to get married.'

It soon becomes obvious to Moshe that Peter isn't Jewish. 'Now look, Peter,' says Moshe, 'you seem a great person and I can see why my Naomi has fallen for you. But you must understand that we only want Naomi to marry a Jewish boy. Please don't take it personally – it's what my wife and I want.'

'I fully understand, sir,' says Peter. 'Naomi and I realised this would be the situation and so I've told her I'm willing to convert to Judaism. If I did this, would you then give us your blessing?'

Moshe thinks for a while, then replies, 'Yes, I would.'

Over the following 12 months, Peter gets circumcised, joins Moshe's *shul,* goes to Hebrew classes, attends *shabbes* services and finally takes a six-week trip to Israel. But when he returns to make arrangements for the wedding, he learns that Naomi has fallen out of love with him. She doesn't now want to marry him. Peter is devastated and goes to Moshe to see whether he can help.

'Moshe,' he says, 'I agreed to convert and become a real Jew – and I have. I've been circumcised, I've regularly attended *shabbes* services and I can speak Hebrew as well as anyone. I know all the Jewish customs and I can tell wonderful Jewish jokes. I'm a *mensh*, but Naomi doesn't want me. What on earth can I do?'

'Marry a *shiksa* like all the other Jewish boys,' replies Moshe.

* * *

The blind date

Yitzhak is on his way to pick up his blind date. Little does he know that he has been paired up with Estelle who, if truth be told, is definitely not one of the world's best-looking women – in fact, quite the opposite.

Yitzhak picks her up as arranged outside the train station and as soon as she gets into his car, he knows he has made a big mistake. He is so embarrassed to have Estelle in his car with him and so afraid that one of his friends might see them together and think he's gone blind that he drives to a dark, desolate spot by a nearby river and turns off the engine.

Unfortunately, Estelle jumps to the wrong conclusion. She thinks Yitzhak wants to make love to her. So she begins to talk dirty and use all her sexual wiles to try and get Yitzhak in a ravenous mood for sex. But he just sits staring out of the window, wishing time would fly.

Finally, after half an hour of trying – and boy, how she talked and talked – Estelle asks him, 'Don't you want it?'

And Yitzhak replies, 'I feel like I already had it.'

* * *

The snare

Sarah and Benjy have been dating throughout their college years but at no time did Benjy talk once to Sarah about marriage. But now they have graduated, Sarah's mother, Kitty, has a quiet talk with her daughter.

'Darling,' says Kitty, 'although Benjy is an absolutely smashing young man, I think you've been too patient with him. He'll make a marvellous husband but he needs a bit of pushing. You must now use every opportunity to hint at marriage.'

The following weekend, Benjy takes Sarah to Minky's Kosher Chinese Restaurant. As he reads the menu, he casually asks her, 'Sarah darling, how do you want your rice? Boiled? Or fried?'

Without hesitating, Sarah looks up at him, smiles sexily and replies, 'Thrown.'

* * *

The compliment
Benny says to his girlfriend, 'You're more beautiful than any stamp in my collection.'

'Philately will get you nowhere,' she replies.

* * *

The boyfriend
Time for a true story. A psychoanalyst told a reader last weekend that a patient of his – who is Jewish, married, has two kids, a house in the suburbs with a two-car garage etc – all of a sudden finds out that he's gay. He goes to his mother and says, 'Mum, I just found out I'm gay and I have a boyfriend, his name is Heinrich.'

His mother says, 'Vot, you're going with a Nazi?'

* * *

Boyfriend advice
One day, Sadie and Rose are talking about men.

'I have a question for you,' says Rose.

'So ask it, already,' says Sadie.

'OK,' says Rose. 'If I meet a stranger at a party and I think that he's attractive, do you think it's OK to ask him straight away whether he's married?'

'No, certainly not,' replies Sadie, 'you should wait until morning.'

* * *

Promises, promises

Jonathan and Renee are on their very first date. As they are walking to the cinema, Renee says, 'If you give me a kiss, Jonathan, I promise faithfully that I'll be yours for ever and a day.'

Jonathan replies, 'Thanks for the early warning, Renee.'

* * *

Good dinner dates

Hannah is talking to her best friend Sharon. They are both still single. 'After my recent experiences with some of my dates, Sharon, I firmly believe men are like a fine wine.'

'Why do you say that?' asks Sharon.

'Well,' replies Hannah, 'they start out as grapes and it's up to women like us to stomp the crap out of them until they turn into something acceptable to have dinner with.'

* * *

Well, that's nice

Rebecca takes her boyfriend Howard to see her parents, to allow them to 'pass judgement' on him.

'Hello Howard,' says her father, 'it's nice to meet you. Where do you live?'

'Near Finchley,' he replies.

'Near Finchley?' interrupts Rebecca, 'He's too modest, Dad. He owns a 10-bedroom mansion with five acres of land in Hampstead Garden Suburb.'

'Well, that's nice, Howard,' says her father. 'So what do you do for a living?'

'Oh, I own a bit of property,' he answers.

'A bit of property?' interrupts Rebecca again. 'Why, Howard owns 10 per cent of the Brent Cross shopping centre and much of the new City Docklands development.'

'Well, that's nice, Howard,' says her father. 'So what are your future prospects?'

'Oh, I'm planning to expand a bit,' replies Howard.

'Expand a bit?' interrupts Rebecca for the third time. 'Why, Howard's just about to purchase the old London Stock Exchange tower so that he can convert it into the world's most expensive hotel.'

'Well, that's nice, Howard,' says her father.

Just then Howard sneezes and reaches into his pocket for his handkerchief. Rebecca's mother immediately asks him, 'Have you got a cold, Howard?'

Before he can answer, Rebecca says, 'A cold? Don't be silly Mum, Howard's got full-blown pneumonia.'

* * *

Shortest fairy tale ever
Once upon a time a man asks a Jewish Princess, 'Will you marry me?'

She says, 'No.'

And the man lives happily ever after.

The end.

* * *

Five pieces of advice for women
1. It's important to find a man who helps you around the house.
2. It's important to find a man that can make you laugh.
3. It's important to find a man you can count on and who doesn't lie to you.
4. It's important to find a man who loves you and spoils you.
5. It's important that these four men don't know each other.

* * *

How to impress a woman
Wine her. Dine her. Call her. Hug her. Support her. Hold her. Surprise her. Compliment her. Smile at her. Listen to her. Laugh with her. Cry with her. Romance her. Encourage her. Believe in her. Cuddle her. Shop with her. Give her jewellery. Buy her flowers. Hold her hand. Write love letters to her. Go to the ends of the earth and back again for her.

How to impress a man
Show up naked. Bring him chicken wings. Don't stand in front of the TV.

Marriage Brokers (*Shadchen*)

Music wins the day
Lionel is a well-educated bachelor who feels ready to marry and settle down, but he's shy and finds it difficult to meet women. So he's developed a great love of classical music and spends much of his spare time going to concerts. Meanwhile, Lionel's parents have been searching for a suitable *shiddach* for him. Then one day, to their great relief, two potential candidates come on to the scene at the same

time (just like London buses). After talking to the two young ladies, his father has a word with Lionel.

'Lionel, I think I may have found you a wife. I have been in touch with two very acceptable but quite different girls for you to choose from and both say they are ready to marry. Let me show you their photos.'

The first photo is of a beautiful woman. 'Rebecca informs me,' says her father, 'that she has a talent for cooking great kosher food – her *matzo*-ball soup is supposed to be superb. She also keeps fit with aerobics and Israeli dancing. But she left school at 15 and admits to having no talent whatsoever for music.'

He then shows Lionel a photo of an ugly woman. She has what looks like a moustache on her top lip, her neck is as thick as a wrestler's, she has cross-eyes, her nose is crooked and her lips are almost non-existent.

'Now Sadie,' says his father, 'might not be great-looking but she comes from a fine, noble family, has a first-class degree from Oxford University and has a wonderful operatic voice. She'll be famous one day – she showed me a poster of a concert she's giving soon at the Royal Opera House, Covent Garden.'

Lionel studies the two photos. Although Rebecca is gorgeous, his keen love of music wins him over and he chooses Sadie. Within weeks, they marry.

On the first morning of their honeymoon, Lionel awakes before Sadie. He takes one look at that face staring up at him from their pillow, shakes Sadie and cries out, 'Sadie, for goodness' sake, sing a little something!'

* * *

Not a lot to ask

Hannah goes to see a *shadchen* hoping that he has someone on his books who would meet her needs. She says to the *shadchen*, 'I'm looking for a husband. Can you please help me find someone suitable?'

'I'm sure I can help,' replies the *shadchen*. 'May I ask what your requirements are?'

'Well,' says Hannah, 'he needs to be handsome in a masculine kind of way and he needs a good sense of humour. He must be polite and courteous and have a knowledge about most subjects. He needs to sing and dance well and he must always be willing to accompany me wherever I decide to go during my leisure hours. And I want him to tell me interesting stories when I need some conversation and be quiet when I need to rest.'

The *shadchen* smiles and says, 'I understand exactly what you need. You need a good television.'

* * *

The perfect woman

Avrahom and Rivkah are quite worried about their 30-year-old son Jacob. They're a *chassidic* family and they feel that Jacob should have found a wife by now and had many children. So one day, Avrahom announces, 'I've been in touch with a *shadchen* to help us find a wife for our Jacob, and he's coming here tonight.'

'*Oy veh*,' says Jacob.

The *shadchen* arrives and immediately starts asking questions to enable him to find the right kind of daughter-in-law. At the end of his visit, the *shadchen* says to them, 'You've answered my questions and I've been able to put together a "shopping list" of your requirements. I know what you want.'

'So do you have someone who meets our requirements?' asks Avrahom, hopefully.

'I think I might have the perfect woman,' replies the *shadchen*. 'I'll be back tomorrow night with some news.'

The next night, the *shadchen* returns and with a smile announces, 'What a wonderful woman I've found.'

'So make with the details, already,' says Avrahom.

'Well,' says the *shadchen*, 'I think this woman will be perfect for Jacob. She's the right age; she keeps a glatt kosher home; she attends *shul* regularly; she *davens* by heart; she just adores children and wants to raise a large family; she's a marvellous cook; and on top of all that, she's very, very beautiful.'

On hearing this, Avrahom and Rivkah begin to discuss the prospects of an early wedding. But then Jacob, who up to now has remained silent, asks the *shadchen*, 'Is she also good in bed?'

The *shadchen* thinks for a moment, then replies, 'Well Jacob, some say yes...and some say no.'

* * *

Marriage proposals

Sarah is talking to her friend Estelle. 'I just don't know what's the matter with you, Estelle. You're nearly 30 years old and you're still not married. Don't you want a husband?'

'Of course I do,' replies Estelle.

'Then I don't understand. You've got great looks and a neat figure, so why haven't you had any proposals?'

'But you're wrong there,' replies Estelle. 'I've been asked to get married dozens of times.'

'Really?' says Sarah. 'By whom, may I ask?'

'By my parents, who else?' replies Estelle.

The Path of True Love

A year in the life

As Sadie and Manny are leaving the shopping centre, they see their neighbour's son Paul and his fiancée Sharon just going in.

'Did you see that?' Sadie says.

'See what?' asks Manny, pretending not to know what Sadie is referring to.

'Paul's fiancée, that's who,' Sadie says. 'She's dressing all wrong. She's probably 37-23-35 and with big breasts like hers, she shouldn't be wearing such a skimpy see-through top. And such a tight leather skirt she's wearing – I don't know how she can breathe properly. And it's so short, it make her legs look too long. I know she's got a beautiful face but I don't think blonde, dyed hair suits her. Believe me, Manny, that marriage won't last more than one year.'

With a deep sigh, Manny replies, 'Please God I should have such a year.'

* * *

The wig

Lionel is getting quite bald and his elder daughter's wedding is coming up. All his friends and family will be there – and, well, even men can be vain. He gets fitted with an expensive toupee.

On the wedding day, everything goes well. Nevertheless, Lionel thinks that everyone must have seen his toupee. Next day, his youngest daughter sees his worried look and says, 'What's the matter, Daddy? Why are you so sad?'

'I'm not really sad, darling,' he replies, 'it's just that I'm sure everyone yesterday saw that I was wearing a wig.'

'No they didn't, Daddy,' she says. 'No one I told knew.'

* * *

Feelings

Sharon tells her best friend, Ruth, 'I've broken off my engagement to Moshe.'

'Oh Sharon,' says Ruth, 'I'm so sorry. Why?'

'Because my feelings towards Moshe have changed – they just aren't the same any more,' replies Sharon.

'So tell me,' whispers Ruth, 'are you giving him back the engagement ring?'

'No, I'm not,' replies Sharon. 'My feelings towards the ring haven't changed.'

* * *

Wedding plans

Victor and Faye are discussing their impending wedding and during their conversation, the subject of children comes up.

Faye says, 'Oh Victor, I just can't wait to marry you and have at least three children. I've always wanted a large family.'

'That's too many, darling,' says Victor. 'Two is perfectly ample for me.'

Faye then spends 10 minutes trying to change Victor's mind but to no avail. Victor thinks he's ended the conversation when he announces, 'In fact, after our second child, I'll just have a vasectomy.'

Without a moment's hesitation, Faye responds to this challenge by saying, 'Well, I hope you'll love the third one as if it's your own.'

* * *

The charges

Sarah and Max get married. On their wedding night, just when Max is highly aroused, Sarah surprises him by demanding £25 for their lovemaking. Max readily agrees.

Over the next 30 years, this scenario is repeated each time they make love – and lovemaking is very frequent, because they are both passionate people. Max always regards the payment as a cunning way to let Sarah buy new clothes and go regularly to the hairdressers.

One day, Sarah arrives home just after lunch to find Max at home. He is stressed out and in tears. He tells her, 'My company's been taken over and I've been made redundant. What on earth will I do? I'm not young any more and finding another job quickly will be difficult.'

Without saying a word, Sarah opens her bureau and hands Max her building society passbook. When he opens it, he's surprised to see it showing deposits plus interest over 30 years totalling nearly £1 million. Sarah then hands him share certificates worth nearly £2 million and says, 'Darling Max. For the last 30 years, I've been carefully investing my "£25 lovemaking charges" and what you see is the result of my investments. So we don't need to worry about money.'

When he hears this, Max gets even more distraught and agitated than before, so Sarah asks him, 'Why are you so upset at such good news, Max?'

Max replies, '*Oy veh*. If I had known what you were doing, I would have given you all of my business!'

* * *

Family growth

Abe's father is a widower and a multi-millionaire. He also has a terminal illness and is likely to pass away soon. Abe, a single man, decides he needs a woman with whom to enjoy his soon-to-be-received fortune – and where better to find one than in a singles bar?

Luckily, on his first visit, Abe meets Rifka, a woman whose beauty literally takes his breath away.

'I'm just a standard kind of a nice guy,' he says to her, 'but in a week or two's time my dear father is expected to die and I'll inherit over £20 million.'

Rifka goes home with Abe and the following day becomes his stepmother.

* * *

I'm not sure

Abe is enjoying his 80th birthday party with family and friends. Even Rabbi Landau is present. Abe is so happy that he decides now is the time to let out his secret and to everybody's surprise, announces his forthcoming marriage to 50-year-old Hetty.

Everyone comes up to wish them *mazeltov* – and to exchange all the old jokes. Such as:

'Abe, where will you both live?'

'We'll be looking for a house near a school.'

And:

'Abe, did you know that lovemaking is dangerous for the elderly?'

'Yes, but I hope Hetty will survive it.'

Later, Rabbi Landau takes Abe aside and says, 'Don't be offended, but I must ask you a few questions. Do you really love Hetty?'

'To tell you the truth, Rabbi, I'm not sure,' Abe replies.

'Well, is she a good cook? Is her chicken soup special?' asks Rabbi Landau.

'I'm not sure, I've never seen her in the kitchen, Rabbi,' Abe replies.

'Is Hetty rich?' asks Rabbi Landau.

'I'm not sure about her finances, we've never discussed money,' replies Abe.

'So, she must be…good in bed. Is that so?' asks Rabbi Landau, timidly.

'I've no idea at all Rabbi; how does one tell before marriage?' answers Abe.

'But if you don't know whether you love her, if you're not sure whether she's a good cook, if you don't know whether she's rich, and if you've never made love to her, why on earth do you want to marry her?' asks Rabbi Landau.

'She can drive at night,' replies Abe.

* * *

A promiscuous riddle
Q: How do you stop a Jewish girl being promiscuous?
A: Marry her!

* * *

A marriage riddle
Q: Who was it who asked a Princess seven times to get married?
A: Her mother.

* * *

The wrong one
Naomi's husband dies and all of a sudden she's on her own to bring up Leah, her 10-year-old daughter. After some time has passed, she starts looking for a partner – not an easy task – but then Mr Shapiro comes on to the scene. He's much older than Naomi but is wealthy and presentable, so Naomi accepts his invite for a meal at Ben's Kosher Kitchen. They have a good time and start seeing each other on a regular basis. She likes him very much and is glad things are getting

serious between them – after all, Leah could do with a new father figure around the house.

When it's time to introduce Mr Shapiro to Leah, she decides to invite him over for a *shabbes* dinner. He accepts and at once Naomi begins to worry about the one thing that could ruin her chances of marriage – Mr Shapiro has a large wart on his nose. She is worried that Leah will not only stare at it but also laugh at it. No matter how hard she tries, she can't get the scene out of her mind.

Friday arrives and she's in such despair that she decides to tell Leah what's troubling her. As they are setting the table, she says, 'Please Leah, I want you be on your very best behaviour tonight and…oh yes, one other thing, darling, don't say a thing about the wart on Mr Shapiro's nose. I don't want him upset.'

'OK, Mum, I won't mention it, I promise,' says Leah.

In the event, the meal is a great success. Conversation flows easily and Leah behaves impeccably, not a word out of place. Naomi breathes a massive sigh of relief when Leah asks to be excused, just before dessert. As Leah closes the door behind her, Naomi turns towards Mr Shapiro and asks, 'So Mr Shapiro, would you like cream or custard on your wart?'

* * *

The world's shortest fairy story
Once upon a time, Leah asks Bernie, 'Will you marry me?'

Bernie says, 'No,' and Leah lives happily ever after – she goes shopping whenever she wants, drinks martinis, meets her women friends regularly, always has a clean house, has no men's clothes strewn all over the place, never has to cook, never has her blankets pulled off her, stays slim, never has to feign a headache, never has to watch sports on television and farts whenever she wants.

The End.

* * *

So you've found your true love and decide to marry her – 1
It is customary for the groom to buy his bride a diamond engagement ring. In traditional circles, this kind of custom is called *yehareg ve-al ya'avor* – that is to say, highly recommended. Our sages have also established a formula to determine how much one should spend on the ring. It is:

Take the amount you can just about afford.

Multiply by 18.

That is how much you must spend.

* * *

So you've found your true love and decide to marry her – 2
The ring symbolises many things. For example:

A ring has the form of a link in a chain. This symbolises that marriage chains a man and deprives him of his liberty. As our sages teach, 'Who is a free man? One who eludes marriage.'

A ring is a circle that has no beginning and no end, which is how marriage feels after a couple of years. This also alludes to Torah study, which is also endless, all the more so because a man won't learn much once he marries.

* * *

You have my blessing
Renee has been going out with Lionel, the latest of her many boyfriends, for three weeks and this time she really believes something will come of it – especially as he has just asked to meet her parents. So that afternoon, Renee goes to her father and says, 'Daddy, when Lionel arrives, there's a very good chance that he's going to come to you to ask for my hand in marriage.'

Her father jumps up from his chair and shouts out '*Mazeltov!*' but before he can get too excited, Renee says, 'But Daddy, you must promise me something. All you need to say to him is a simple, "Yes, you have my blessing." I beg you, Daddy, please don't do what you did last time with my previous boyfriend.'

'So just what did I do last time?' asks her father, innocently.

'Well,' replies Renee, 'you fell on your knees, grabbed his hand and shouted out, "Oh, thank you my lovely *boychick*! Thank you, thank you! You're my salvation!"'

* * *

The fortune teller

Daniel proposes to his girlfriend Rachel. 'Will you marry me, darling?'

With tears in her eyes, she replies, 'Oh yes, yes, Daniel. Of course I will. And I want you to know that when we get married, I'll be there to share all your worries and troubles and help lighten your burden.'

'I'm so glad you want to be my wife,' says Daniel smiling, 'but as for your offer to share all my worries and troubles, you won't have to because I just don't have any.'

'Well,' says Rachel, 'that's because we aren't married yet.'

* * *

The pre-nuptial agreement

Sam and Leah, both in their eighties, are discussing the possibility of getting married. Leah says, 'If I marry you, Sam, I'll want to keep my au pair. She's fantastic.'

'That's OK with me,' replies Sam.

'And I'll also want to keep my Lexus,' Leah continues.

'That's also fine with me. It won't be a problem,' says Sam.

'And not only that,' says Leah, 'I'll want to have sex six times a week, without fail.'

'That's no problem with me,' says Sam. 'Put me down for Mondays.'

* * *

Marriage reminiscences

Rivkah awakens one night to find that her husband Howard is not in bed with her. She goes downstairs to look for him and finds him sitting at the kitchen table with a cup of coffee in front of him. He appears to be in deep thought, just staring at the wall. She watches as he wipes away a tear from his eye and takes a sip of his coffee.

'What's the matter, dear?' she asks tenderly, 'Why are you down here in the middle of the night?'

Howard looks up from his coffee. 'Do you remember, Rivkah, how young we both were when we first started dating?'

'Yes, I remember,' Rivkah replies.

Howard's voice is brimming with emotion. 'Do you also remember when your father caught us in the back seat of my car making love?'

'How could I forget?' says Rivkah.

'And do you remember he put a gun against my head and said, "Either you marry my daughter or I'll see to it that you go to jail for 30 years?"'

'I remember that well,' Rivkah softly replies, taking hold of his hand.

Howard wipes away a tear and says, 'I would have got out today.'

* * *

An American marriage

Lionel, from London, is taking his university gap year in America and he's visiting as many places there as he can. But while spending some time in Oklahoma, he meets and falls deeply in love with a Cherokee girl. Not long after, they decide to get married and Lionel rings his mother to tell her the good news.

'Mum, I've found my future wife and we're getting married over here. I'm going to send you the air tickets to join us.'

'*Mazeltov*, Lionel,' his mother says. 'I'm so pleased, but is she…Jewish?'

'No, Mum,' Lionel replies, 'she's not. But she promises to act as a Jewish wife.'

'*Oy*,' his mother wails, 'I've always wanted you to marry a lovely Jewish girl.'

'You can't have everything, Mum,' Lionel says. 'And another thing I must tell you. She lives on a reservation and that's where we'll be living after we marry.'

'I can't take any more of this,' cries his mother. 'I don't want the tickets and I don't want to speak to you again.' And with that she slams down the phone.

Almost a year later, Lionel rings his mother and tells her that they are expecting a baby. His mother doesn't slam down the phone but says, very politely and unemotionally, 'That's nice, son, I'm happy for you both.'

Eight months later, Lionel again rings his mother and says, 'Mum, I just want to say that last night my wife gave birth to a beautiful, healthy baby boy. I also want you to know that we've agreed to give our son a Jewish name.'

Upon hearing this unexpected news, his mother shouts out with happiness. 'Oh Lionel, *bubbeleh*, this is wonderful news,' she cries. 'I've been waiting for this moment all my life. You've both made me more happy than you could ever know.'

'That's fantastic, Mum,' replies Lionel. 'I'm so glad that you and I are back together as mother and son.'

'And what,' asks his proud and happy mother, 'is my lovely grandson's name going to be?'

Lionel replies, proudly, 'Smoked Whitefish.'

* * *

An observation on marriage

When Jewish women get married, they often find that, unfortunately, they have exchanged the attentions of many men for the inattention of one man.

* * *

The inexperienced couple

Yitzhak and Leah decide to marry. However, they are both so inexperienced that neither knows what they have to do on their wedding night. So they go to Rabbi Bloom for advice.

After hearing their story, Rabbi Bloom takes them upstairs to his bedroom and says to Leah, 'I want you to get undressed and get on my bed. I'll get undressed too and then I'll be able to show you both exactly what you will have to do on your wedding night.'

So Leah gets undressed as she was told and gets up on the bed. Rabbi Bloom then begins to demonstrate, with Leah, the steps and actions involved in making love. From start to finish!

As soon as Rabbi Bloom finishes, he starts getting dressed, saying to Yitzhak, 'Well, that's what you have to do, Yitzhak. You can see that it has worked by the lovely glowing look on Leah's face. So now I suggest you take her home and practise what I've shown you.'

But then Leah interrupts and says, 'Hold on Rabbi, could you please show Yitzhak again what to do? He's a little forgetful....'

* * *

Breaking the bad news

The time comes for Monty to break the news to his fiancée, Leah. 'Darling,' he says, 'I have some bad news. I'm breaking off our engagement.'

'Oh why?' she sobs.

'Because I'm going to marry another woman.'

'Why? Can she cook better than me?' sobs Leah.

'No, not even on her best days,' Monty replies.

'And will she buy you expensive presents like I always do? Will she take you on holidays and pay for the trips as I do?'

'No, she can't – she's not rich like you, she's very poor.'

'Well then,' sobs Leah, 'is it the sex? Has she done things to you better than I've done?'

'Absolutely no,' replies Monty, 'nobody makes love better than you.'

'Then what on earth can she do that I can't?' Leah asks.

'Sue me for child support,' replies Monty.

* * *

Wedding-night advice

Joe is talking to his soon-to-be-married son Abe. 'Let me give you some advice, Abe. On my wedding night, I took off my trousers, handed them to your mother and said, "Here, try these on." Your mother did as she was told and said, "These are too big – I can't wear them." So I said to her, "And don't you forget it. I wear the trousers in our house and always will." Ever since that night, we have never had any problems.'

Abe thinks this is such good advice that on his honeymoon, he takes off his trousers and says to his bride, 'Here Rifka, try these on.'

She does, then says, 'But these are too large – they don't fit me.'

Abe says, 'Exactly. I wear the trousers in our house and always will. I don't want you to ever forget that.'

So Rifka takes off her panties, hands them to Abe and says, 'Here, you try on mine.'

Abe tries but has to admit, 'I can't get into your panties.'

Rifka responds, 'Exactly. And if you don't change your smart-ass attitude, you never will.'

* * *

A letter to an agony aunt

Dear Naomi

I am getting married next month to a gorgeous girl called Miriam and our reception is going to be held at the renowned Dorchester hotel in London.

Because my family's invitation list totalled 120 people – more than her parents were expecting to pay for – Miriam's mother Rachel invited me to her house to see what could be done. When I got there, Rachel and I went through my list and we managed to trim it down to 101, including my rabbi. Rachel said she could accept this number. She is not only young and attractive but also very understanding.

Then, out of the blue, Rachel shocked me. She said that she fancied me and that before I became a married man, she would like to have sex with me. She then turned around and started walking upstairs to the bedroom. Halfway up the stairs, she turned around and told me that if I wanted to leave, I knew where the front door was.

I stood there for a few minutes and then made my decision. As I headed out the front door, there was Max, my future father-in-law, leaning on my Lexus. Smiling, Max said to me, 'Mazeltov, you've passed our little test.' He then explained that they just wanted to be sure I was a good Jewish boy and would be faithful to their little girl. We then shook hands.

So Naomi, the question is, should I tell Miriam what her parents did and that I thought their test insulted my character? Or should I keep quiet, knowing that the reason I went to my car was to get a condom?

Relieved of north London.

Spouses

Silence is not golden

Bernie and Estelle have a big argument that ends with neither one speaking to the other. This 'silence' goes on for three days. But then Bernie realises he needs Estelle's help because he has an early-morning flight to catch. However, he still can't bring himself to talk to her, so he writes a note and leaves it on her pillow.

It says, 'Please wake me at 5am. I have to catch an early plane.'

Next morning, Bernie wakes up and finds to his horror that it is 9am. He hears Estelle busy in the kitchen and there is a note on his pillow.

It says: 'It's 5am. Wake up.'

* * *

Looking for Freda

Isaac arrives home one afternoon and can't see his Freda anywhere. So he shouts out, 'Oh darling, my sweet honey bun, I'm home. Where are you?'

He hears Freda reply from somewhere, 'I'm hiding.'

So Isaac shouts out, 'Oh darling, my sweetheart, I've got a lovely surprise for you. Where are you?'

Again he hears Freda reply, 'I'm hiding.'

Isaac then shouts out, 'Oh darling, my loved one, I've bought you that diamond and platinum bracelet you've always wanted from Mappin & Webb. Where are you?'

This time he hears Freda shout back, 'I'm hiding – I'm hiding in the bedroom wardrobe.'

* * *

Good answer

Hyman wakes up one morning with a hangover. He forces his eyes open and looks around his bedroom. First thing he sees is a bottle of aspirin and a glass of water on his bedside table. His clothes are on a chair next to the bed, cleaned and ironed and the bedroom itself is airy, sweet smelling and spotlessly clean. He takes two of the aspirins and slowly walks downstairs. Everything is exceptionally clean and tidy. Downstairs, on the kitchen door, is a note which reads,

'Darling, your breakfast is on the hob. I had to leave early to go shopping. See you soon. Love you. Freda XXXXX.'

Hyman goes into the kitchen and finds his son Paul watching TV while eating his cereal. And there, waiting for him on the hob, as the note said it would be, is his breakfast – scrambled eggs, tomatoes, baked beans and toast. And there is a clean, folded, unread *Times* newspaper on his chair.

Hyman asks, 'Paul, what on earth happened last night? I can't remember a thing.'

'Well, Dad,' Paul replies, 'you came home at one o'clock in the morning very drunk and singing rude songs very loudly. You were sick in the hallway and then you fell over and went to sleep when you tripped over the dog.'

Hyman is very confused. 'Paul, I don't understand – why is everything so clean and tidy, including my clothes, and why is my favourite breakfast waiting for me? From what you've just told me, I don't deserve any of this.'

Paul responds, 'Oh that's easy to explain, Dad. When Mum dragged you upstairs to the bedroom and tried to take off your trousers, you shouted angrily at her, "Leave me alone, I'm a married man."'

* * *

Isn't knowledge wonderful?

Hymie is sitting on a bench with his friend Monty. Neither has spoken for 10 minutes when Hymie suddenly says, 'Do you know what, Monty?'

'No, what, Hymie?'

'Mine Rivka', continues Hymie, 'is very knowledgeable. She reads *The Times* newspaper every day from front to back; she watches the news on TV every hour; she reads all kinds of books and she regularly goes to evening classes. She is so up-to-date about current affairs that she can talk all night on any subject.'

'So what?' says Monty, 'Mine Sadie doesn't need a subject.'

* * *

I'm ashamed

Howard is one of the laziest men around and refuses to look for a job. One day, as he is lying flat out on the couch, his wife Becky says to him, 'I'm so ashamed of the way we live, Howard.'

'What do you mean by that?' Howard asks.

'Surely I don't have to remind you', she replies, 'that we are so poor, my mother buys our kosher food, my father pays our mortgage and your sister buys our clothes. Why, even your aunt has just bought us a car. Aren't you just a little bit ashamed?'

Howard sits up on the couch and replies, 'You should be ashamed too. Benjy and Jacob, your two worthless brothers, have never given us a penny.'

* * *

What an angel
Sadie has been married for five years and is pleased when her husband Issy starts to call her an 'angel'. She likes compliments as much as the next woman, but after it goes on for a few weeks, Sadie asks Issy, 'Why do you call me an angel, dear?'

'Because', replies Issy, 'you're always up in the air, you're continually harping on about something and you never have a thing to wear.'

* * *

Hot, hot, hot
'Please, Leah, please.'

'Oh leave me alone, Moshe.'

'But it won't take long.'

'If I do, I won't be able to sleep afterwards.'

'Well, if you don't, I won't be able to sleep either.'

'Why do you have to think of such a thing just before I go to sleep?'

'Because I'm hot, hot, hot, that's why, Leah.'

'You always get hot at the wrong times, Moshe.'

'If you really loved me, you wouldn't be making me beg you.'

'Well, if you really loved me, you'd be more considerate.'

'Don't you love me any more?'

'Of course I do, Moshe, but let's forget it for tonight.'

'Oh please, Leah.'

'OK, OK, I'll do it – anything for a quiet life!'

...

'What's keeping you?'

'I can't find it.'

'Oh, for heaven's sake, Leah, feel for it.'

'There! Now are you satisfied?'

'*Oy veh*, that's good.'

'Is it up far enough?'

'Yes, oh yes.'

'Now go to sleep and when you next want the window open, open it yourself.'

* * *

Jewish husbands and wives

- He will pay £2 for a £1 item he needs, whereas she will pay £1 for a £2 item that she doesn't need.
- She worries about the future until she gets a husband, whereas he never worries about the future until he gets a wife.
- He is successful if he can make more money than she can, whereas she is successful if she can find such a man.
- To be happy with him, she must understand him a lot and love him a little, whereas to be happy with her, he must love her a lot and not try to understand her at all.
- He will live longer than single men do, but then he's a lot more willing to die.
- She marries him expecting him to change (but he doesn't), whereas he marries her expecting that she won't change (but she does).
- She has the last word in any argument, whereas anything he says after that is the beginning of a new argument.

* * *

A rose by any other name

Sarah is married to a well-known horticulturist and is both proud and flattered when one day he creates a new type of rose and names it after her. But her happiness is soon cut short when she reads the rose's description in the catalogue: 'No good in a bed, but fine up against a wall.'

* * *

The body scan

David asks his wife Renee, 'I was just wondering, darling, what part of me do you like the most? Is it my handsome, rugged face or my hard, muscular body, or what?'

Renee scans him from head to toe, then replies, 'I like your sense of humour.'

* * *

What I want in a wife

Lionel tells his friend Sidney that he's at last looking for a wife.

'So what kind of wife are you looking for?' asks Sidney.

'Well,' replies Lionel, 'she needs to be ultra beautiful, she needs to be very kind to me, and she needs to have lots of money.'

'But you can't marry three women at the same time,' says Sidney.

* * *

Important instruction for men

I strongly recommended that you never criticise your wife. Just remember that if she were perfect, she would have married someone much better than you.

* * *

Women's questionnaire

A recent study was set up for women, asking them how they felt about their arse.

- 85 per cent of women think their arse is too big.
- 10 per cent of women think their arse is too small.
- The other 5 per cent say that they don't care – they love him and would have married him anyway.

Making Love

Love bragging

Victor, Cyril and Abe meet up for a chat and a coffee. Victor says, 'Do you two know that last night I made love to mine Leah three times and this morning, as soon as I awoke, she told me how much she loved me.'

'*Mazeltov*,' says Cyril, 'but last night I made love to mine Sarah four times and this morning, as soon as I awoke, she told me I must be the world's greatest lover.'

Abe doesn't say a word and just takes another sip of his coffee. So his two friends ask him how many times he made love last night.

'Vell if you must know,' replies Abe, 'I made love to mine Becky vonce.'

'Only once?' says Cyril, 'And what did Becky say to you this morning?'

'She said, "Don't stop!" '

* * *

Keeping the family together

Ethel goes to see Dr Myers and tells him that she is feeling constantly tired and exhausted, especially after making love.

'So how often do you make love, Ethel?' asks Dr Myers.

'I make love every Monday, Wednesday and Friday, Doctor,' she answers.

'Well,' says Dr Myers, 'maybe you should cut out Wednesdays?'

'No, that's not really a good idea,' says Ethel, 'that's the only night I'm home with mine Arnold.'

* * *

It's obvious

It is Friday and to his surprise, Max is told that he is being promoted to manager. He is also given the afternoon off. When he gets home to his sixth-floor flat and tells his wife Helen the good news, they decide to celebrate by making love. But what are they going to do about their nine-year-old son Sam?

'I know,' says Max, 'let's put Sam out onto the balcony and get him to report to us on everything he sees happening in the neighbourhood. That'll keep him busy.'

'Good idea, darling,' says Helen and 10 minutes later, Sam begins his reporting at the same time she and Max begin their lovemaking.

'OK, Dad,' reports Max, 'they're towing away Mr Shineman's 4x4 from in front of his flat.'

A few moments later, Max says, 'A fire engine has just stopped outside the Himmelfarbs' shop.'

Then he shouts out, 'Looks like the Levys are going to the *shul.*' Followed quickly by, 'My friend David's riding his new red two-wheeler bike across the main road.'

And then, 'Mr and Mrs Abrahams are having sex.'

At that, Max and Helen sit up in bed and shout out, 'How do you know that, Sam?'

'Because,' Sam replies, 'their son Paul, like me, is standing on their balcony reporting what he sees.'

* * *

A fall-off in performance

Sadie, an elderly lady, goes to see her doctor. 'Doctor,' she says, 'I really believe the romance is going out of my marriage.'

'Why do you say that, Sadie?' asks the doctor.

'Because mine Moshe is not (if you excuse me) performing very well in bed these days.'

'Sadie,' he asks, 'how old are you?'

'I'm 80, Doctor,' she replies.

'And how old is your Moshe, Sadie?' asks the doctor.

'*Kin-a-hora*, he's a healthy 88 years old,' she replies.

'Well, Sadie,' says the doctor, 'I don't think you need worry. Sexual performance always begins to drop off in men of advanced years. It's normal. But tell me, when did you first notice Moshe's failing performance?'

Sadie replies, 'I noticed it twice last night, Doctor, and once again this morning.'

* * *

Regular sex

Hyman and Sadie, an elderly couple, go for their annual medical. Hyman goes in first and after examining him, Doctor Cohen says, 'You appear to be in good health, Hyman. Do you have any medical concerns you would like to discuss?'

'Yes I do,' says Hyman. 'After I have sex with mine Sadie, I'm usually hot and sweaty and then, after I have sex with her the second time, I'm usually cold and chilly.'

'That's odd,' says Doctor Cohen, 'I'll ask Sadie about it when I check her out.'

Soon it was Sadie's turn. After examining her, Doctor Cohen says, 'Everything appears to be fine, Sadie. Do you have any medical concerns that you would like to discuss with me?'

'No, Doctor,' she replies.

Doctor Cohen then says, 'Hyman has an unusual problem. He claims that he is usually hot and sweaty after having sex with you the first time and then cold and chilly after the second time. Can you think of why this might be?'

'Oh that stupid *shmuck* of a husband of mine,' Sadie replies, 'it's because we have sex only twice a year – once in the summer and once in the winter.'

* * *

Dangerous liaison

Eighty-seven-year-old Nathan is sitting at the bar of his local senior citizens' dance club when in walks Fay. 'What a beauty,' he says to himself. He can't believe his luck when she walks over and starts chatting to him. It is love at first sight for both of them. After dating for only a few weeks, they decide to get married. On their wedding night, they consummate their marriage with a long and passionate sexy romp. As soon as it ends, Fay notices that Nathan is very quiet and still. She then realises that her new husband has died just as he reached his climax.

At Nathan's funeral, one of Fay's friends comes over to her and says, 'I was so shocked to hear the news, Fay. Whatever happened?'

'Nothing much,' Fay replies, 'he came and he went.'

* * *

Revenge

Moshe comes home early from work one day and discovers his wife Clare in bed with his neighbour. He's angry and bitter and feels very humiliated. So he goes over to his friend Henry's house and says, 'I'm going to poison her, Henry.'

'I wouldn't do that, Moshe,' says Henry. 'The police will quickly discover it's you and you'll go to jail for a very long time. Better you should *shtup* her to death. It'll be over in 12 months, I guarantee.'

Moshe takes Henry's advice and starts to make love to Clare every morning, noon and night without fail. After this has been going on for about a year, Henry goes to visit them.

Clare answers the door and Henry is immediately taken aback by how well she looks. She is literally glowing with health. She takes him into the lounge and there sitting on the sofa is Moshe. And *oy veh*, does Moshe look bad! His skin is pale, his eyes are sunken in their sockets, he's lost most of his hair and he's shaking all over. When Clare goes into the kitchen to make some tea, Henry says to Moshe, 'So how come you're looking so ill and yet Clare seems so well?'

'Shhh,' replies Moshe, 'don't talk so loud. She doesn't know it yet but she's only got a few more weeks to live.'

* * *

A loving riddle
Q: Why do Jewish women *shtup* with their eyes closed?
A: They hate to see their husbands having a good time.

* * *

A good solution
It's a lovely Sunday morning and Issy wakes up, puts on his dressing gown and goes downstairs, where his wife Rose is in the kitchen making breakfast.

'So what's for breakfast, dear?' he asks, as he enters the kitchen.

Rose walks over to him and says, 'Before I answer that, you've got to make love to me right now.'

Thinking it's his lucky day, Issy does as he's told and makes love to Rose. When it's over, Issy asks, 'Darling, why did you want to make love at this very moment? You've never wanted to do that before.'

'Because I'm making you eggs and the egg timer's broken,' Rose replies.

* * *

That's the way to do it
After 15 years of marriage, it's got to the stage where Victor and Rivkah have no choice but to book an appointment to see Levy, the well-known marriage guidance counsellor. When they arrive, Levy asks them to explain their problem. Rivkah immediately launches into a seemingly never-ending tirade, going on and on about Victor's selfishness, his lying, his bullying, his controlling, his spending money on worthless goods, his never saying anything nice about her, their arguments, his lack of love for her...but Levy has heard enough, already. He gets up, goes over to Rivkah, pulls her from her chair, embraces her and kisses her passionately on the lips. That stops her in her tracks. Levy then rips off her clothes and makes love to her on his desk. When it's over, Rivkah sits back down in her chair with a dazed but very satisfied look on her face.

Levy turns to Victor and says, 'You see? That's what your wife needs, and she needs it at least three times a week. Do you think you can do that?'

Victor thinks for a moment, then replies, 'Well, I can certainly get her here on Monday and Thursday, Doctor, but on Friday I play golf.'

* * *

Did the earth move for you?
Even though they know San Francisco is due for another big earthquake, Lionel and his wife decide to go there to celebrate their silver wedding anniversary. Unluckily, at midnight on their first night, they experience their first violent earthquake. It wasn't the BIG one, though, and when morning comes, Lionel goes down to hotel reception to find out more about the event. As he's waiting to be seen, another hotel guest walks up to him and says, 'Say, mister, did you feel the earthquake during the night?'

'I sure did,' replies Lionel. 'My wife and I are here on holiday from London and I never realised a quake could be so terrible. I thought the hotel was going to collapse on top of us.'

'So what were you doing during the earthquake?' asks the other guest.

'Well, if you must know,' replies Lionel, smiling, 'while the earthquake was actually taking place, I was experiencing my best sexual performance ever.'

'*Mazeltov*,' says the other guest. 'What did your wife think about it?'

Lionel replies, 'Well, it damn near woke her up!'

* * *

Fitness counts

Jed and Solly, both in their fifties, have been working in the same office for many years and have become close friends. One Monday, despite his age, Jed boasts to Solly about his sexual endurance the night before.

'I did it three times with my wife last night, Solly,' says Jed, matter-of-factly.

'*Oy yoy yoy*! Three times,' gasps Solly, admiringly. 'How on earth did you manage that?'

'It wasn't too difficult,' replies Jed, modestly. 'After my wife and I made love for the first time, I took a 10-minute nap. Then I made love to her again, followed by another 10-minute nap. And then we made love for the third time. I can't describe how I feel, Solly. I woke up this morning feeling like a stallion.'

'What a good method,' says Solly. 'I must try it. Mine Sadie won't believe what's happening to her when I manage to *shtup* her three times in one night. It will be a *mekheiyeh* for both of us.'

So that night, Solly surprises Sadie. He makes love to her, then takes a 10-minute nap, makes love to her again, takes another nap, this time for 15 minutes, and then makes love to her for a third time. Then, with a smile on his face, he rolls over and falls fast asleep.

Solly wakes up feeling absolutely marvellous. He gets dressed and leaves for work. Rather than get on his usual bus, he takes a leisurely stroll to his office. This makes him 30 minutes late. When he arrives, his boss is waiting for him.

'What's the matter, Mr Jones?' he asks, 'I've been working for you for nearly 25 years and I've never once been late. Surely you're not going to reprimand me for a measly 30 minutes?'

'What do you mean 30 minutes?' says Mr Jones. 'Where were you yesterday?'

* * *

I might be six minutes late

Cyril gets a new job at Rothschild's Bank and immediately gets on well with his fellow investment bankers. So much so that a group of them who meet for a round of golf every Sunday ask Cyril whether he'd like to join them this Sunday at 10am.

'I'd love to,' replies Cyril, 'thanks for asking. But I might be six minutes late.'

'No problem,' they reply.

Cyril turns up on Sunday exactly at 10am, golfs right-handed and posts the lowest score. They congratulate him and invite him to join them again next Sunday.

'I'll be there,' Cyril says, 'but I might be six minutes late.'

The following Sunday, Cyril turns up exactly at 10am, golfs left-handed and posts the lowest score. They again congratulate him.

This continues for a number of Sundays, with Cyril always saying that he might be six minutes late, and always posting the lowest score, whether he golfs left- or right-handed.

One Sunday, in the bar after their round of golf, his

colleagues ask, 'Cyril, we hope you don't mind us asking, but every Sunday you tell us that you might be six minutes late, but you never are. And then, whether you play left- or right-handed, you still post the lowest score. What's it all about?'

'It's no great deal,' replies Cyril. 'I'm very superstitious. Every Sunday, when I awake, I look over at my beautiful wife Freda. If she's sleeping on her left side, I golf left-handed and if she's sleeping on her right side, I golf right-handed.'

'But what if your Freda is sleeping on her back?' they ask.

Cyril replies, 'Then I'm going to be six minutes late.'

* * *

The doctor's advice
Right up to the time he gets married to the lovely Hannah, Avrahom has never been with a girl. So it's not surprising that on his wedding night, poor Avrahom can't do anything right for Hannah. Two weeks go by and he still doesn't really know what to do in bed. Totally frustrated, Hannah suggests to Avrahom that he has a chat with their doctor. He agrees and two days later he's talking to Dr Myers.

'So what should I do, Doctor?' asks Avrahom.

'It's quite simple, Avrahom,' advises Dr Myers. 'Next time you're in bed with Hannah, you should place your hand gently on her stomach and say something like, "Darling, I love you so much," and everything will be OK from that moment onwards.'

Avrahom goes home feeling more confident.

Later that night, soon after they get into bed, Avrahom places his hand on her stomach and says in a very romantic voice, 'Darling, I love you with all my heart and I always will.'

Hannah can't believe the change in Avrahom and decides to take things further, so excitedly she whispers back, 'Lower Avrahom, lower!'

So our Avrahom repeats, but this time in a much lower voice, 'Darling, I love you with all my heart....'

Wedding Anniversaries

Anniversary surprise

It's Henry and Diane's second wedding anniversary and for a surprise, Henry decides to send some flowers to her office. He even instructs the florist to write on the card: 'From Henry. Happy Anniversary. Year Number 2.'

Diane is thrilled with the flowers, but not so pleased with the card. It reads: 'From Henry. Happy Anniversary. You're Number 2.'

* * *

The anniversary card problem

Max is in the newsagent's looking for a suitable wedding-anniversary greeting card. He's been there for over 45 minutes, but he's not having any luck. An assistant notices Max lingering over one card after another and, being a helpful kind of person, goes over to him to see if she can help. 'Is there a problem, sir?' she asks.

'Yes, there is,' replies Max. 'I can't find a card that mine Sarah will believe.'

* * *

Living in the past

Morris and Ruth have just celebrated their 25th wedding anniversary. That night, as they are getting ready for bed, Morris looks carefully at Ruth.

'What are you staring at?' Ruth asks.

'Darling,' he replies, 'I've been thinking. When we got married 25 years ago, we lived in a small apartment, we drove a cheap Ford car, we watched TV on a small 15-inch black-and-white television and we couldn't afford a proper bed so we had to make do with a sofa-bed. However, despite all of that, I was proud to be sleeping with a sizzling 25-year-old blonde. Now, however, we have a large house in Hampstead, we drive a Lexus, we have a 42-inch Sony LCD television set with Sky digital and we have a king-sized water bed. But here's my problem – I'm now sleeping with a 50-year-old woman. You're obviously not holding up your side of things and I don't know what to do.'

Ruth, being a very reasonable and sensible lady, says to Morris, 'I've got a solution to your problem, Morris. Go out and find a sizzling 25-year-old blonde. When you find one, I'll make sure that you'll once again be living in a small apartment, driving a cheap Ford, sleeping on a sofa bed, and watching a 15-inch black-and-white television set.'

* * *

I wish you long life

Rivka and Bernie have been married for 50 years and are being interviewed by a reporter from the *Jewish Chronicle*.

'So Rivkah,' asks the reporter, 'I know today is your golden wedding anniversary, but how old, exactly, are you?'

'I am 78 years old,' replies Rivkah, 'and *kin-a-hora* I should live to be 100.'

'Well I hope your wish comes true,' says the reporter. He then turns to Bernie and asks, 'And how old are you, Bernie?'

'I'm also 78 years old,' replies Bernie, 'and please God I should live to be 101.'

'But why', asks the reporter, 'do you want to live one year longer than your wife?'

'Well, to tell you the truth,' replies Bernie, 'I would like to have at least one year of peace and quiet.'

* * *

Our little secret

Harry and Kitty are celebrating their 60th wedding anniversary with a party for their family and friends. During the party, Max and Betty walk over to them and say, '*Mazeltov*. We're so pleased for you both. But you must let us in on your secret – how have you managed to stay married for so long, especially in this day and age?'

Harry turns to Kitty and asks, 'OK for me to reply to this?'

Kitty replies, 'Yes, dear.'

'Well,' continues Harry, 'our secret is quite simple. On the very day we got married, Kitty and I came to an agreement that we've stuck to all these years. We decided that I would make all the major decisions and Kitty would make all the minor decisions. And I can truthfully say that over the 60 years of our marriage, I have never needed to make a major decision.'

Gifts

A jewel of a present

Sam is out shopping when he meets his friend Abe outside the jeweller's. Sam notices that Abe has a small gift-wrapped box in his hand.

'So what have you just purchased, Abe?' Sam asks.

'Well, now that you've asked,' replies Abe, 'it's my Rifka's birthday tomorrow and when I asked her this morning what she wanted for her birthday she said, "Oh, I don't know, dear, just give me something with a lot of diamonds in it."'

'So what did you get her?' Sam asks.

Abe replies, smiling, 'I bought her a pack of cards.'

* * *

Ooops – 1

Joshua is mega-rich and is always lavishing expensive presents on his wife, Naomi. But today, Joshua is in big trouble. He has forgotten that it's their wedding anniversary. *Oy veh*!

Naomi looks him in his eyes and says, in a very serious manner, 'Tomorrow, Joshua, there had better be something for me outside our garage that goes from 0 to 200 in next to no time at all, or else….'

Naomi gets up early next morning, opens the front door and finds a small package outside the garage. She opens it and finds, of all things, brand new bathroom scales.

The *levoyah* is on Sunday and Naomi is sitting *shivah* for the whole week.

* * *

Sheer love

Monty is in a department store to buy his wife Leah a 70th birthday present. He looks around the ladies' underwear department and decides to buy some sheer lingerie for her, so he goes over to a salesgirl to explain what he wants. She shows him many different types, ranging in price from £35 to £280. The most sheer item is, of course, the most expensive, but as nothing is too good for his Leah, he chooses the £280 item. He pays for it and the salesgirl gift-wraps it nicely for him.

When he gets home, Monty kisses Leah and says, 'Happy birthday, darling, this is for you.'

Leah opens the package, smiles and says, 'Thanks for such a nice surprise.'

'I'm glad you like it,' says Monty. 'Why don't you put it on now and model it for me?'

'OK,' she says and goes upstairs with her present. But as soon as she sees the receipt, which Monty had forgotten to remove from the bag, she says to herself, 'It's really such a waste of money. It's so sheer that it might as well be nothing. I won't need to put it on – Monty won't notice if I do the modelling naked. Then I can return it tomorrow and keep the £280 refund for better things.'

Soon, Leah comes downstairs, naked, and starts to do some poses for Monty. Monty looks carefully at Leah and says, '*Oy veh*! For £280, you'd have thought they would have ironed it for me.'

PS: Monty never saw the frying pan as it hit him on the back of his head. The *levoyah* is on Thursday.

Conflicts and Tussles

Late home

Morris and Sadie are having matrimonial problems. Morris runs a small video rental shop and he regularly comes home late from work. As a result, Sadie has to throw away his dinner most nights. Realising her unhappiness, Morris constantly promises her that he will be home in time for dinner, but somehow something always crops up to keep him working late. He really loves Sadie but, after all, times are hard and he has to make a living as well. He just can't help it.

One morning, Sadie says, 'Morris, if you're not home by 7pm tonight, then I will never cook for you again and our marriage will be in jeopardy.' This ultimatum frightens Morris and he is determined to be home on time for once. So he closes his shop an hour early and sets off for the station. But before he gets there, he is hit by a car and is taken to hospital. Fortunately, his injuries are not too severe and he's quite quickly released. Nevertheless, a trip to hospital, plus tests, X-rays and waiting for a doctor takes time and he doesn't arrive home until 9pm.

Sadie is fuming mad. 'What time do you call this?' she shouts. 'You said you would be home by 7pm.'

'I know I did, darling,' he replies, 'but I have an excuse. I was run over by a car on my way home to you.'

'*Nu*, so it takes two hours to get run over?'

* * *

The homecoming

As usual, Sidney arrives home at 6.30pm, takes off his coat, turns on the TV and sits down in his favourite chair. This time, however, he turns to Leah and says, 'Make me a cup of tea straight away before it starts.'

Leah is surprised by this but makes him his cup of tea anyway. Sidney finishes his tea then turns to Leah and says, 'Make me another cup of tea straight away. I think it's going to start very soon.'

This time Leah is quite angry, but still makes him another cup of tea. Sidney empties his cup then again turns to Leah and says, 'Quickly, another cup before it starts.'

At this, Leah loses her cool. 'That's the last straw, you rude, inconsiderate pig,' she shouts. 'You come home, don't say one word to me, put your fat *toches* in your armchair and then expect me to act like your servant. Does it ever occur to you that I might be tired, with all the cleaning, washing, ironing, shopping and cooking I do to keep this house of ours spotlessly clean? I don't think you ever give me a thought. Selfish, that's what you are. You don't need a wife, you need a slave, you need someone to....'

Sidney sighs, 'Oh dear, it's started.'

* * *

What's in a name?
Benny is talking to his best friend Sam. 'Don't tell anyone, Sam, but mine Sadie once again had a headache last night.'

'Really?' says Sam.

'Yes,' replies Benny, 'it's been like this for some weeks now and I've been thinking that they must have named a Jewish holiday after my sex life.'

'Which one?' Sam asks.

'Passover.'

* * *

Absolutely certain
As soon as Rabbi Levy enters his office, there's Arnold waiting for him.

'I need your advice, Rabbi,' says Arnold.

'OK, Arnold, how can I help, what's bothering you?' asks Rabbi Levy.

'Rabbi,' asks Arnold, 'is it right for one man to make money from another man's errors?'

'No, Arnold, it certainly isn't,' replies Rabbi Levy.

'Are you absolutely sure about that?' asks Arnold.

'About that, Arnold, I'm absolutely positive,' replies Rabbi Levy.

'I'm so pleased to hear you say this, Rabbi,' says Arnold. 'So could you please return the £300 I gave you to marry me to my wife Sadie?'

* * *

Eagle eyes
Issy comes home from work. As usual, he drops his jacket on the chair in their hallway. As usual, his wife Freda picks it up. Just as she's about to hang it up in the cloakroom, she notices something on the jacket.

'Issy,' she shrieks at him, 'There's a long grey hair on your jacket. You've been to your mother's to get sympathy again, haven't you?'

* * *

Try harder
Becky is having lunch with Hannah, the world's most perfect 'Princess'. Becky says, 'My Moshe is just impossible. Absolutely nothing pleases him. Tell me, Hannah, is your Hymie hard to please?'

Hannah shrugs and replies, 'I wouldn't know. I've never tried.'

* * *

A painful riddle
Q: What does Sadie do with her headache each morning?
A: She sends him to work.

* * *

She, not me
Peter, Chris and Abe have all recently got married and are bragging about how they have given their new wives household duties.

Peter says, 'I told my wife on our first day of marriage that she, not I, was going to do all the dishes and house cleaning. It took a couple of days, but on the third day I came home to a clean house with all the dishes washed and put away.'

Chris says, 'I went a bit further. I told my wife that not only was she to do all the cleaning and the dishes but she, not I, was to do the cooking as well. Like Peter, it was on the third day that I came home to a clean house, dishes were done and I had a huge dinner on the table.'

Abe says, 'I married a Jewish girl and I told her in no uncertain terms that she, not I, had to keep the house clean, dishes washed, lawn mowed, laundry washed and hot meals on the table as soon as I got home. Like you two, it wasn't until the third day that things got better. By then, most of the swelling had gone down and I could see a little out of my left eye, enough to fix myself something to eat, load the dishwasher with my dirty washing and start mowing the lawn.'

* * *

Terms of endearment
Shlomo and Hetty are having breakfast one morning when Hetty suddenly says, 'You don't talk nicely to me any more Shlomo, not the way you used to when we first got married. I don't think you love me.'

'Don't love you?' Shlomo growled. 'There you go again saying I don't love you. Don't you know that I love you more than life itself? So please shut up now and let me get on with reading the morning papers.'

* * *

Not like me
Max leaves his house to hail a taxi and almost immediately finds one. As he gets in, the cabbie says, 'Perfect timing, just like Hymie.'

'Who's Hymie?' asks Max.

'Hymie Gold, of course,' says the cabbie. 'Now there's someone who got what he wanted – like a taxi just when he needed it. Not like me – I always have to wait ages when I need something.'

'No one's perfect,' says Max.

'Except Hymie,' says the cabbie. 'Hymie was a great

athlete and could have been a champion in any sport. Not like me – I'm just a couch potato.'

'So am I,' says Max.

'And', says the cabbie, 'Hymie danced like Astaire. Not like me – I've got two left feet.'

'Sounds like Hymie was really someone special,' says Max.

'You can say that again,' says the cabbie. 'He even remembered everyone's birthday. Not like me – I always forget important birthdays and anniversaries. And Hymie could fix anything in the house. Not like me – if I change a fuse, the whole neighbourhood has a power failure.'

'Wow,' says Max, 'there aren't many men around like Hymie.'

The cabbie continues, 'And Hymie knew how to treat a woman. He could always make her feel good and never answered her back even if she was in the wrong. Not like me – I'm always getting into arguments with my wife.'

'What an amazing person,' says Max. 'How did you meet him?'

'Well, I never actually met Hymie,' replies the cabbie.

'Then how do you know so much about him?' asks Max.

'I married his widow,' replies the cabbie.

* * *

Angry Henry
Henry is *broyges* with his wife and is telling his friend Barry why. 'My Diane's becoming a real sex object these days,' says Henry.

'So what's wrong with that? Why are you complaining?' asks Barry.

'Because,' replies Henry, 'every time I suggest we have sex, she objects.'

* * *

Kite flyer
Issy has taken to flying kites, but he's Jewish so he's not very good at it. In fact, today he's having trouble controlling his kite – it's bobbing and weaving all over the sky. His wife Sarah, observing the scene from the window, calls out to him, 'Issy, I think it would be better if you had a piece of tail.'

Issy replies, 'When I asked you for that a little while ago, you told me to go fly a kite.'

* * *

The quarrel
Moshe and Hetty have been married for 10 years. One day, after their usual quarrel, Hetty says, 'You know, Moshe, I was a fool when I married you.'

'Yes, dear,' replies Moshe, 'but I was in love and I didn't notice it.'

* * *

Home truth
When Shlomo arrives home one evening, he finds his wife Sarah crying.

'What's the matter?' he asks her.

'I went to Dr Myers today for a check up on my blood pressure and after he'd finished, he said I can't make love to you.'

Morris asks, 'How'd he find out?'

* * *

The cooking lesson

Hannah is frying some eggs for her Sam's breakfast when he suddenly enters the kitchen and goes over to the cooker.

'Careful with the eggs,' Sam says, 'be careful…Now put in some more butter…*Oy veh*, you're cooking too many eggs at once…There's too many of them…So turn them already, turn them now…We need some more butter, but where are we going to get more butter? …They're going to stick…I said they're going to stick…Careful…I said be careful…Are you crazy?…You never listen to me when you're cooking, never…Hurry up, turn them now…Don't forget to salt them, you know how you always forget the salt…Use the salt now, use the salt, the salt, I said!'

Hannah stares at him, 'What on earth is wrong with you this morning? Don't you think I know how to fry a couple of eggs?'

Sam calmly replies, 'I just wanted to show you, dear, what it feels like when I'm driving with you in the car.'

* * *

Ooops – 2

Mervyn and Kitty are sitting in an expensive kosher restaurant, enjoying their salt beef and *latkes*, when Mervyn notices Kitty staring at a man at the next table. The man looks decidedly drunk, so Mervyn asks Kitty, 'You've been watching that man for some time now. Do you know him?'

'Yes,' she replies, 'he's my ex-husband.'

'Has he always been a heavy drinker?' Mervyn asks.

'No, not always,' Kitty replies, 'but he's been drinking like that ever since I left him six years ago.'

'That's remarkable,' says Mervyn, 'I didn't think anybody could celebrate that long.'

Kitty hasn't spoken to Mervyn since.

* * *

Knowing the rules

Naomi, recently married, meets her friend Emma out shopping.

'Hi Naomi,' says Emma, 'how's marriage treating you?'

'Not too bad, Emma,' replies Naomi, 'but tell me something – I seem to have forgotten the proper procedure. When one first gets married, how long should one wait before starting to point out to one's husband what disgusting habits he has?'

* * *

Abe and his wife Freda

Abe welcomes the slight impediment in Freda's speech because every now and then she has to stop to breathe.

On the other hand, Freda doesn't hate Abe enough to give him back his diamonds. She says, 'I know money can't buy me happiness and I'm suffering, but at least I'm suffering in comfort.'

* * *

Nothing ever changes

Daniel arrives home from work at 5pm and as soon as he steps through his front door, his wife Judith starts having a go at him. 'Why don't you ever wipe your feet before walking into the house?…I thought you said you were coming home at lunchtime today…Where's the shopping I asked you to get on the way home?…You left the toilet seat up again this morning…Don't you ever think of buying me *shabbes* flowers, like you used to do?'

This incessant criticism, nagging and complaining goes on for nearly two hours – nothing Daniel says or does seems to be right by her. By 7pm, Daniel has had enough. But he knows better than to have a go at Judith so he tries a more tactical approach.

'Darling,' he says, 'please – let's start again. I'll go back outside and shut the door. Then I'll open the door and come in. We can then pretend I've just come home. What do you think?'

'OK,' she replies.

So Daniel puts on his coat, goes outside, shuts the door, waits a minute, opens the door, and steps in with a smile on his face. He immediately announces, in a musical tone, 'Oh darling, I'm home.'

'And just where have you been?' says Judith. 'It's past seven o'clock!'

* * *

What a lovely sunny day

One morning, as soon as Isaac and Fay wake up, Isaac opens the curtains and says, 'Oh my, what a lovely sunny day it is today.'

The following day, as they are sitting on their terrace having tea and biscuits, Isaac looks up at the sky and says, 'What a beautiful sunny day it is today, dear.'

The next day, as they're driving into town to do some shopping, Isaac looks out the window and remarks, 'Isn't it a lovely sunny day today?'

By now, Fay is getting a bit *farmisht* by Isaac's regular ravings about the weather. So she says to him, 'What's with you? Are you going *meshugga*? What's with all the talk about sunny days?'

'It's because', replies Isaac, 'you told me once that one sunny day you're going to leave me and you're never coming back.'

* * *

A mourner's lament

As Leah is visiting her late father's grave, she passes close by a woman who is sobbing and wailing at another grave. Leah can easily hear the woman saying, 'Oh why, oh why did you die? Why did you have to die?' This question is repeated many times.

After paying her respects to her father, Leah is leaving the cemetery when she again passes the sobbing woman. She is still wailing, 'Why, oh why did you have to die?'

Leah feels pity for this woman and walks over to try to comfort her. 'Pardon me, I hope you don't mind me coming over, but I heard your cries of pain and anguish. I assume the deceased was a relative of yours?'

'No, she's not,' says the other woman, 'in fact, I never met her.'

'Then why are you so sad?' asks Leah. 'Who was she? Who is buried in this grave?'

'My husband's first wife,' replies the woman.

* * *

Resolving any problem

One day, Jacob asks his wife Yetta, 'You always carry a photo of me in your handbag. What on earth would you want with my photo?'

'Well,' replies Yetta, 'whenever I encounter a problem, no matter how impossible it might seem at first, I look at your picture and the problem doesn't seem a problem any longer – it just melts away.'

Jacob smiles with pride when he hears this. 'It doesn't really surprise me, Yetta,' he says. 'Haven't I always told you how miraculous and powerful I am for you?'

'Yes, I know you have,' replies Yetta, 'but the way it works is like this – when I take your photo out of my handbag and look at your face, I say to myself, "What problem can there be that's greater than this one?"'

* * *

Marriage research

Isaac has been quietly perusing a document for some time and his wife Rose is getting curious. So she asks him, '*Nu*, so what are you reading, Isaac?'

'Our *ketubah*,' he replies.

'But you've been staring at it now for nearly an hour,' she says.

'I know,' Isaac replies. 'I'm looking for something.'

'So what are you looking for, Isaac?' asks Rose.

'An expiry date,' he replies.

* * *

Home comforts

Maurice and Estelle are not having a good sex life. After yet another listless lovemaking session, Maurice decides to confront Estelle. 'How come you never tell me or indicate when you have an orgasm?'

Estelle looked at Maurice with contempt and replies, 'You're never home.'

* * *

Death wishes

Even though it is Issy and Yetta's 40th wedding anniversary, they still have their inevitable, regular quarrel. Only this time, it is more serious than ever before.

Issy shouts, 'When you die, Yetta, I'm going to get you a headstone that says, "Here Lies Yetta – Cold As Ever."'

'Oh yes?' she replies. 'When you die, Issy, I'm going to get you a headstone that says, "Here Lies Issy – Stiff At Last."'

* * *

Because I'm a man, that's why!

• Because I'm a man, when I catch a cold I need someone to bring me chicken soup and take care of me while I lie in bed and moan. You're a woman – you never get as sick as I do, so for you this isn't a problem.

• Because I'm a man, I can be relied upon to purchase basic groceries, like milk or *chollah*. Don't expect me to find exotic items like 'cumin' or 'tofu'. For all I know, these are the same thing. And never, ever expect me to purchase anything for which 'feminine hygiene product' is a euphemism.

• Because I'm a man, I don't want to visit your mother or have her come visit us or talk to her when she calls or think about her any more than I have to. Whatever you got her for Mother's Day is OK – I don't need to see it. And don't forget to pick up something for my mother too.

• Because I'm a man, you don't have to ask me if I liked the film. If you're crying at the end of it, chances are I didn't. And if you're feeling amorous afterwards, then I'll certainly remember the name and recommend it to others.

• Because I'm a man, I think what you're wearing is fine. I thought what you were wearing five minutes ago was also fine. Either pair of shoes is fine. With or without the belt, it looks fine. Your hair is fine. You look fine. Can we just go now?

* * *

For all you Moshes, an explanation to help you understand 'woman-speak'

FINE: This is the word she uses to end an argument when she feels she is right and you need to shut up. Never use 'Fine' to describe how she looks, as this will cause you to have one of those arguments.

FIVE MINUTES: This is half an hour. It's equivalent to the five minutes that your football game is going to last before you take out the rubbish, so it's an even trade.

NOTHING: This actually means something and you should be on your toes. It's usually used to describe the feeling she has of wanting to turn you inside out and upside down. It usually signifies an argument that will last 'Five Minutes' and end with 'Fine'.

GO AHEAD (With Raised Eyebrows): This is a dare, one that will result in her getting upset over 'Nothing' and end with the word 'Fine'.

GO AHEAD (Normal Eyebrows): This means 'I give up' or 'Do what you want because I don't care'. You'll get a 'Raised Eyebrow Go Ahead' in just a few minutes, followed by 'Nothing' and 'Fine' and she'll talk to you in about 'Five Minutes' when she cools off.

LOUD SIGH: This is not actually a word, but is a nonverbal statement often misunderstood by men. It means that she thinks you're an idiot at that moment and wonders why she's wasting her time standing there and arguing with you over 'Nothing'.

SOFT SIGH: Again, this is a nonverbal statement, not a word, and means that she's content. Your best bet is not to move or breathe and she'll stay content.

THAT'S OK: This is one of the most dangerous statements that she can make to you and means that she wants to think long and hard before paying you back for whatever it is that you've done. It's often used with the word 'Fine' and in conjunction with a 'Raised Eyebrow'.

GO AHEAD: At some point in the near future, you're going to be in some serious trouble.

PLEASE DO: This is not a statement, it's an offer. She is giving you the chance to come up with whatever excuse or reason you have for doing whatever it is that you've done. You have a fair chance with the truth, so be careful and you shouldn't get a 'That's OK'.

THANKS: She is thanking you. Don't faint. Just say 'You're welcome'.

THANKS A LOT: This is very different to 'Thanks'. She will say 'Thanks A Lot' when she's really ticked off at you. It signifies that you've offended her in some callous way and will be followed by the 'Loud Sigh'. Be careful not to ask what is wrong after the 'Loud Sigh' as she will only tell you 'Nothing'.

* * *

For all you Sadies, an explanation to help you understand 'man-speak'

IT'S A GUY THING: There's no rational thought pattern connected with this and you have no chance at all of making it logical.

CAN I HELP WITH DINNER?: What he really wanted to say was, 'Why isn't dinner already on the table?'

UH HUH; SURE, HONEY; OR YES, DEAR: This is a conditioned response and means absolutely nothing.

IT WOULD TAKE TOO LONG TO EXPLAIN: This is another way of saying, 'I have no idea how it works.'

I WAS LISTENING TO YOU. IT'S JUST THAT I'VE THINGS ON MY MIND: What this really means is, 'I wasn't listening to you because I was wondering if that blonde over there was wearing a bra.'

TAKE A BREAK, DARLING, YOU'RE WORKING TOO HARD: What he really wanted to say was, 'I can't hear the football match on the TV. Please turn off the vacuum cleaner.'

THAT'S INTERESTING, DEAR: This is another way of saying, 'Are you still talking?'

YOU KNOW HOW BAD MY MEMORY IS: This means, 'I remember all the words to "My Way"; the name of the first girl I kissed; and the registration numbers of every car I've owned – but I forgot your birthday.'

I WAS THINKING ABOUT YOU SO I GOT YOU THESE FLOWERS: This really means, 'The girl selling flowers on the corner was a real beauty, so I bought some from her.'

HEY, I'VE GOT MY REASONS FOR WHAT I'M DOING: But what he didn't add was, 'And I sure hope I think of some pretty good reasons soon.'

WHAT DID I DO THIS TIME?: What he really wanted to say was, 'What did you catch me at this time?'

I HEARD YOU: What this means is, 'I haven't the foggiest clue what you just said and I'm hoping desperately that I can fake it well enough so that you don't spend the next three days yelling at me.'

YOU KNOW I COULD NEVER LOVE ANYONE ELSE: This really means, 'I'm used to the way you shout at me, and I realise it could be worse.'

YOU LOOK TERRIFIC: What he really wanted to say was, 'Please don't try on one more outfit, I'm absolutely starving.'

* * *

Houses of Ill Repute (and *Kurvehs*)

Room service

Jacob is staying at a London hotel and decides to phone his friend. He calls the operator and in broken English with a heavy Eastern European/Yiddish accent, he asks, 'Can you get me please 266418.'

Ten minutes later, Jacob hears a knock on his door. When he opens it, he sees two gorgeous, sexy women standing there.

One of them says to him, 'Was it you who ordered two *shikses* for one night?'

* * *

The money maker
Leah and Sam, both in their seventies, are in financial difficulty. Their savings accounts have been slowly dwindling over recent years and now they have very little left. Sam, of course, blames Leah.

'It's your fault, Leah,' he says, 'you overspend week after week. Now you'll personally have to go out and find some more *gelt*.'

'But how do you expect me to make money at my age?' asks Leah.

'Well, you could go out on the streets and hustle,' replies Sam.

So at 6am next morning, Leah wakes up and goes to work. She doesn't return until 1am next morning. Sam notices that she is tired-looking, dirty and dishevelled – a complete wreck, in fact.

'Well Leah, how did you do?' asks Sam.

'I made £22.50,' she replies.

'So tell me, already,' asks Sam, 'who gave you the 50p?'

'Everyone gave me 50p,' Leah answers.

* * *

Why do you want to be that?
Three 12-year-olds, Benjy, Sidney and Oliver, are sitting on the balcony of Benjy's sixth-floor flat discussing the jobs they'd like to do when they grow up.

'I want to be an actuary,' Sidney says.

'Why do you want to be that?' the other two ask.

'Do you see that silver car down there?' Sidney replies. 'Well that's a Lexus IS250 and all actuaries drive Lexus cars.'

'Well,' says Oliver, 'I want to be a footballer.'

'Why do you want to be that?' the other two ask.

Oliver points to the car next to the Lexus and says, 'That car's a Bentley and all good footballers drive Bentley cars.'

Benjy says, 'When I grow up I want to be a *kurveh*.'

'Why do you want to be that?' the other two ask.

'Because my dad says my older sister is a *kurveh* and that Lexus and that Bentley are both hers.'

* * *

The *chassid*'s visit

When Shlomo and Moshe, two *chassids*, meet in town one Monday morning, Moshe is very surprised to see that Shlomo is all dressed up in his special *shabbes* clothes. He's wearing his *kippa*, his *tzitzit* is showing, he has a *siddur* and *tallis* bag under one arm and a *tefillin* bag under the other.

So Moshe asks, '*Oy veh*, Shlomo, where are you going all dressed up like that? It's not *shabbes*, you know.'

'Sssshhh,' replies Shlomo, 'I don't want anyone to know, but as I've never been to a brothel before, I thought I'd try one out.'

'OK, but what's with your *shabbes* gear and prayer tools?'

'Well,' replies Shlomo, 'if I like it there, I might decide to stay over the weekend.'

* * *

Farewell message

Boris, a *kunyehlemel*, is making his way to a *shivah* house by bus. But he gets confused, gets off at the wrong stop and ends up in a red light district. This doesn't deter Boris, however. Thinking he's in the right road, he finds the house number he's looking for and rings the doorbell. The door opens and there stands a voluptuous woman.

She immediately grabs hold of his arm, *schleps* him in, takes him upstairs and gives him sex. When the deed is done, Boris leaves the room. He's halfway down the stairs when the woman shouts to him, 'Excuse me, mister, haven't you forgotten something?'

Boris thinks for a second, then replies, 'Oh yes – I wish you long life.'

* * *

The *chassid*

A *chassid* arranges for a hooker to come to his room for the evening. They undress, get into bed and make mad, passionate love. Then the *chassid* jumps up, runs over to the window, takes a deep breath, runs out the door, returns, jumps back into bed with the hooker and repeats the performance.

The hooker is impressed with the gusto of the second encounter. The *chassid* then jumps up, runs over to the window, takes a deep breath, runs through the door, returns, jumps back into bed with the hooker and starts again.

This sequence is repeated four times. The hooker is totally amazed. Then after the fifth encore, she decides to try it herself. So she jumps up, goes to the window, takes a deep breath, runs through the door...and finds the other nine members of the *minyan*.

Unfaithfulness

Sneaky

Sam goes into a barber's shop and asks, 'How long before I can get a haircut?'

Issy looks around his shop and replies, 'About 30 minutes.'

Sam thanks him and leaves.

Two days later, Sam again enters the shop, 'How long before I can get a haircut?'

Issy looks around at the shop full of customers and says, 'About 45 minutes.'

Sam again thanks him and leaves.

A week later, Sam sticks his head into the shop and asks, 'How long before I can get a haircut?'

Issy looks around his shop and says, 'About 35 minutes.'

Sam once again thanks him and leaves.

Issy is bewildered by this strange behaviour, so he says to his assistant, 'Could you please follow that man and let me know where he goes. He keeps asking me how long he would have to wait for a haircut but doesn't return.'

Five minutes later, his assistant comes back, laughing aloud. Issy asks him, 'So where did the guy go when he left here?'

The assistant looks at Issy and replies, 'Your house.'

* * *

Who was it?

Yitzhak returns from a four-week business trip to New York and finds out that his wife Sadie has been unfaithful during his time away.

'Who was it?' he yells at Sadie. 'Was it that bastard Sam?'

'No,' replies Sadie, 'no, it wasn't Sam.'

'So was it Abe, that degenerate old man?'

'No, it certainly wasn't him.'

'Then it must have been that simpleton Moshe.'

'No, it wasn't Moshe either,' replies Sadie.

Yitzhak is now very angry and his blood pressure is sky high. 'What's the matter?' he cries out, 'Are none of my friends good enough for you?'

* * *

Death in the family

Becky meets her best friend while she's out shopping. 'Rebecca, did you know that Naomi passed away last week?'

'No, Becky, I didn't know,' replies Rebecca. 'How did Abe, that stupid husband of hers, take it?'

'Hard, Rebecca, very hard,' says Becky, 'but not as hard as Isaac, their lodger, whom everyone knew was having an affair with Naomi. Rumour has it that when Naomi died, Isaac just went to pieces. He couldn't eat, he couldn't sleep and he just sat around the house crying buckets.'

'So then what happened?' asks Rebecca.

'I'll tell you what happened,' answers Becky, 'a few days after the funeral, that stupid Abe said to Isaac, "Stop your crying, Isaac. Don't worry. I'll get married again!"'

* * *

True news story: birthday

Really, it's true. A woman decided to give her husband a laugh for his birthday so she came up with this practical joke – she would make him believe that he had won top prize in the lottery. (1) She gave one of her friends her husband's address, date of birth and lottery numbers and asked him to ring her husband at work on his birthday and pretend to be a lottery official. (2) With the help of a printer, she produced a letterhead containing the official lottery logo. (3) She told all of her husband's workmates of her joke and swore them to secrecy.

So, on his birthday, her husband got a phone call telling him of his win, quickly followed by a hand-delivered lottery letter confirming the win. All his workmates rejoiced with him. Then his wife arrived unannounced at his office and saw the celebrations taking place.

'Why didn't you ring me as soon as you found out you had won?' she teasingly said to him with a smile.

He replied, 'You stupid cow. I've been having an affair with your best friend for the last two years and now that I am worth over £6 million, I'm leaving you. Goodbye.'

* * *

The surprise

Maurice comes home one day to find his wife Hannah, an English teacher, in bed with his best friend.

'Darling,' Maurice cries, 'how could you? After all the years we've been together, I come home from work to find you like this. I am surprised.'

'No, no, my dear,' says Hannah, 'you are amazed. I am surprised.'

* * *

The homecoming surprise

Yitzhak was not the kind of person you would expect any sympathy from. Whenever something bad happened to anyone, he would always shrug his shoulders and say, 'Well, look on the bright side – it could have been worse.'

One day, something terrible happened to the married couple living next door to Yitzhak – the husband came home early from work and caught his wife in bed with another man, so he shot both his wife and her lover, then killed himself.

Soon, crowds began to gather in the street and many were in a state of shock. But as usual, Yitzhak shrugged his shoulders and said, 'Well, look on the bright side – it could have been worse.'

They all recoiled in horror. 'Don't be so stupid,' they told him, 'how on earth could it have been any worse?'

Yitzhak replied, 'Well, if the husband had come home early yesterday instead of today, I would be dead now.'

* * *

The stupid golfer

Hymie is an avid golfer (if truth be known, he's a golf fanatic). Every Sunday morning he gets up at 6am because he has an early tee time. He then plays golf all day long.

One Sunday morning, Hymie gets up early as usual, dresses quietly so as not to disturb his Leah, gets his clubs out of the study and goes to his car. But it's raining torrentially, there is snow mixed with the rain and the wind is blowing at 50 mph. So he goes back into the house, finds a weather website on the internet and discovers that it's going to be terrible weather all day long.

He then puts his clubs back into the study, quietly undresses, slips back into bed, cuddles up to Leah's back and whispers, 'The weather's terrible.'

Without moving, Leah replies, 'Can you believe my *meshugga* Hymie is out golfing?'

* * *

The marathon

Sadie is having a daytime affair while her husband Cyril is at work. One wet and rainy day she's in bed with her boyfriend Morris when to her horror she hears Cyril's car pull into the driveway. She looks out the window and yells to Morris, 'Quick, jump out the window, my husband's home early!'

'I can't jump out the window – it's raining,' says Morris.

'If my Cyril catches us together, he'll kill us both,' she says. 'He's got a jealous temper and a large gun. The rain is the least of your problems.'

So Morris gets out of bed, grabs his clothes and jumps out the window. As he begins running down the street in the pouring rain, he discovers he's run right into the middle of a marathon. There's not much he can do but continue to run alongside the real runners. Being naked, with his clothes tucked under his arm, he tries to blend in as best he can. After a while, a group of runners who have been studying him with some curiosity jog closer.

'Do you always run in the nude?' asks one of them.

'Oh yes,' replies Morris, gasping for air, 'it feels so wonderfully free.'

Another runner moves alongside. 'Do you always run carrying your clothes with you under your arm?'

'Oh, yes,' Morris answers, breathlessly, 'that way I can quickly get dressed at the end of the run and get in my car to go home.'

Then a third runner casts his eyes a little lower down and asks Morris, 'Do you always wear a condom when you run?'

'Oh no,' replies Morris, 'only when it's raining.'

* * *

Conversation in a restaurant

'What would you do if I suddenly died, Maurice?' says Sadie, 'Would you marry again?'

'No, Sadie, definitely not,' replies Maurice.

'Why ever not?' says Sadie. 'Don't you like being married?'

'You know I do,' replies Maurice.

'Then why do you say you wouldn't get married again?' asks Sadie.

'OK, Sadie, I was wrong,' replies Maurice, trying to end the conversation. 'Yes, I would get married again.'

Sadie then puts on a sad look and continues his 'interrogation'. 'You really would remarry?'

Maurice doesn't answer this but just groans very quietly.

'So would you live with her in…our house?' asks Sadie.

'Why not?' replies Maurice, beginning to enjoy himself, 'It's paid for, there's no outstanding mortgage.'

'And would you take my photos out of our silver frames and replace them with her photos?' asks Sadie.

'Yes, why not,' replies Maurice, 'that would seem like the correct thing to do.'

'And would you sleep with her in our marital bed, where we conceived our children?' asks Sadie.

'So where else do you think we would sleep?' replies Maurice.

'And would she use my golf clubs?' asks Sadie.

'Oh no,' replies Maurice, 'she's left-handed.'

Silence fills the air, then…'Oh, shit,' says Maurice.

* * *

Lost and found

Nathan goes to *shul* one *shabbes* and Rabbi Bloom almost faints when he sees him – Nathan has never sat foot inside a *shul* since his *Bar mitzvah*. At the end of the service, Rabbi Bloom goes over to Nathan and says, 'I'm very pleased to see you here today, what made you come?'

Nathan replies, 'I'll be honest with you, Rabbi. I lost my favourite hat about three months ago and I really miss it. A friend of mine told me that Kenneth Gold has a hat just like mine. My friend also told me that Gold comes to *shul* every *shabbes*, always takes off his hat before the service begins, leaves it in the cloakroom at the back of the *shul* and replaces it with his *yarmulke*. So I was going to leave after the *Torah* reading and steal Gold's hat.'

Rabbi Bloom says, 'Well Nathan, I notice that you didn't steal Gold's hat after all. While I'm very glad, please tell me why you changed your mind.'

'Well, Rabbi,' replies Nathan, 'after I heard your sermon on the Ten Commandments, I decided that I didn't need to steal Gold's hat.'

Rabbi Bloom smiles and says, 'I suppose you decided against it after you heard me talking about "Thou Shalt Not Steal"?'

'Not exactly, Rabbi,' replies Nathan. 'After you talked about "Thou Shalt Not Commit Adultery", I remembered where I left my hat.'

* * *

Where have you been?
Although married, Moshe is infatuated with his secretary Mary, so one lunchtime, he takes a chance and says to her, 'Let's go back to your place.'

To Moshe's surprise, Mary smiles and says, 'What a good idea, Moshe. Yes, I'd love to.'

They get to her house and make mad, passionate love all afternoon. Then, totally exhausted, they fall asleep and don't wake up until 7pm.

'*Oy veh*,' shouts Moshe, jumping out of her bed, 'just look at the time.'

As he's getting dressed, Moshe tells Mary to take his shoes into the garden and rub them thoroughly into the wet mud and grass. She does what she's told even though she doesn't know why. Moshe finishes dressing, puts on his shoes and drives home. As soon as he opens his front door, there's his wife Rifka waiting for him.

'So, where have you been?' demands Rifka, angrily.

'Darling, I can't lie to you,' replies Moshe. 'I've been having an affair with my secretary and we've been making love all afternoon. Then I fell asleep and didn't wake up until 7 o'clock.'

Rifka takes one look at his shoes and says, 'You lying *momzer*. You've been playing golf again.'

* * *

Special offers
Sam is hungry and stops off for a bite to eat at Minky's Kosher Salt Beef Bar. When the waiter asks him whether he'd like a drink to start, he orders a Maccabi beer. 'A good choice, sir, we have a special offer on this beer tonight – it's only going to cost you 1p.'

'That's really cheap,' exclaims Sam,

Then Sam quickly looks through the menu and says, 'I'd

like a big plate of your best salt beef with *latkes, haimisher* cucumbers and English mustard.'

'Certainly,' replies the barman, 'but that's going to cost you real money.'

'So how much is real money?' asks Sam.

'Five pence,' replies the waiter.

'Five pence?' says Sam. 'That's ridiculous. You'll loose money on this. I'd like to talk to the owner. Where is he?'

'He's upstairs with my wife,' replies the waiter.

'What's he doing upstairs with your wife?' asks Sam.

'The same thing as I'm doing to his business,' replies the waiter.

* * *

A cheating riddle

Q. How does a Jewish wife cheat on her husband?

A. She has a headache with the postman.

* * *

What a spectacle!

Rifka is a simple young housewife who enjoys many simple things in life. One day, as she is walking through a department store, Rifka notices a pair of X-ray glasses on special sale. She is not convinced that such a thing can really work, but the store assistant convinces her that they are indeed X-ray glasses. So she buys a pair.

As soon as she leaves the store, Rifka opens the package, puts on her new X-ray glasses and immediately sees everyone around her naked. She removes them and everyone has their clothes on. She puts them on and everyone is naked again.

'How cool,' she thinks. 'I can't wait to get home to show them to Gary.'

So she decides to cut her shopping and finish it the next day. When she arrives home, she finds Gary and the young lady from next door in bed together. She puts on the glasses and they are naked. She takes off the glasses and the two are still naked. She puts them back on and they are still naked. Rifka then says, 'Bother, I just paid £50 for these glasses and they've broken already!'

* * *

The secret message

Benny has been having an affair with Gina, his Italian secretary, for several years. One night, during one of their clandestine 'meetings', Gina shocks him by telling him that she is pregnant and that he is the father. Not wanting to ruin his marriage, Benny says, 'I've done very well in business, as you know, and I'm prepared to pay you a large sum of money if you'll go to Italy to secretly have your baby. Furthermore, if you'll stay in Italy to raise the baby, I'll also provide generous child support until the baby turns 18. What do you say?'

Gina thinks for a while then replies, 'OK, Benny. You're an honest man and I trust you. I'll move back to Italy and live with my parents. But how will you know when the baby is born?'

'To keep it discreet,' he tells her, 'simply send me a postcard with the word SPAGHETTI written on the back. I'll then immediately arrange for child support payments to begin.'

One day, about nine months later, Benny comes home to his confused wife. 'Darling,' she says, 'you received a very strange postcard today.'

'OK, let me see it,' he says.

His wife hands him the postcard and as she watches him read the card, he turns white and faints.

Written on the card is: SPAGHETTI, SPAGHETTI, SPAGHETTI. TWO WITH MEATBALLS, ONE WITHOUT.

* * *

The fishing trip

Jonathan phones home and tells his wife Rachel, 'Darling, my boss has just asked me to go fishing with him. We're leaving this afternoon and several of our top clients are joining us there. This is a fantastic opportunity for me to get that promotion I've been waiting for, so could you please pack my small suitcase for me. Put in enough clothes for a week, including my new blue silk pyjamas and get out my rod and tackle box. We're leaving the office in about 30 minutes and we'll stop by the house to pick up my things.'

Rachel thinks this a bit odd, but nevertheless does what her husband asks. One week later, Jonathan returns home looking quite tired. Rachel welcomes him back and asks him if he caught many fish.

'Yes, darling,' Jonathan replies, 'lots of salmon and rainbow trout. We ate all we caught. But why didn't you pack my blue silk pyjamas like I asked?'

'But I did,' Rachel replies innocently, 'they were in your tackle box.'

Moral: Men shouldn't think they can outsmart women!

* * *

Einstein's late night

Einstein the scientist starts getting home later and later in the evenings. Then one day, he comes home at 2.30am. His shirt is torn, there are lipstick stains on his neck, and his wiry hair is even more dishevelled than it usually is. As soon as he sets foot inside his house, his wife jumps out from behind the front door, grabs hold of him, shakes him and shouts, 'So why have you once again come home so late?'

'Well,' he replies, 'as I was leaving work at 5.30pm today, I met some friends and they persuaded me to go with them and have a few quick drinks. We then met some good-looking young ladies inside the bar and…well, to be honest, we all started to drink more than we could handle, as you can probably see. But I managed to sober up just enough to see how late it was. So I called a taxi and…here I am.'

'You're a liar,' she screams at him, 'you were in the lab again working on your stupid relativity theory, weren't you?'

* * *

A wives riddle

Q: What's the difference between an Italian wife, a French wife and a Jewish wife?

A: When an Italian wife is having an affair, she says, '*Mamma mia.*' When a French wife is having an affair, she says, 'Ooh-la-la.' And when a Jewish wife is having an affair, she says, 'Issy, the ceiling needs painting.'

Separation and Divorce

Getting back

Issy goes to see Rabbi Levy.

'Rabbi,' he says, 'you remember Sarah and I got divorced last year?'

'Yes, Issy, I remember.'

'Well, Rabbi, the thing is, my friends are telling me that Sarah is feeling very sorry she divorced me. They think she wants to get back with me. What do you think I should do?'

'Nothing,' said Rabbi Levy, 'do absolutely nothing.'

'You seem so sure about this, Rabbi. Why?'

'Yes, Issy, I am,' replied Rabbi Levy. 'You see, wives are very much like fishermen – complaining about the one they caught, and bragging about the one that got away.'

* * *

Knowledge is a wonderful thing
Rose has filed for divorce. When she and Sam finally attend the court hearing, the judge asks her, 'So what do you find wrong with your husband?'

'Well, among other things, your Honour, he lies; he's aggressive; he steals my money; and he's poor in bed. In fact he's a bit of a *shlemazel*.'

'Those are serious allegations,' says the judge. 'Can you prove them?'

'Prove them?' replies Rose. 'I don't have to, your Honour. Everyone knows what Sam is like.'

'If you knew all of this,' asks the judge, 'why on earth did you marry him?'

'But I didn't know it before I married him,' replies Rose.

Sam then shouts out, 'She did too, your Honour.'

* * *

Reasons for divorce
Rose goes to see Max, her solicitor, and says, 'I want to divorce my Harry.'

'Why do you want to do that?' Max asks. 'I thought you said he was a man of rare gifts.'

'He is,' replies Rose, 'he's never given me a present in 20 years of marriage.'

'Very funny, Rose. Is there another reason why you want a divorce?' asks Max.

'Yes there is,' replies Rose. 'I want a divorce because of his appearance.'

'That's an unusual reason,' says Max.

'Not really,' says Rose. 'Harry hasn't put in an appearance at home for four years.'

* * *

I know everything

Sharon is driving her six-year-old daughter Emma to her friend's house for tea. On the way, Emma asks, 'How old are you, Mummy?'

'Why darling,' says Sharon, 'you're not supposed to ask a woman her age. It's not polite.'

'OK,' says Emma, 'how much do you weigh, Mummy?'

'Really, Emma,' says Sharon, 'that's a very personal question.'

Emma carries on, 'Why did you and Daddy get divorced, Mummy?'

'OK, that's enough questions for today, darling. Anyway, we're here now. Let's take you inside.'

Later, Emma and her friend are playing upstairs while their mothers are finishing tea. 'My mummy won't tell me anything about her,' Emma says to her friend.

'All you need do,' says her friend, 'is look at your mum's driver's licence. It's just like a report card – it has everything you need to know about her on it.'

Later, when she returns home, Emma says, 'I know how old you are, Mummy, you're 30.'

Sharon is surprised. 'How did you know that, darling?'

'I also know, Mummy, that you weigh 10 stone 3 pounds.'

Sharon is even more surprised. 'How did you find that out, darling?'

'I know everything, Mummy,' says Emma. 'I even know why you and Daddy got divorced.'

'OK,' says Sharon, 'so tell me why we got divorced.'

'Because you got an F in sex.'

* * *

Calculating your age

Sadie is divorcing her husband Moshe. After two months of waiting, her case is finally being heard in court.

The judge asks Sadie, 'So how old are you?'

'I'm 40 years old, your Honour.'

The judge replies, 'Please answer my question honestly. How old are you?'

'I'm 40 years old, your Honour,' answers Sadie again.

'Well,' says the judge, 'you're not being truthful. It's written down here that you were born in August 1940 and that means you're over 60.'

'But your Honour,' replies Sadie, 'I'm not counting the last 20 years with my husband.'

'Why not?' asks the judge.

'You call that living?' replies Sadie.

* * *

The whole divorce

Rivkah is in court, finalising her divorce. As soon as she signs the last paper and realises her divorce is complete, she says out loud, 'At last, now all I have to do is arrange for a *Get*.'

The judge hears her and asks, 'Mrs Gold, what do you mean by "*Get*"?'

Rivkah replies, 'Well your Honour, a *Get* is a religious ceremony that's required under the Jewish religion in order to receive a divorce.'

'You mean like a *Brit Milah*?' asks the judge.

'Yes,' Rivkah replies, 'it's very similar. But in a *Get*, you get rid of the whole *shmuck*.'

* * *

A holy event
Did you hear about Rivkah, who divorced her bagel-maker husband and remarried a poet?

She went from batter to verse.

* * *

Relative problems
Renee is talking to her friend Talya. 'So Talya,' she says, 'you're telling me that you want to divorce your Mervyn due to incompatibility problems?'

'Yes, you've got it in one,' Talya replies.

'Why? Aren't your relations any good?' asks Renee.

'Well,' replies Talya, 'mine are wonderful, but Melvyn's... *Oy!* what *yachnas* and *krechtzers!*'

* * *

Best airline
Q: What's the best airline to fly if you want a divorce?
A: Easyget.

* * *

Logic wins the day
Rachel and Lionel are in the final phase of getting divorced, but, like many other divorces, it's not plain sailing. They are now in court one last time – the issue being, who is going to keep their one and only child?

Rachel tells the judge, 'Your Honour, as I'm the one who carried my daughter, and as I'm the one who painfully gave birth to my daughter, it's therefore only logical that I should be the one to keep her.'

The judge then asks Lionel, 'Have you anything to say about your wife's logic?'

Lionel thinks for a moment, then rises slowly to his feet and replies, 'Yes your Honour, I do. If we're into logic, then my question is this – if I insert a coin in a Pepsi vending machine and I get my can, whose can is it – the machine's or mine?'

Family Fortunes

Bundles of Joy/The First Cut (and *Mohels*)

A visit to the butcher

Gary goes to Jacob's Butchers for some pickled brisket. As Jacob is wrapping his order, Gary says to him, 'So, Jacob, you can congratulate me. Mine Suzy has just given birth to a beautiful nine-pound baby boy.'

Jacob nods his approval in an absent-minded kind of way and says, 'Nine pounds, eh? With or without bones?'

* * *

A sexual riddle

Q. When a couple have a baby, who is responsible for its sex?
A. I'll lend him my car, the rest is up to him.

* * *

Time and motion

Miriam gets married and a year later goes into hospital and gives birth to triplets. All her family and friends are shocked when they hear the news – they know of no one who has had triplets before.

As soon as she hears the news, Miriam's *shviger* Fay goes to visit her daughter-in-law in hospital. As soon as she arrives, Fay hands over the bunch of grapes and says, 'What a surprise, Miriam. No one on our side of the family has ever had twins before, yet alone triplets.'

'Yes, it was a bit of a shock,' replies Miriam, 'but I'm

getting over it. In fact, my doctor tells me that triplets only happen once every hundred thousand times.'

'*Oy veh*, Miriam,' says Fay, 'how on earth did you find the time to do your housework?'

* * *

The three sons
Issy leaves school and decides to open a small grocery store. He's good to his customers and the store does well. Soon he meets a beautiful girl and within months they are married. A year later, a boy arrives. Issy calls Dr Myers, a *mohel*, who performs the *Bris* and charges Issy £50.

Over the next 12 months, his business begins to take off and Issy opens a large supermarket. It too does well and they buy a nice house near their business. Then a second boy arrives and once again Issy calls Dr Myers, who performs the *Bris* and who this time charges him £250.

Over the next two years, Issy opens more supermarkets and even moves into the catering business. They move home again, this time to a large eight-bedroom house in one of the smartest areas of town. Then, once again, his wife presents him with a son and once again Issy requests the services of Dr Myers, who performs the *Bris*. This time, Dr Myers charges Issy £1,000.

As Issy hands over the cheque, he says to Dr Myers, 'Over the time we've been using you, your charges have increased by far more than inflation. Why should this be so? Is it because I'm wealthy?'

Dr Myers replies, 'No, absolutely not. My £50 charge was for a *Bris*, my £250 charge was for a ritual circumcision and my £1,000 charge was for an extra special *shmuckelotomy*.'

* * *

A cut above the rest

Emanuel the *mohel* comes home early in a nervous state. His hands are shaking violently. He has just performed a circumcision on an elderly man and although it went well he's worried that one day things might really go wrong. He now thinks he should take out some professional insurance and calls Monty, who is an insurance broker.

'Monty,' says Emanuel, 'I need some malpractice cover designed for *mohels*.'

'This I've never heard before,' says Monty, 'but give me a day to investigate.'

Next day, Monty calls back, 'Do you want the good news or the bad news?'

'So give me the good news first,' says Emanuel.

'No regular insurance company will offer you such insurance. But Lloyds of London will insure you for up to £1 million at a premium of £500 per year.'

'*Nu*, and the bad news?' asks Emanuel.

'There's a two-inch deductible.'

* * *

The rabbi and the bear

Rabbi Bloom from London is visiting two friends in America. One is a priest and the other a Pentecostal preacher. As soon as they meet up, they start to talk shop. Their discussion centres on whether preaching to people is really that hard. They quickly agree that a real challenge would be to preach to a bear and they decide to experiment. Each will go into the woods, find a bear and preach to it.

A week later, they're all together to discuss the experience. Father Carroll, who has his arm in a sling and is on crutches, speaks first. 'Well,' he says, 'I went into the woods, found a bear and began to read to him from the Baltimore Catechism. Unfortunately, the bear wanted nothing to do with me and begun to slap me about. I quickly grabbed my holy water and, the saints be praised, he became very subdued. My bishop is coming out next week to give him his first communion and confirmation.'

Reverend Billy Bob speaks next. He is in a wheelchair, with an arm and both legs in casts. 'Well, brothers, you know that we don't sprinkle – we dunk. I found a bear and began to read to him from God's Holy Word. But that bear wanted nothing to do with me. So I took hold of him and we began to wrestle. Up and down the hills we wrestled until we come to a creek, where I quickly dunked and baptised him. He immediately became very subdued and we spent three days in fellowship, praising God's Holy Word.'

They both then look down at Rabbi Bloom who is lying in a hospital bed, is wearing a full body cast, is in traction and has IVs and monitors running in and out of his torn body. Rabbi Bloom looks up at his two friends and says, 'When I found a bear, I found preaching to him very easy. But *oy veh*, did he get touchy about the circumcision!'

* * *

The *Bris*

The *Bris* is over. Baby Sam has been circumcised and the rabbi, family and friends have all left the house. Moshe and Sadie are quietly sitting in their lounge when their four-year-old son Benny comes crying into the room. Sadie asks him what is wrong.

Benny sobs, 'In his speech, Rabbi Bloom said he wants us brought up in a Jewish home – and I want to stay with you guys!'

* * *

A marketing rabbi
Did you hear about the famous *mohel* Rabbi Bloom, who ran his own PR company? He saved his own clippings.

* * *

New knowledge
Five-year-old Benny comes home from Hebrew school one day and says to his parents, 'I learned something interesting at school today.'

'That's nice, Benny,' says his father. 'What did you learn today?'

Benny thinks for a moment, then replies, 'Daddy, have all the men in our family had their willies criticised?'

His mother laughs out loud. 'Oh Benny, darling, the word is "circumcised", not "criticised", but either way the answer is still "YES!"'

* * *

A fairy-story riddle
Q: What's the name of the fairy story about an uncircumcised troll?
A: Rumpled Foreskin.

* * *

A doctor's solution
Ruth's baby boy is born with only one eyelid. '*Oy veh*! What am I going to do?' she says to her doctor.

'Don't worry,' he replies, 'after the *Bris*, we will take the little bit of skin from down there and make him a nice new eyelid.'

'But if you do that,' says Ruth, 'won't it will make him cock-eyed?'

'On the contrary,' says the doctor, 'it will give him good foresight.'

The nurses' visits

When Lionel was born, his parents decided not to have him circumcised, despite objections from their rabbi. So Lionel spends the first 18 years of his life avoiding talking about his lack of Jewishness. Then one day he decides to solve the problem – he books himself into hospital to be circumcised.

The day following his operation, Bernie, one of his friends, stops by to see how Lionel is doing. While he's sitting with Lionel in his private hospital room, Bernie's amazed at the frequency with which different nurses enter Lionel's room. Some come with fresh glasses of water, some with bowls of fruit and some with magazines and books. Some offer to make his bed again, some retake his temperature and blood pressure, and some offer to give him a relaxing massage.

'You lucky so-and-so,' says Bernie, 'what's with all this attention from the nurses? You look OK to me.'

'I feel OK too,' replies Lionel, with a large smile on his face, 'but when the nurses heard that my circumcision required 25 stitches, they immediately formed a little fan club for me.'

* * *

A nursery riddle

Q: How can you tell a Jewish baby boy in a nursery?
A: He's the one with the heartburn.

* * *

Childhood

Thinking ahead

Little Simon has been naughty and is sent to bed by his father. He has only been in bed for a few minutes when he shouts downstairs, 'Daddy, oh Daddy.'

'What do you want?' asks his father.

'I'm thirsty, Daddy,' replies Simon. 'Can you bring me up a glass of water?'

'No,' says his father, 'you had your chance earlier. Now get to bed and turn off the light.'

A few minutes later: 'Daddy, oh Daddy.'

'WHAT DO YOU WANT?' shouts his father.

'I told you, Daddy, I'm very thirsty. Can I please have a drink of water?'

'I've already told you the answer. If you ask again, you'll be punished.'

Again, a few minutes later: 'Daddy, oh Daddy.'

'WHAT IS IT THIS TIME?' shouts his father.

'When you come upstairs to punish me, Daddy, can you bring a drink of water with you?'

* * *

Strongmen

Little Isaac and his friend John were having an argument about whose father was the strongest. John says, 'Do you know the North Sea? Well, my dad's the one who dug the hole for it.'

Isaac replies, 'That's nothing! Do you know the Dead Sea? Well my dad's the one who killed it.'

* * *

Entry to heaven

Fay's son Harry is always getting into mischief, and she is getting quite exasperated by his antics. One day, Fay says to him, 'Harry, how do you expect to get into heaven when you're always so naughty?'

Harry thinks about this question for a little while, then replies, 'Well, Mum, I'll run in and out and in and out and I'll keep on slamming the gates of heaven until the angel at the gates says what you always say to me: 'For heaven's sake, Harry, come in or stay out.'

* * *

House move

Little Esther is talking to her friend Rebecca. 'Have you moved into your new house, Rebecca?'

'Yes,' replies Rebecca, 'we moved in last Sunday.'

'Do you like it?'

'Oh yes, it's a much bigger house than the one we had before. We all now have our own bedrooms. All except my poor mum – she's still in with Dad.'

* * *

Playtime learning

Four-year-old Moshe is playing in his garden with his friend Mary. They're splashing around in his paddling pool and quickly get thoroughly soaked, so they decide to take off their wet clothes. Moshe looks at little Mary, then looks down at himself, and then says, '*Oy*, I just didn't realise there was so much difference between Catholics and Jews.'

* * *

OK for Daddy

Little Henry is on the beach with his parents in Eastbourne when he says to his mother, 'Mummy, can I go swimming in the sea?'

'No, *bubbeleh*,' she replies, 'the water is too deep and too rough for you.'

'But Daddy has just gone in,' says Henry.

'I know, darling, but your daddy's insured.'

* * *

Aren't children fantastic?

- Little Moshe got lost at the Maccabi club and found himself in the women's changing room. When he was spotted, the room burst into shrieks, with ladies grabbing towels and running to hide. Moshe watched in amazement and shouted, 'What's wrong, haven't you ever seen a little boy before?'

- While working for my *shul* delivering lunches to elderly Jewish women living at home, I used to take my four-year-old daughter Esther with me. She was always intrigued by the various appliances of old age, such as walking sticks, zimmer frames and wheelchairs. One day I found Esther staring at a pair of false teeth soaking in a glass of water. As I braced myself for the inevitable barrage of questions, she merely turned and whispered, 'The tooth fairy will never believe this.'

- When four-year-old Sam opened the family Bible, something fell out of it. He picked up the object and looked at it. It was old leaf that had been pressed between the pages. 'Mummy, look what I found,' he said. 'What have you found, *bubbeleh*?' I asked. Sam replied, 'I think it's Adam's underwear.'

* * *

Inevitable changes

Little Sam and Melissa are very good friends. They attend the same school, are in the same class and every day without fail follow the same lunchtime routine – they sit down together, open their lunch boxes together and both eat chicken sandwiches (their favourite) together.

Five years later, they're still following the same routine. But then one day, as Sam is eating his chicken sandwich, he's shocked to see that Melissa is eating a smoked salmon sandwich.

'Missy,' says Sam, looking upset, 'you're not eating a chicken sandwich. I thought you said you would only ever eat chicken.'

'I still love chicken, Sam,' replies Melissa, 'but I have to stop eating it.'

'Why?' asks Sam.

Melissa points to her lap and replies, 'Because I'm starting to grow feathers down here.'

'I don't believe it,' says Sam. 'Show me.'

'OK,' says Melissa and she lifts up her skirt and lowers her panties.

Sam looks very closely and after a few seconds says, 'I see them too, Missy. I think you're right to stop eating chicken.'

Their new lunchtime routine continues for another six months, with Sam eating chicken and Melissa eating smoked salmon. Then one day he brings in a peanut butter sandwich.

'Missy,' he says, 'I've given up chicken. I'm growing feathers down there too.'

'Can I see?' asks Melissa.

'OK,' says Sam and he pulls down his trousers and pants.

'You've left it very late, Sam,' she says. 'You've already started to grow the *polkeh* and also the *matzoh* balls for the chicken soup.'

* * *

Why I love children

Rivkah is trying hard to get the tomato ketchup to come out of the bottle. As she is banging the bottom of the bottle the phone rings, so she asks her four-year-old Faye to answer it.

'Mummy, it's the rabbi,' shouts Faye. But before Rivkah can get to the phone, Faye says to the rabbi, 'My mummy can't come to the phone to talk to you right now. She's hitting the bottle.'

* * *

Things children say

- Sam watches his mother breastfeeding his new baby sister. After a while he asks, 'Mummy, why have you got two? Is one for hot and one for cold milk?'
- Sarah asks her *bubbeh*, 'How old are you?' *Bubbeh* replies, 'I'm so old, darling, I just don't remember any more.' So Sarah says, 'If you don't remember, you must look in the back of your panties. Mine say "Five to six".'
- Little Issy is in his bedroom looking worried. When his mother asks what is troubling him, he replies, 'I don't know what'll happen with this bed when I get married, Mummy. How will my wife fit in?'
- Howard is listening to his father reading him a Bible story. 'The man named Lot was warned to take his wife and flee out of the city but his wife looked back and was turned to salt.' Concerned, Howard asks, 'What happened to the flea, Daddy?'

* * *

Who will buy?

One afternoon, little Benjy returns home from school and finds his father in the lounge watching an auction of racing horses on the TV sports channel. As Benjy stares at the screen, he can't help noticing a man moving from one horse to another, running his hands up and down the horse's legs, rump and chest. After a few minutes of this, Benjy asks, 'Daddy, why is the man doing that?'

'Because', replies his father, 'when you're buying horses, you have to make sure that they're healthy and in good condition before you buy.'

Benjy looks a bit worried. 'Daddy,' he says, 'I think Uncle Hymie wants to buy Mummy.'

* * *

Not seeing eye to eye
There are three brothers called David, Henry and Alan. One day, they meet Peter, who has just moved into the house next door to them. Unfortunately, Peter is cross-eyed.

'What's your name?' Peter asks David.

'Henry,' replies Henry.

'I wasn't talking to you,' Peter says to Henry.

'But I didn't say anything,' says Alan.

* * *

What *saychel*! And in someone so young!
One morning, young Benjy is watching, fascinated, as his mother smoothes some Nivea cream on her face. 'Why are you doing that, Mummy?' he asks.

'To make myself beautiful, that's why,' replies his mother, who then begins removing the cream with a tissue.

'What's the matter, Mummy?' asks Benjy. 'Are you giving up?'

* * *

The latest doll

Little Emma is talking to Naomi, her best friend. 'My mum has just bought me the latest Barbie doll for my birthday. It's a Jewish mother Barbie doll.'

'Oh you lucky thing,' says Naomi. 'So what does the doll do, Emma?'

'When you press her button,' replies Emma, 'she cries out, "*Oy veh*, enough with the button already!"'

* * *

Courtesy seating

Young Benny arrives home from school and says to his mother, 'Mummy, when Daddy was taking me to school on the bus this morning, he asked me to give up my seat to a lady who was standing next to us. So I did. But do you think I should have given up my seat?'

'Well Benny,' replies his mother, 'I think it was a very nice thing to do. I always appreciate someone giving up their seat for me when all the seats are taken.'

'I know that, Mummy,' says Benny, 'but I was sitting on Daddy's lap at the time.'

Bar Mitzvahs and *Bat Mitzvahs*

Bar mitzvah present

Avrahom is a 12-year-old known for his total lack of religious study, so when his *Bar mitzvah* day arrives, Rabbi Bloom is not about to let this go without comment. Avrahom performs his *Bar mitzvah* as best he can with his minimal preparation and when it comes time to receive his presents, Avrahom gets what most *Bar mitzvah* boys are given: a daily prayer book; a set of Jewish Festivals prayer books; a *kiddush* cup from the congregation's ladies' guild; an encyclopaedia – *The History of the Jewish People from Bible Times to the Present*; and a Bible (Old Testament).

Rabbi Bloom then addresses the *Bar mitzvah* boy, 'My dear Avrahom. You have received today a number of treasures of Judaism in book form that will surely enrich your life and make it holy in the eyes of God. I also have a gift for you.'

With that, Rabbi Bloom pulls out an umbrella from behind the lectern and says to Avrahom, 'I present you with this umbrella because I want to give you something that at least I know for certain you will open.'

* * *

No help needed

Issy, a reform Jew, is invited to his nephew's *Bar mitzvah*. The invitation also says that they would like him to do an *aliyah*. Not being a regular *shul* goer, he learns how to do it. Everyday he practises, '*Barachu et hashem hamevorach ...baruch hashem hamevorach leolam vaed.*'

On the day before the *Bar mitzvah*, he practises it one more time and when he goes to sleep that night, he is confident that he knew it well.

The day of the *Bar mitzvah* arrives and soon it is his turn in the *shul*. He goes up and says, '*Barachu et hashem hamevorach.*'

Everyone behind him then says, '*Barachu hashem hamevorach leolam vaed.*'

'SHUT UP,' he shouts out, 'I can do it myself!'

* * *

The gold spoon

As the catering staff are clearing up after Benjy's *Bar mitzvah* party, they notice that one of the gold spoons is missing – and it's the one from where Rabbi Bloom sat. So they tell the hosts, Moshe and Sadie, of the disappearance.

'Can you believe it, Sadie?' says Moshe, 'But how can we call our Rabbi a *gonif*? We'll just have to keep quiet about it.'

Twelve months later, while out buying bagels one Sunday morning, Moshe finds himself next to his rabbi.

'Moshe, I'm glad we've met,' says Rabbi Bloom. 'What's the problem, why have you been avoiding me?'

Moshe replies, 'Now that you ask, Rabbi, I've been avoiding you ever since we discovered one of our gold spoons missing from Benjy's party.'

Rabbi Bloom says, 'But why didn't you ask me about this? I put the spoon in Benjy's *tefillin* bag. He obviously hasn't opened it since his *Bar mitzvah* day.'

* * *

The *Bar mitzvah* space boy

Abe has done very well in business and has amassed a small fortune. Now he's looking to create the most unique and spectacular *Bar mitzvah* ever for his son David. But what should it be? He dismisses the *Bar mitzvah* safari – too many families have already done it. But then, after much investigation, Abe is sure he has cracked it – he'll rent a spaceship and David can be the first *Bar mitzvah* space boy. He starts on the plans immediately.

In due course, the spaceship takes off with his family and friends (and his rabbi, of course) on board. When they return, the media are there to find out how the journey has gone.

The first person off the shuttle is the *bubbeh*.

'How was the service, grandma?' asks the *Jewish Chronicle* reporter.

'OK,' she replies.
'And how was David's speech?'
'OK.'
'So how was the food?'
'OK.'
'Everything was just OK? Why aren't you more enthusiastic? What went wrong?'
'There was no atmosphere,' she replies.

* * *

Mistaken identity

One morning, Hannah is on a bus on her way to the shopping centre when she notices a man sitting opposite her. 'Hello,' she says to him, 'do you recognise me?'

'No I don't,' he replies.

'Are you joking?' says Hannah. 'Are you really saying you don't remember me?'

'Madam,' he replies, 'I've never seen you before.

'*Oy veh*, you're going to be so embarrassed when I tell you who I am,' says Hannah.

'OK,' he says, 'why do you think you know me?'

'Because I went to your *Bar mitzvah*, that's why,' replies Hannah.

'You've made a mistake then,' he says, 'because I'm not even Jewish.'

'You're not Jewish?' says Hannah. 'Then please give me back my present.'

* * *

Great for a *Bar mitzvah/Bat mitzvah* speech

'And to my dear parents. From the moment I came into this world, you've "washed" over me – or is it "watched" over me – I forget which. Probably both.'

* * *

The *Bar mitzvah* invitation

Dear ....

It is with great stress (emotional and physical) and unbelievable financial hardship beyond your comprehension that Rebecca and I cordially invite you to join us in *kvelling* over our wonderful son, Jonathan Sam, as he is called up to read the *maftir and haftorah* on his *Bar mitzvah* day.

Jonathan Sam's special service takes place on *Shabbes*, 19 May at the local synagogue. We realise this service might take place on the day of the biggest football match of the season, but you can always tape it – the match, that is, not the service.

The service commences at the ungodly (please excuse the language) hour of 9 o'clock in the morning and we would like you to be there at this time, even though you don't really need to be there until 10.30am, when the real action starts.

The service lasts for three hours and we hope you will be able to survive our rabbi's speech and our *chazan*'s voice. If you do, you can skip the *kiddush* (which is usually only biscuits and grape juice), which will take place in the Ladies' Guild room. This is just for those not invited to our main affair, which takes place later on that evening.

So please join us at 7pm for an over-the-top, *shmaltzy*, ostentatious semi-kosher evening meal at the MCC (Mishegass Country Club). Rebecca wants me to mention that we had to join the MCC just to book their hall and, *oy veh*, you wouldn't believe how much they charged us.

We've booked lots of expensive and noisy entertainment, including Minky's Kosher Jammers Orchestra (with six singers) and Moshe the Jester.

Apart from Jonathan Sam's friends, the guests will include 50 unruly teenagers, no doubt wearing expensive outfits and fake bling, and 70 middle-aged adults with lots of botox and real bling. At least a quarter of the guests will be hormonally and/or chronologically challenged, while others will act stupid while under the influence of the Palwin table wine we've ordered. And no doubt many will complain about the food (we would hope that you won't be one of them).

Please have the courtesy to complete the enclosed RSVP card in the next few days. I don't want to receive it at the last minute – I just can't take any more stress. Also note that if you indicate on the card that you will be attending, I will have no choice but to invoice you £100 per person if you subsequently don't show up for any reason.

In terms of what present to give Jonathan Sam, may we suggest it should be: flat; made of paper; with a signature and account number on it; and presented inside a small white envelope. Any other types of gift are a waste of your time and ours.

We hope you can make it.

PS: Please bring your own *kippot*, as I don't have any money left to buy these.

Parents

Conversation with mother

'Can I leave the children with you tonight, Mum?'

'Why, are you going out?'

'Yes I am.'

'So aren't you going to tell your mother who you're going out with?'

'Oh I'm just going out with a friend.'

'I don't know why you left your husband, he was so good to you.'

'But you know I didn't leave him, Mum, he left me!'

'I think you let him leave you and now you go out with anybody.'

'I don't go out with anybody. So, can I bring the children over or not?'

'I never left you to go out with anybody except your father.'

'There are many things that you did that I don't do.'

'So, what are you hinting at?'

'Nothing, Mum. I just need to know if I can bring the children over tonight.'

'You're staying the night with him? What would your husband say if he knew?'

'My ex-husband wouldn't care. From the day he left, he never slept alone!'

'So, you're going to sleep over at this loser's place?'

'He's not a loser.'

'Any man who goes out with a divorcee with children is a loser.'

'I don't want to argue with you, Mum – should I bring over the children or not?'

'Poor children, with such a mother.'

'A mother such as what?'

'With no stability. No wonder your husband left you.'

'MUM. ENOUGH IS ENOUGH, ALREADY!'

'Please don't scream at me. You probably scream at this loser too.'

'So now you're worried about the loser?'

'Ah, you admit he's a loser, then. I guessed he was a loser straight away.'

'Goodbye, Mother.'

'Wait! Don't hang up. What time are you bringing them over?'

'I'm not bringing them over because I'm not going out.'

'But darling, if you don't go out, how do you expect to meet anyone?'

* * *

The son

Victor and Rivkah have always wanted a son to join their two stunningly gorgeous teenage daughters and so they try one last time for 'their boy'. After months of trying, Rivkah gets pregnant and nine months later delivers a healthy baby boy.

Victor is at first ecstatic but as soon as he sees his son he is horrified – it's the ugliest baby he's ever seen. He turns to Rivkah and says, 'This can't be my son, Rivkah. Anyone can tell this just by looking at the two beautiful daughters I've fathered. Have you been unfaithful to me?'

Rivkah smiles sweetly and replies, 'No, not this time.'

* * *

The promotion

Moshe is the owner of Shmatters R Us, Ltd, a hugely successful chain of upmarket menswear shops. One day, Moshe calls in one of his staff and says, 'Bernie, when you first joined the company, you started as tea boy. Then, within three weeks, I promoted you to assistant to the catering manager and three months later you became junior buyer. I promoted you again six months later to chief buyer and two years after that you became our general manager. I've now decided to retire and after careful deliberation I've decided to give you my job as chairman and managing director of the company. What do you say about that?'

'That's fine,' says Bernie.

'Is that all you've got to say?' asks Moshe.

'No, you're right, I'm sorry,' replies Bernie, 'I should have said, "Thank you, Dad, that's fine."'

* * *

The quick thinker

Ethel and Leah meet while they're out shopping and sit down on a bench to chat. After a few minutes have gone by, Ethel suddenly says, '*Oy veh*, Leah, just look at the face of that poor boy coming towards us. His mouth is so misshapen that it makes his lips stand out. And his chin – what a double chin it is. His eyes look at each other and he's already losing his hair.'

'That boy you've been describing, Ethel, that boy coming towards us, he is none other than mine son Henry,' says Leah, with tears in her eyes.

'Oh, is that Henry?' replies Ethel. 'On him it looks good.'

* * *

Motherly advice – 1

'Mountains, shmountains. Stay away – you want a nosebleed?'

* * *

Mother's 11th commandment

Of the beasts of the field, and of the fishes of the sea, and of all foods that are acceptable in my sight, you may eat – but not in the living room.

Of the cereal grains, of the corn and of the wheat and of the oats, and of all the cereals that are of bright colour and unknown provenance you may eat – but not in the living room.

Of frozen dessert and of all frozen after-meal treats you may eat – but absolutely not in the living room.

Of the juices and other beverages, yea, even of those in non-spill cups, you may drink – but not in the living room (and neither may you carry such therein).

Indeed, when you reach the place where the living-room carpet begins, of any food or beverage there you may not eat, neither may you drink. But if you are sick and are lying down and watching something, then may you eat in the living room.

* * *

Innocent conversation

Leah and her best friend Talya, both four years old, are having a chat in the playground of their school. Leah is talking very excitedly because her mother is getting remarried on Sunday and she's telling Talya all about her new father.

'And my new daddy is also very rich,' says Leah, 'he's a chartered accountant.'

'So what's your new daddy's name?' asks Talya.

'His name is Benny Gold,' replies Leah delightedly.

On hearing this, Talya's little face lights up. 'He's lovely, Leah. You'll really, really like him,' she says.

'Do you know him?' asks Leah.

Talya nods, 'Yes, he was my daddy last year.'

* * *

The storm

One evening, as Ruth is tucking her son Sam into bed, a flash of lightning lights up the room and a loud clap of thunder soon follows. She hopes Sam won't react to the storm and is about to turn off the light when Sam asks, in a frightened voice, 'Mummy, can you sleep with me tonight?'

Ruth smiles and gives Sam a big comforting hug. 'I can't *bubbeleh*,' she says, 'I have to sleep in Daddy's room.'

After a few seconds of silence, Sam says, in a shaky voice, 'The big sissy.'

* * *

Would a Jewish mother say such things?
- 'If you're good, I'll buy you a motorbike for your birthday.'
- 'Of course it's OK to walk to school. There are only three main roads to cross.'
- 'Get closer to the screen. How can you see the TV sitting so far back?'
- 'There's no need to wear a jacket tonight, it's not that cold out.'
- 'Could you turn the music up a bit louder, please, so I can enjoy it too?'
- 'Run and bring me the scissors darling. And hurry up.'
- 'I don't have a tissue with me. Why don't you just use your sleeve?'
- 'Well, if Sam's mother says it's OK, then that's good enough for me.'
- 'If your wife wants you to move overseas to live near her family, it's OK with me, darling.'
- 'You really don't have to call me every week. I know how busy you are.'
- 'Just live with him, you don't have to marry him.'
- 'Mother's Day, schmother's day, just go to the cinema and enjoy yourselves.'
- 'You're really so lucky to have your in-laws. They're very nice people.'
- 'Could you leave the lights on please – it makes the house more cheerful.'

* * *

New policy
There's a new car insurance policy written especially for Jewish mothers. It's called the 'My Fault' policy.

* * *

A Jewish mother riddle
Q: What are the two most important things a Jewish mother needs to know about sex and marriage?
A: Who is having sex? Why aren't they married already?

* * *

About Jewish mothers
• Mothers only offer advice twice: when you want it and when you don't.
• A mother's love is a better cure than chicken soup, but chicken soup is cheaper.
• Your mother is the only person who knows more about you than you know about yourself.
• If you can't remember whether or not you called your mother, you didn't.
• The motherly advice you ignore will always turn out to be the best advice she ever gave you.
• If you forget, your mother will remind you of all your mistakes so you don't repeat them.
• Anything you do can be criticised by your mother – even doing nothing.
• You can't 'out mother' your mother. Don't even try.
• Never lie to your mother. And if you do, never think you got away with it.
• The harder you try to hide something from your mother, the more she resembles a webcam.
• The older you are, the more you feel like a child around your mother.
• Mother's way is best. If you don't believe it, ask her.

* * *

Protective

Little Sam is bored. So he goes over to his mother and asks, 'Mum, can I go outside and watch the solar eclipse?'

'OK, *bubbeleh*,' says his mother, 'but don't go too close.'

* * *

Confused identity

Cyril buys a new telephone-answering machine with a pre-recorded message in a man's voice, but he forgets to tell his elderly mother. Soon after the phone is connected, it rings and Cyril decides to test it out by letting the machine answer. After the pre-recorded message, there's a pause and the caller hangs up without leaving any message. The phone soon rings again, and the same thing happens.

When the phone rings for a third time, Cyril hears, 'Cyril, this is your mother, I think. If I am, please call me.'

* * *

Motherly advice – 2

Probably the only good advice that your mother gave you was this, 'So go already! You might meet somebody!'

* * *

A pullover riddle

Q: What is a Jewish pullover?
A: It's what Jewish children wear when their mothers are feeling cold.

* * *

A woman's poem
He didn't like my salt beef
And he didn't like my cake.
My *kichel* were too hard...
Not like his mother used to make.
I didn't make the *borsht* right
He left the *cholent* stew.
I didn't wash his *gatkes*...
The way his mother used to do.
I pondered for an answer
I was looking for a clue.
Then I turned around and gave him a *potch*...
Like his mother used to do.

Grandparents

Growing old riddle – 1
Q. *Bubbeh*, can a pea last for 1,000 years?
A. It seems that way sometimes, darling.

* * *

Growing old riddle – 2
Q. *Bubbeh*, which of your five senses has diminished as you've gotten older?
A. My sense of decency, darling.

* * *

Growing old riddle – 3
Q. *Bubbeh*, as you've grown older, have you tended to gesture more or less with your hands while talking?
A. Darling, ask me one more 'growing old' question, and I'll give you a gesture you won't forget in a hurry.

* * *

The home help

Naomi was happily married with two lovely boys. When she gave birth for the third time, her mother came over to stay with the family to help out. The two boys were excited that their *bubbeh* was coming – they always got on well with her.

The first thing *Bubbeh* did was to go out and buy some of her own favourite cleaning materials so that, throughout her stay, Naomi's house would be spotless. *Bubbeh* scrubbed the kitchen, bathrooms and toilets, vacuumed the carpets and polished the silver. Soon, the smell of *Bubbeh's* cleansers, polishes and air fresheners was everywhere.

After two months, *Bubbeh* went back to her own house, her job done. A few days later, Naomi used one of *Bubbeh*'s cleansers to remove a greasy mark from her kitchen worktop. She had just put away the cleanser when her youngest son came into the kitchen and said, 'Where's *Bubbeh*, Mummy?'

'She's back at her own house now,' said Naomi, 'don't you remember we took her to the station?'

'Then why do I smell her perfume?' he asked.

* * *

The birthday pullover

It's Victor's birthday in a few days time and his *bubbeh* goes out to buy him a present. She finds a menswear shop that is having a half-price sale and buys a luxurious rollneck pullover for him. Unfortunately, the pullover is for a size-14 neck and Victor is a size 18.

When Victor receives his present, he immediately tries it on. He then writes a thank-you note to his *bubbeh*. This is what he writes: 'Dear *Bubbeh*, Thanks a lot for the beautiful pullover. I'd write more but I'm all choked up.'

* * *

Bubbeh's favourite sayings (translated from the Yiddish–Russian slang)

The length of 'a minute' depends on which side of the toilet door you are.

(To her daughter): 'Please lower your voice to a plain scream.'

(About results of her facelift): 'Now I've got only one wrinkle and I sit on it.'

* * *

Insomnia cure

Dr Myers has been looking after one of his patients, 80-year-old Freda, for most of her life. But he retires and passes all his patients over to the newly qualified Dr Faith, who has just joined the practice. One of the first things Dr Faith does is to ask to see Freda and that she should bring with her a list of all the medicines that have been prescribed for her. Eventually, Freda has her appointment.

As Dr Faith is looking through Freda's list, he is shocked to see that she has a prescription for birth control pills.

'Mrs Cohen,' he says, 'do you realise that these are birth control pills?'

'Yes doctor,' replies Freda, 'they help me sleep at night.'

'Mrs Cohen,' says Dr Faith, 'I can assure you that there is absolutely nothing in birth control pills that could possibly help you sleep better at night.'

When she hears this, Freda reaches over to Dr Faith, lovingly pats him on his knee and says, 'Yes, Doctor, I know that, but every morning I get up very early, grind up one of the pills and mix it in the glass of orange juice that my 16-year-old granddaughter Suzy drinks when she awakes. Believe me doctor, this helps me sleep at night.'

* * *

What are *bubbehs* and *zaydehs*?
The following were taken from papers written by children:
* A *bubbeh* and *zaydeh* is a lady and a man who have no little children of their own. They like other people's.
* A *zaydeh* is a man *bubbeh*.
* *Bubbehs and zaydehs* don't have to do anything except be there when we come to see them. They are so old they shouldn't play hard or run. It is good if they drive us to the shops and give us money to spend.
* When they take us for walks, they slow down past things like pretty leaves and caterpillars. They also show us and talk to us about the colour of the flowers.
* They don't say, 'Hurry up!'
* Usually *bubbehs and zaydehs* are fat, but not too fat to tie your shoes.
* They wear glasses and funny underwear and can take their teeth and gums out.
* *Bubbehs* and *zaydehs* don't have to be smart.
* When they read to us, they don't skip anything. They don't mind if we ask for the same story over again.
* Everybody should try to have a *bubbeh* and *zaydeh*, especially if you don't have television, because they are the only grown-ups who like to spend time with us.
* They know we should have a snack before bedtime and they kiss us even when we've been naughty.

* * *

The lost girl
One Sunday, little Rachel and her *bubbeh* go out shopping to buy a present for Rachel. Unfortunately, while shopping, Rachel gets separated from her *bubbeh* and immediately starts to cry. A security guard sees the sobbing little girl and takes her to the lost-and-found office. When they ask

Rachel for her name, she replies, 'Shana Punam Kenahorah Poo Poo Poo.'

They again ask her for her name and she repeats, 'My name is Shana Punam Kenahorah Poo Poo Poo.'

So the office puts out the following message over the tannoy,

'We have in our lost-and-found office a cute brown-eyed, blonde-haired little girl who has lost her grandmother. If you are that grandmother, please come and claim your granddaughter, "Shana Punam Kenahorah Poo Poo Poo".'

Five *bubbehs* immediately come running to claim her.

* * *

A wise man
Hymie is talking to Max. 'I wish my *zaydeh* were still alive today,' he says.

'Why's that, Hymie,' asks Max.

'Because he always had pearls of wisdom to pass on to me,' replies Hymie.

'So was he a wise man?' asks Max.

'Wise?' replies Max. 'Of course he was wise. I remember once we were sitting on a park bench watching some mothers and their children playing around and enjoying themselves when he turned to me and said, "Hymie, be sure to marry a Jewish girl with small hands."'

'"Why, *Zaydeh*?" I asked.'

'"Because they'll make your pecker look bigger," he answered.'

* * *

Appearances are deceptive

Cyril was the black sheep of his family and decided to live in a nudist colony. One day, he was surprised to receive a letter from his grandma. In her letter, she told him that she was the only one who still wanted to remain in contact with him and she asked him to send her a current photo of himself in his new neighbourhood. The only recent photo he had of himself was one of him in the nude. Too embarrassed to remind her that he now lived in a nudist colony, Cyril cut the photo in half but accidentally sent her the bottom half of the photo. When he realised he'd sent the wrong half, he got quite worried, but then remembered how bad his grandma's eyesight was and assumed she wouldn't notice.

Some weeks later, Cyril received a reply from his grandma. It said: 'Thank you, *bubbeleh*, for the photo. But please, for your grandma, change your hairstyle – it makes your nose look short. Love Grandma.'

* * *

Zaydeh's lament

It's a very cold day when Daniel arrives at his grandparents' house. He's greeted by his *bubbeh* and taken into the lounge. 'Where's *Zaydeh*?' he asks.

'He's in the garden,' she replies.

'But it's cold outside, *Bubbeh*,' he says. So Daniel goes into the garden and is shocked to see his grandfather sitting on a terrace chair with nothing on below his waist. '*Zaydeh*,' he cries, 'what on earth are you doing undressed on such a cold day like this?'

His grandfather stares into the distance then turns to Daniel and replies, 'Well, last week I sat out here with no shirt on and I got a stiff neck. This is your *bubbeh*'s idea.'

Mothers-in-Law

Yes it's true
Nathan meets his friend Harry in the bagel factory. 'I hear that your mother-in-law has sold her house and moved in with you. Is this true, Harry?'

'Yes it's true,' replies Harry.

'And I also hear that she's recently become quite ill,' says Nathan.

'Yes it's true,' replies Harry.

'In fact, I hear that she's so ill that she's been taken into hospital,' says Nathan.

'Yes it's true,' replies Harry.

'So how long has she been in hospital?' asks Nathan.

'In two days' time, please God, it will be two weeks,' replies Harry.

* * *

The family question
Howard is visiting his prospective in-laws for the first time. As soon as he arrives, the father asks him, 'Young man, can you support a family?'

Howard is surprised by this question and replies, 'Well sir, to be truthful, I can't. But I'm only planning to support your daughter – the rest of you will have to do whatever you can without my help.'

* * *

Birthday wishes
Maurice and Hettie are out shopping one morning when Hettie says, 'Darling, it's my mother's birthday tomorrow. What shall we buy for her? She said she would like something electric.'

Maurice replies, 'How about a chair?'

* * *

Jewish cannibals

Two Jewish cannibals are stewing a pot of food over a fire.

'*Oy veh*,' says the first cannibal, 'I really do hate my mother-in-law.'

The second cannibal replies, '*Nu?* So leave her and just drink the chicken soup and *lockshen*.'

* * *

Family love

It's dinner time and Jeremy is finding it hard to get through his chicken soup. To be honest, he really doesn't much like its taste or consistency. His wife Sarah sees her Jeremy struggling with it and so asks him, 'What's wrong with the soup, Jeremy?'

'Although you're the best cook in the world, darling,' replies Jeremy, 'when it comes to chicken soup, you've got a lot to learn. I don't want to upset you, but I just don't like your soup. My mother Miriam makes the best chicken soup in the world. Why don't you ask her for her recipe?'

'*Oy veh*, Jeremy,' replies Sarah, 'you know how Miriam hates me. She would never tell me such a thing.'

'But your mother Hetty also makes an excellent chicken soup,' says Jeremy. 'Surely she must have told you how.'

'Jeremy,' says Sarah, 'this was the recipe she gave me. I guess my mother hates you just as much as your mother hates me.'

Domestic Animals

Canine agent

One day while out walking, Max sees a sign in front of a house: 'Talking Dog for Sale'. He's curious, so he rings the bell. The owner tells Max the dog's name is Cindy. He then takes Max into the back garden, where a Cavalier King Charles spaniel is sitting.

'Do you really talk?' Max asks Cindy.

'Yes, of course I do,' Cindy replies.

'So what can you tell me about yourself?'

Cindy looks up at Max and says, 'I discovered this special gift of speech when I was young and as I've always wanted to help my country, I told MI5 about it. In next to no time, they had me flying all over the world, sitting in rooms not only with royalty and world leaders but also with spies. No one figured a dog could be eavesdropping, so I was their most valuable spy. But all the jetting around really tired me out. I wasn't getting any younger and I wanted to settle down. So I resigned and signed up for a job at Heathrow airport to do some undercover security work, mostly wandering near suspicious people and listening in to their conversations. As a result, I uncovered some incredible plots and deals and received seven doggie awards. I had a husband and many puppies. Now, I'm retired.'

Max is amazed and asks the owner how much he wants for Cindy.

The owner replies, 'Twenty pounds.'

Max says, 'This dog is amazing. Why on earth are you selling her so cheap?'

The owner replies, 'Because Cindy is a liar – she didn't do any of the things she told you.'

* * *

The singer

Leah walks into a pet shop in and says to Hymie, the owner, 'I want to buy a canary.'

'We have many types,' says Hymie. 'Is there any particular one you're after?'

'Yes,' replies Leah, 'it's got to be a very good singer. I'm prepared to pay good *gelt* for a great singing bird.'

'Lady, I've got the very one,' says Hymie. 'I've been in this business for a long time and this bird has the best singing voice I've ever heard. We don't call it "Pavarotti" for nothing. I'll get it for you.'

As he begins to climb a ladder to reach a small cage on the top shelf, Leah says, 'I hope you're not wasting your time. Just because you're climbing a ladder like a monkey won't make me feel obliged to buy this canary if it's not a real singing canary.'

Hymie brings down the cage, places it on the shop counter and says to Leah, 'Just you listen.'

With that, the bird begins singing one beautiful song after another. Pleasantly surprised, Leah murmurs, 'What *mazel* – this canary really can sing.'

But then, a few seconds later, Leah shouts out, '*Oy veh*, this canary's only got one leg. Are you trying to cheat me, or what?'

Hymie calmly looks at Leah and replies, 'Lady, do you want a singer or a dancer?'

* * *

Horse for sale

Moshe goes to an outdoor sale. As he is walking around the grounds, he sees a sign saying: 'Luigi has nice things for sale'.

He goes up to Luigi's pitch and immediately sees that Luigi owns a horse. Moshe has always wanted his own horse, so he says to Luigi, 'Excuse me but do you want to sell me your horse?'

Luigi replies, 'I would sell it but it no looka so good.'

Moshe says, 'Well he looks fine to me. How much do you want for it?'

Luigi says, 'But as I tella you, I canna sell him to you – he no looka so good.'

Moshe says, 'OK, I'll give you £1,000 for your horse. Final offer. What do you say?'

Luigi shrugs his shoulders and agrees. After writing out a cheque, Moshe gets on the horse and gallops off. But after no more than one minute of riding, the horse suddenly rides straight into an oak tree at speed and is killed.

Moshe is lucky to be alive and goes straight back to Luigi. 'You thieving son of a bitch, you sold me a blind horse.'

Luigi replies, 'I tella you, he no looka so good.'

* * *

Naomi's toy

Little Naomi lives near a fire station. One day, one of the firemen is surprised to see Naomi glide slowly past the station in a small red fire engine. It is an expensive toy. It has little ladders hooked up on either side, an extendable ladder on top and a garden hose coiled up at the back. Naomi is sitting in the driver's seat wearing a yellow fireman's helmet and the fire engine is being pulled by both her dog and her cat. The fireman walks over to her.

'Wow,' he says, 'you've got a real nice fire engine, missy. I wish I had one like this.'

'Thank you,' says Naomi, 'it's my favourite toy.'

But then the fireman is shocked when he notices how Naomi has connected her pets to the fire engine – she's tied one rope to her dog's collar and a second rope to her cat's testicles.

'I have an idea,' he says to her, 'if you were to tie that rope around your cat's collar instead, I think you would go even faster.'

After thinking about this for a little while, Naomi replies, 'You're probably right, but then I wouldn't have a siren.'

* * *

The new dog

Rachel is walking down the street and meets her friend Naomi. Rachel is very surprised to see that Naomi is walking a dog.

'So what's with the dog, Naomi?' asks Rachel. 'I've never seen you with a dog before. Is it new?'

'Yes it is,' replies Naomi. 'I got this dog for my husband. I wish I could make a trade like that every day.'

* * *

Up on the roof

Daniel and Howard are brothers and both live in a smart area of town. But there the similarity ends – Daniel lives with and looks after their elderly mother and Howard lives with his cat Peachy.

Howard is besotted by Peachy. His whole life is based around her. So when his boss tells him at short notice that he must go to New York to sort out a problem there, he doesn't know what to do. He can't take Peachy with him, he can't leave her behind on her own and he can't refuse to go to New York. He eventually decides to trust Daniel with Peachy while he's away. So just before he leaves, Howard goes round to Daniel and explains in great detail what to do. He hands over the cat plus one week's worth of cat medicine and top-grade cat food, says goodbye to Peachy and then leaves.

The phone calls begin as soon as he arrives in New York. Howard phones Daniel morning, noon and night to make sure Peachy is all right. But on the fourth day, when he calls and asks how Peachy is getting along, Daniel replies, 'I'm afraid Peachy is dead, Howard.'

Howard is immediately besotted with grief. In between his sobs, he says, 'That was most cruel, Daniel. You know how much I loved Peachy. Why couldn't you have broken it to me gently?'

'How could I have done that?' asks Daniel.

'Well,' says Howard, 'when I called, you could have said, "Well, she's OK but she's up on the roof." Then, when I called the next time, you could have said, "She fell off the roof and she's at the vet's." And then, the next time, you could have said, "I'm sorry, but she passed away peacefully." At least then I would have been a little prepared for the bad news.'

'Yes, you're right, I'm so sorry,' says Daniel.

Howard then asks, 'By the way, how's Mum?'

'She's...OK,' replies Daniel. 'She's up on the roof fixing a tile.'

A Medical Compound

The Body and its Functions

The indiscretion

Rebecca walks into an up-market car showroom. As she is browsing around, she spots a special-looking car and walks over to inspect it. Rebecca opens the driver's door and bends down to feel the fine leather upholstery. Suddenly, a loud fart escapes her.

Rebecca is very embarrassed and looks nervously around, hoping that no one has noticed her little 'indiscretion'. But as luck would have it, when she turns back to the car, there, standing next to her, is a salesman.

'Good afternoon, madam, can I be of service?'

Very uncomfortably, Rebecca asks, 'Yes. What is the price of this lovely car?'

'If you farted just touching it, madam,' he replies, 'you will shit yourself when you hear the price.'

* * *

Scientific fact

Did you know that the human body has a nerve that connects the eyeball to the *toches*? It is called the anal optic nerve. If you don't believe it, pull a hair from your *toches* and see if it doesn't bring a tear to your eye.

* * *

The big sit

Kitty and Freda, both in their eighties, are returning from their visit to a shopping centre. They have been sitting on a bench for over 30 minutes waiting for their bus when Kitty turns to Freda and says, 'You know, Freda, I've been sitting here so long, my *toches* has fallen asleep.'

Freda turns to Kitty and says, 'I know, I heard it snoring!'

* * *

Incident in a theatre

Moshe and Sadie are in the theatre when Moshe suddenly leans over to Sadie and whispers in her ear, 'I just did a silent fart. What do you think I should do?'

Sadie whispers back, 'I think you should put a new battery in your hearing aid.'

* * *

Tit for tat

Sadie, an elderly, rather poorly dressed lady, is in a lift in a department store on her way down to the ground floor. On the fourth floor, a beautiful young woman gets into the lift, wearing what to Sadie is an expensive perfume. The woman turns to Sadie and says, arrogantly, 'Balenciaga, £100 an ounce!'

On the third floor, another beautiful woman smelling of expensive perfume gets into the lift, very arrogantly turns to Sadie and says, 'Christine Dior, £150 an ounce!'

When the lift reaches the ground floor, as she leaves the lift, Sadie looks both beautiful women in the eye, bends over, farts and says, 'Broccoli – 75p a pound.'

* * *

The misdemeanour

Sarah is on a dinner date. When she gets to the restaurant, she is shown to her table. Her date has not yet arrived. She puts down her handbag and waits. After 10 minutes he still hasn't arrived so she decides to tidy herself up to make sure that she looks perfect for him. She bends down and starts rummaging through her handbag, looking for her mirror. Unfortunately, as she is bending down, she accidentally lets go a loud *fortz* just as a waiter is walking by. Sarah immediately sits up straight. She's embarrassed and red-faced and sure that everyone in the restaurant heard her 'misdemeanour', so she quickly turns to the waiter and shouts, 'Stop that!'

The waiter looks at her and, keeping a straight face, says, 'Of course, madam, which way was it headed?'

* * *

The flower streaker

Rachel and Fay, two old ladies, are sitting on a bench near a flower show.

Fay leans over to Rachel and says, 'Don't you think life has got very boring? I just don't seem to have fun any more. You know what? For £10, I'd take off my clothes and run naked right through that stupid flower show over the road.'

'You're on,' says Rachel, holding up a £10 note.

So Fay fumbles her way out of her clothes as fast as she can. Then, completely naked, she streaks across the road and into the front door of the flower show, leaving Rachel wondering what will happen next. Rachel doesn't have long to wait. She hears a huge commotion inside the town hall, followed by loud applause. Then Fay, still naked, bursts out of the building and, followed by a cheering crowd, runs back over to her friend.

'*Nu*, so what happened?' asks Rachel.

'I won the first prize as Best Dried Arrangement,' replies Fay.

* * *

Satisfaction guaranteed

One day, 60-year-old twins Joshua and Shlomo are having a chat about their sex lives. Joshua says, 'I must be honest with you Shlomo, I just can't seem to satisfy mine Esther these days. I try hard, but I don't succeed.'

'I don't have that problem, Joshua,' says Shlomo. 'Every night, just before mine Sadie and I get into bed, I get totally undressed in front of her and say, "Well, take a look. Are you satisfied?" Sadie just shrugs and replies, "Yes." And that's it.'

* * *

It doesn't compare

Faye is on a Caribbean cruise to celebrate her 80th birthday. She is standing with some other passengers at the front of the ship and thinking of the film *Titanic*. It's very windy up front and she has to hold tightly on to her hat to stop it from blowing away.

Daniel is also at the front of the ship and notices something. So he walks over to Faye and says, 'Excuse me madam, but did you know the wind is blowing your dress up over your waist?'

'I know, thank you,' replies Faye, 'but there's not much I can do – I need both my hands to hold on to my hat.'

'Look, lady,' says Daniel, 'I'm sorry if this embarrasses you, but you're not wearing any underwear and your... ahem...private parts are exposed.'

Faye looks down for a few seconds, then looks up at Daniel and says, 'Thanks for pointing that out, but everything you see down there is 80 years old, whereas I only bought this hat last week.'

* * *

Things to come

As little Joshua is being given a bath by his mother, he starts to closely examine his testicles.

'Are these my brains, Mummy?' he asks.

'No, darling,' she replies, 'not yet they're not.'

* * *

The operation results

Immediately following his expensive private operation, Victor awakes and sees his surgeon standing near his bed. He says to the surgeon, 'Well, how did it go then?'

'Victor,' replies the surgeon, 'I have some good news and some bad news for you. The good news is that we were able to save your testicles.'

'Good,' says Victor, 'and what's the bad news?'

'They're under your pillow in a plastic bag,' replies the surgeon.

* * *

The record breaker

Maurice the mortician is working late one night when they bring him the body of a Mr Schwartz to examine. Schwartz is to be buried early the next day. As he examines the body, Maurice can't help but notice that Schwartz has the biggest *shlong* he's ever seen.

'I'm sorry, Schwartz,' says Maurice, as he carefully removes the organ with his scalpel, 'but I can't send your "pride and joy" to be buried with you. This piece of flesh needs to be saved for posterity.' He then stuffs it into his briefcase and takes it home with him.

The first person he shows it to is his wife. 'Darling,' he says, 'I've got something to show you that you won't believe.' He then opens up his briefcase.

'*Oy veh zmir*,' she cries out, with tears running down her face, 'Schwartz is dead!'

* * *

Birthday wishes

Bennie wakes up one morning with a smile on his face – because today he is 90 years old. He gets out of bed, looks down at his toes and says, 'Hello toes, how are you today? Did you know that you're now 90? Oh, the times we used to have together. Do you remember when we used to take a walk in the park every Sunday afternoon? Or the weekends we rock-and-rolled on the dance floor with all the young ladies? So, happy birthday toes.'

Bennie then looks down at his knees and says, 'Hello knees, how are you today? Did you know that you're now 90? Oh, the times we used to have together. Do you remember when we always used to march in all the parades we could find? Or all the Israeli dancing we used to do with all the beautiful ladies in Roberto's class? So, happy birthday knees.'

Bennie then looks down at his crotch and says, 'Hello Willie, you little traitor. If you were alive today, you'd be 90 years old.'

* * *

The burial

Two Jews who work for Chevra Kadisha, preparing bodies for burial, receive a new corpse. One of them opens his eyes wide and, pointing to the man's penis exclaims in amazement, '*Nu* Yossle, have you ever seen something like this?'

To which Yossl replies, 'Abraham my friend, mine is exactly the same.'

Abraham, greatly surprised, inquires, 'So large?'

Yossl replies, 'No, so dead!'

* * *

Proof of age

David reaches 60 years of age and is now entitled to a Freedom Pass (for free travel on London buses and tubes). So he goes to the Post Office to pick up his pass. After queuing for nearly 20 minutes, he finally gets to the counter and says to the lady clerk, 'Could I please have a Freedom Pass.'

'OK,' says the clerk, 'but first I need to see either your passport or your driver's licence so that I can verify your age.'

After fumbling in his pockets for a while, David says to the clerk, 'I'm very sorry, but I've left my documents at home. They're still sitting on my sideboard.'

But before David can leave, the clerk says to him, 'Don't go. Maybe I can check your age another way. Please open your shirt.'

David does what he's asked and opens his shirt, revealing a large mass of silver curly hair.

'That silver hair on your chest is proof enough for me,' says the clerk with a smile and promptly processes his application.

When David gets home, he can't wait to tell his wife Andrea about his experience with the lady clerk at the Post Office. Andrea listens to his story then says, 'You should also have pulled down your trousers and pants. She would then have given you a disability pension as well.'

* * *

Frightened Isaac

In 1967, Isaac joins the Army. On his first day of service, he gets issued with a comb and later on in the afternoon, the Army hairdresser cuts off all his lovely thick brown hair. Isaac is not at all happy with this. His hair was his pride and joy.

On Isaac's second day of service, he gets issued with a toothbrush and later on in the afternoon, the Army dentist extracts four of his teeth. Isaac is very angry with this, as he felt these teeth were perfectly sound.

On Isaac's third day of service, he gets issued with a jock strap.

Forty years later, the Army is still searching for Isaac.

* * *

The dust cloud
It's 6.30am and the alarm clock goes off in Hymie and Becky's bedroom. Hymie awakes and starts to get ready for work. He takes a pair of fresh underpants from his wardrobe and is surprised to see white powder fall from them. So he shakes them a bit and creates a mini dust cloud.

'Becky,' he says to the figure still in bed, 'why did you put talcum powder in my underwear?'

Becky replies, 'I didn't, darling. It's not talcum powder, it's "Miracle Gro".'

* * *

Yiddish proverb
When the penis stands, the brains get buried in the ground.

* * *

It's wonderful
While out shopping with her grandchildren, Hannah is forced to let her small grandson pee in the gutter. As she watches him do his thing, Hannah can't help but praise aloud, in no uncertain terms, what she sees.

'Oh, how gorgeous, how cute, how wonderful, and how BIG it is!'

Standing on the other side of the road is Moshe and he's been witnessing the event over the road. He shouts over to Hannah, 'Lady, if you're such a *maven*, such an expert in such male things, why don't you come over here and give me an estimate also?'

* * *

The bridge club

Sharon runs a local bridge club, which is renowned for the quality of its players. One evening, just before the players are due to arrive, she gets a last-minute call from one of them saying that she is sick and won't be coming in. Unable to get a replacement at such short notice, Sharon persuades her husband Brian, a mediocre player with a bad attitude, to make up the foursome.

During the evening's play, Brian gets up and goes to the toilet, leaving the door ajar. Soon, everyone can hear him peeing. Embarrassed, Sharon calls out, 'Brian, would you please close the toilet door?'

But Brian's partner says, 'Never mind, Sharon, it's the first time since we started playing that I've known what the man has in his hand.'

* * *

Where is a man's brain?

No one knows how it happened but once upon a time a female brain cell, by mistake, ends up in a man's head. She looks around nervously, but all around her is empty and quiet.

'Hello?' she cries out, but she gets no answer.

So she cries out a little louder, 'Is there anyone here?' but still she gets no answer.

Feeling very much alone and getting quite scared, she yells out at the top of her voice, 'Hello, hello, is there anyone here?'

Then, at last, she hears very faint voices from a long way away…'Hello, we're all down here!'

* * *

Life's problems
It's Tuesday and today's the day that Hannah and Becky go to their local swimming pool for their weekly exercise. As they are undressing, Hannah looks down at Becky's body, points and asks, 'I've always wanted to ask you this, Becky, but how come most of the hair on your head is grey, but down there your hair is a lovely auburn?'

'Because down there I've got no worries,' replies Becky.

Dental Issues

Career change
Leah meets her friend Hannah in the bagel shop and asks, 'Hannah, so how is your grandson the proctologist doing?'

Hannah sighs, 'Well Leah, my grandson Paul is no longer a proctologist. He decided to become a dentist a few months ago.'

'A dentist?' says Leah, 'So why has Paul changed his career?'

'Let's face it,' replies Hannah, 'everyone starts off with 32 teeth but have you ever heard of anybody who has more than one *toches*?'

* * *

How do the dentures feel?
Abe's eating a bagel for his mid-morning snack and breaks his dentures. He searches Yellow Pages for a dental technician, but everyone he calls quotes him an exorbitant price. 'I just don't understand you, Abe,' says his wife Sarah, 'we have a newly qualified dentist in the family, so why don't you call your nephew Arnold? I know you don't think much of him, but I'll bet he'll give you a better deal than those *gonifs* you've just spoken to. Why don't you go see him, he's only five minutes away?'

'*Oy veh*, Sarah,' replies Abe, 'you know I think Arnold is a *shmuck*. I wouldn't want to put any dentures he makes in my mouth.'

But Sarah doesn't let up and 30 minutes later, Abe is discussing new dentures with Arnold. 'I can make you a new set for only £100,' says Arnold, 'which is a special rate just for the family.'

A week later, Abe has his first fitting and just as he thought, they're uncomfortable. Over the weeks that follow, Abe regularly visits Arnold for adjustments. Sometimes Arnold adds some material, sometimes he grinds away some material and sometimes he bends some material, but to no avail – Abe never feels they fit perfectly. Then, suddenly, Abe stops coming and Arnold thinks he is at last happy with his dentures.

Two months later, by chance, they meet in the street. 'Hi, Uncle Abe,' Arnold says, 'it's good to see you again. How do the dentures feel?'

'Let me answer that by telling you a true story,' replies Abe. 'For the past three weeks, we've been on a Caribbean cruise. While there, I hire a boat to do some deep-water fishing and immediately I hook this great big 350-pound tuna. This is a very powerful fish and immediately begins to swim away from me. As I'm struggling to hold him, my 200-metre fishing line runs out and I'm nearly jerked over the side. Then the tuna turns around and starts swimming back towards me at great speed and now I'm frantically reeling in the line. Then I notice that somehow the loose line, which has been falling in the boat, has wrapped itself around my shorts, trapping my testicles. Before I can take any action, the tuna turns around for a second time and starts swimming even faster away from the boat.

'Arnold, believe me, just then, for the first time in many, many weeks, I didn't feel your dentures!'

Health, Physicians and Medicals

The benefit of private medical insurance

Benjy is getting chest pains and goes to see his doctor. After examining him, the doctor says, 'There are two different opinions on how best to treat you. I'm convinced that you need a triple heart bypass operation. However, your private medical policy says all you need to do is take this £10 tube of chest ointment and rub it in twice a day.'

* * *

To be a doctor

A Jewish doctor needs three things to be successful:

To have grey hair, to look distinguished.

To be moderately overweight, to look prosperous.

To have painful haemorrhoids, to have a constant look of grave concern.

* * *

Inflation

Sol and Abe, both elderly, meet one day in a shop.

'So, how's by you, Abe?' asks Sol.

'It could be worse, Sol. I'm surviving. And what about you?' asked Abe.

Sol replies, 'I've been ill quite a lot recently and it's costing me a lot of money. I have no private medical insurance and in the last five months, I've spent over £6,000 on doctors' fees and medicine.'

Abe replies, 'Ach. In the old days, you could be ill for at least two years for that kind of money.'

* * *

The doctor's bill

Morris the tailor is worried because his wife Hetty is very ill and needs a good doctor. Everyone knows that Dr Myers is the best doctor around, so Morris rings him to say that he would like him to treat Hetty.

Dr Myers says, 'OK, but can you afford me? What if I'm unable to save Hetty and you decide not to pay my bills?'

Morris replies, 'I promise to pay you anything, no matter whether you cure Hetty or kill her.'

So Dr Myers agrees to treat Hetty. Unfortunately, Hetty dies soon after.

When Dr Myers's invoice arrives, Morris refuses to pay, despite his promise. After much arguing, they agree to take the issue to their rabbi for a decision.

Dr Myers puts his side of the story to the rabbi. 'He promised to pay me, no matter whether I cured his wife or killed her.'

After a few minutes' deliberation, the rabbi says, 'So did you cure her?'

Dr Myers has to reply, 'No.'

The rabbi then asks, 'So did you kill her?'

'No, I certainly did not,' replied Dr Myers.

'In that case,' says the rabbi, 'Morris owes you nothing – you fulfilled neither of the conditions on which you agreed that your fee should be paid.'

* * *

Problems, problems

Two doctors are having a conversation over lunch. Simon says, 'Every day, Abe, all I hear from my patients are stories of suffering and pain. They describe their back problems, their stomach problems and their headaches. I don't think I can take much more. But what about you, Abe? You always seem so calm. So tell me, how do you cope so well listening to all these problems?'

Abe replies, 'So who listens?'

* * *

Good advice

Abe is in a terrible state and goes to see Dr Myers, his psychiatrist.

'Doctor, I need your help in a big way. I feel very suicidal. What should I do?'

Dr Myers replies, 'You must pay me in advance.'

* * *

The cure

Faye goes to her doctors' surgery and is seen by Dr Myers, a new young doctor who has just joined the practice. Within five minutes of talking to the doctor, Faye bursts out of his consulting room and runs crying out loudly down the hall. Fortunately, the receptionist is able to stop her and makes her take a seat. When Faye has calmed down, the receptionist asks, 'Faye, what's the matter? Tell me what's happened.'

After listening to her story, the receptionist says, 'Wait here, Faye, I'll sort this out for you here and now.'

The receptionist strides purposefully down the hall to Dr Myers's room and enters. 'Doctor, what's the matter with you? Mrs Cohen is nearly 60 years old and has two grown-up children and four grandchildren. Yet you just told her that she's pregnant. How could you do such a thing?'

Dr Myers replies, without looking up from making his notes, '*Nu*? Does she still have the hiccups?'

* * *

Miracle cure

Dr Simon is known throughout London as one of the best consultants on arthritis. He always has a waiting room full of people who need his advice and specialist treatment. One day, Hetty, an elderly lady, slowly struggles into his waiting room. She is completely bent over and leans heavily on her walking stick. A chair is found for her. Eventually, her turn comes to go into Dr Simon's office.

Fifteen minutes later, to everyone's surprise, she comes briskly out of his room, walking almost upright. She is holding her head high and has a smile on her face. A woman in the waiting room says to Hetty, 'It's unbelievable, a miracle even. You walk in bent in half and now you walk out erect. What a fantastic doctor he is. Tell me, what did Dr Simon do to you?'

'Miracle, shmiracle,' says Hetty, 'he just gave me a longer walking stick.'

* * *

Medical disciplines

It's the funeral of Moshe the cardiologist and Avrahom and Hymie are there to pay their last respects. Behind Moshe's coffin stands a huge red heart covered in hundreds of flowers. Following the eulogy, the heart suddenly opens, the coffin moves slowly inside and the heart shuts, enclosing Moshe inside the beautiful heart forever. Avrahom immediately bursts out laughing.

'What's so funny?' asks one of the congregation.

'I'm sorry,' replies Avrahom, 'but I can't help thinking of my own funeral – I'm a gynaecologist.'

Hymie, the proctologist, then faints.

* * *

Long-lasting medicine

Sadie is 80 years old and is under the care of Dr Myers. One day, she phones him and says, 'Is it true, Doctor, the medicine you've just prescribed for me must be taken for the rest of my life?'

'Yes Sadie, I'm afraid it is,' replies Dr Myers.

Sadie thought for a while then continued, 'Well then, Doctor, I'm wondering just how serious is my condition.'

'Why do you ask?' says Dr Myers.

Sadie replies, 'Because on the prescription it says, "NO REPEAT PRESCRIPTIONS".'

* * *

Water problems

Ninety-year-old Issy goes to his doctor. 'Doctor, I'm having trouble passing water.'

'How long has this been happening?' asks the doctor.

'I haven't gone in three days,' replies Issy.

'Well,' says the doctor, 'that's not good news.' The doctor opens his drawer and gives Issy a large bottle of pills. 'Take two of these pills as soon as you get home and then take two pills three times a day. Give me a call in three days' time.'

Issy goes home and starts his treatment. Three days later, he calls the doctor as requested.

'Are they working?' asks the doctor.

'No,' replies Issy.

So the doctor tells him to take four pills three times a day and to call him again in three days' time.

Issy does as he is told and three days later he calls the doctor again.

'Are they working?' asks the doctor.

'No,' replies Issy.

The doctor then tells Issy to take 10 pills four times a day and not to stray too far from the toilet. Issy does as requested. Three days later, he calls the doctor again.

'Are they working now?' asks the doctor.

'No,' replies Issy, 'and I'm getting very worried, Doctor. It's been nearly two weeks since I last *pished*.'

The doctor asks, 'How old are you?'

'I'm nearly 91,' replies Issy.

'Well,' says the doctor, 'then there's no need to worry. You've *pished* enough in your life.'

* * *

Medical emergency

Rifka is out shopping in the West End of London one very hot and humid Sunday afternoon when suddenly a man faints at the junction between Oxford Street and Bond Street. Traffic quickly piles up in all directions.

Rifka sees the man collapse and rushes over to help him. But as she kneels down to loosen his collar, a man emerges from the crowd, pushes her aside and says, 'It's all right, darling, I've taken a course in first aid.'

Rifka stands up and watches as he takes the man's pulse and prepares to give artificial respiration. At this point Rifka taps him on the shoulder and says, 'When you get to the part about calling a doctor, I'm already here.'

* * *

The appointment

Harry has a 'malfunction problem' and makes an appointment to see a consultant urologist in Harley Street. When Harry arrives, he notices that the waiting room is already filled with patients. As he walks over to the receptionist to check in, he can't help noticing that she is a very large and unfriendly looking woman who looks just like a Sumo wrestler. He says to her, 'My name is Harry and I've got an appointment with Dr Bard.'

The receptionist replies in a very loud voice that everyone can hear, 'Yes, Harry, your name is on my list. You want to see the doctor about impotence. Is that correct?'

All the patients in the waiting room turn to look at Harry, who is by now very embarrassed. However, he quickly gathers himself together and in an equally loud voice replies, 'No, you're wrong. I've come to enquire about the possibility of a sex change operation, but now I've seen you, I don't want the same doctor that did yours.'

* * *

A doctor's philosophy

Yossi goes to see Dr Levene and says, 'Doctor, I'm suffering terrible pains in the left shoulder.'

Dr Levene replies, '*Nu*, so what do you think? You're going to enjoy them?'

* * *

Problem after problem

Isaac is one of the world's great hypochondriacs. One day he goes to see Dr Myers and says, with a worried look on his face, 'Doctor, you must help me.'

'How can I do that, Isaac?' asks Dr Myers calmly.

'Do you remember those voices in my head I've been complaining about?' says Isaac.

'Yes of course,' replies Dr Myers.

'Well,' says Isaac, 'they've suddenly gone away.'

'So what's the problem, then?' asks Dr Myers.

'I think I'm going deaf,' replies Isaac.

* * *

The medical practice sign

Dr Minky, a psychiatrist, and Dr Lau, a proctologist, open a medical practice. But they have great difficulty in getting the local council to agree to the wording on the sign they want to put up outside their office. These are the signs they try, but which are not accepted by the council:

'Hysterias and Posteriors'

'Schizoids and Haemorrhoids'

'Catatonics and High Colonics'

'Manic Depressives and Anal Retentives'

'Minds and Behinds'

'Lost Souls and Butt Holes'

'Analysis and Anal Cysts'

'Nuts and Butts'

'Freaks and Cheeks'

'Loons and Moons'

Almost at their wits' end, the doctors finally come up with a sign which the council approves. It reads, 'Dr Minky and Dr Lau, Odds and Ends'.

* * *

The doctors' convention

It's 10pm when the phone rings in Dr Minkofsky's house. 'It's Dr Gold,' says his wife, passing him the phone. 'I do hope it's not another emergency.'

Dr Minkofsky takes the phone and says, 'Hi, what's up?'

'Don't worry, everything's OK,' replies Dr Gold. 'It's just that I'm at home with Dr Lewis and Dr Kosiner. We're having a little game of poker and we're short of one hand so we thought you might like to come over and join us.'

'Sure…yes, of course,' replies Dr Minkofsky, putting on a serious voice, 'I'm leaving right now.' And he puts down the phone.

'What's happened?' his wife asks, with a worried look.

'It's very serious,' Dr Minkofsky replies. 'They've already called three doctors.'

* * *

The pain

Moshe is known to all his friends as a hypochondriac. One day he awakes with a pain on his left side and is convinced that his pain is appendicitis. But his wife Sadie tells him that appendices are on the right side of the body.

'Aha,' says Moshe, 'so that's why it's hurting me so much. My appendix is obviously on the wrong side.'

* * *

Health forecast

Benny meets his grandfather in the street one morning. 'Hi *zaydeh*. How are you feeling today?'

'*Oy veh*, Benny, I've got so many aches and pains that if I get a new one, it will have to wait at least a week before I can think of even worrying about it.'

* * *

Operation talk

Freda and Kitty meet at the shopping centre one day for their regular chat. Kitty says, 'Do you know what my doctor told me the other day, Freda?'

'No,' says Freda, 'surprise me!'

'Well, he told me that I needed to have another operation,' replies Kitty.

'So when will you have it?' says Freda.

'I won't,' replies Kitty. 'I told him that because Harry and I have had so many expenses this year, we couldn't afford to pay for an operation.'

'Never mind,' says Freda, 'you'll just have to talk about your old operation for yet another year.'

* * *

The rift

By chance, Esther meets her friend Becky out shopping. 'Well fancy seeing you here,' says Esther, 'I haven't seen you for at least a year. How's everything?'

'Oh fine…I suppose,' replies Becky.

'What do you mean by "I suppose"?' asks Esther.

'Well,' replies Becky, 'my sister Rachel is very ill and is in hospital. I've just come back from visiting her.'

'Oh, I'm sorry to hear it,' says Esther. 'Is Rachel the sister who's not been speaking to you for some time?'

'Yes,' replies Becky, 'she fell out with me some two years ago and she hasn't spoken a word to me since.'

'So why did you visit her?' asks Esther.

'My sister Rachel is almost impossible to deal with,' replies Becky. 'When she's *broyges,* she stays *broyges,* no matter what. But she's very ill and my son Arnold begged me to go see her, and so I did.'

'How did the visit go, then?' asks Esther.

'As soon as I walked into her ward, she said to me, "Becky, don't think that coming here automatically changes anything between us. Nevertheless, I want you to know that if I die, you're forgiven for all you've done to me. But, if I get well, please God, then I'll stay *broyges* with you."'

* * *

After my check-up

Moshe and his friends Abe, Max and Nathan meet for a coffee – as they do every Monday. They sit down and Moshe starts to discuss the importance of regular medical check-ups.

He asks his friends, 'So when did you all last have a medical?' All reply it was years ago. So Moshe tells them of Dr Myers, a wonderful doctor he went to and who gave him the best examination he's ever had. He suggests they each contact Dr Myers and book a check-up ASAP. They agree to do so and take down the doctor's phone number.

The following Monday, Moshe asks his friends, '*Nu*, how went the medicals?'

'After my check-up,' says Abe, 'Dr Myers asked me how old I was. I said I was 70 and he said I could expect to live another 30 years. I was so relieved and happy to hear that.'

'After my check-up,' says Max, 'Dr Myers also asked me how old I was. When I said I was 80 he said I could expect to live another 20 years. You can't believe how fantastic it was for an 80-year-old to hear that.'

Nathan is looking very sad and doesn't say anything at first. But Moshe eventually persuades him to discuss how his medical went. 'Being older than all of you,' says Nathan, 'I have been loath to see a doctor. But when Moshe told us of Dr Myers, I reluctantly booked to see him. After my check-up, the doctor asked me how old I was. When I said I was 90, he looked at me and said, "Thanks for coming. Have a nice day."'

* * *

Her yearly medical

Leah goes to Dr Myers for her yearly examination. He begins by putting her on the scales. 'How much do you think you weigh, Leah?' he asks.

'I am 8 stone 5 pounds,' Leah replies.

But Dr Myers tells her that her weight is actually 9 stone 3 pounds.

Dr Myers then asks, 'How tall are you, Leah?'

'I'm five foot nine,' Leah replies.

But when he measures her, it turns out that she is only five foot six.

Dr Myers then takes her blood pressure. 'Your blood pressure is very high, Leah,' he says.

'It's no wonder,' Leah shouts at him. 'When I came in here I was tall and slender. Now I'm short and fat.'

* * *

A good check-up

Just before her 70th birthday, Kitty says to her husband, 'You know what, Harry? I think I'll go see Dr Besser and get myself checked over. I haven't been to see him for ages.'

'That's a good idea, darling,' says Harry.

Two days later, Kitty is telling Dr Besser why she's come. 'I haven't had a check-up for over 25 years and I think it wise to have one now,' she tells him.

'I agree,' he says. 'Get undressed, put on this gown and go sit down on the bed over there. Then I'll look you over.'

As soon as she's done what he's asked, Dr Besser goes over to her, puts his hand under the gown, lifts her right breast and tells her, 'Say "Ninety-nine".'

'Ninety-nine,' says Kitty.

'Nothing wrong there,' says Dr Besser. He then lifts her left breast and again says to her, 'Say "Ninety-nine".'

'Ninety-nine,' says Kitty.

'This one's fine too,' says Dr Besser. 'Now I'd like to check out your other vitals. Lie down on the bed and put your feet in the stirrups.'

Kitty does what the doctor asked. Dr Besser puts on a rubber glove, rubs on some KY jelly and starts to check out Kitty's private parts for any problem signs. He once again says to her, 'Say "Ninety-nine".'

This time Kitty replies, 'One, two three, four…'

Hospitals and Surgeons

Let's go

The regulations at the hospital require a wheelchair to be provided for all patients being discharged. So when Michelle, a student nurse, is told that the patient in Room 50 is being discharged, she finds a wheelchair and takes it to the room. When she enters, there's Moshe, an elderly man, fully dressed and sitting on the bed with a suitcase at his feet. 'OK, let's go,' she tells him, 'just pop into the wheelchair and I'll take you downstairs.'

Moshe argues with her. 'I don't need your help to go downstairs. I'm not that old, I can do it perfectly well by myself.'

But no matter how hard he insists that he doesn't need her help to leave the hospital, Michelle is more insistent. 'You just have to leave in the wheelchair, no matter how fit you think you are – it's the rules,' she says. 'You can't change them.'

So very reluctantly, Moshe lets Michelle wheel him to the lift. On their way down, Michelle asks him if his wife is meeting him.

'I don't know,' Moshe replies, 'she's still upstairs in the bathroom changing out of her hospital gown.'

* * *

Lunch appointment

Seventy-year-old Sidney opens his eyes and sees a lovely lady in white staring at him. 'Where am I?' he says.

'You're in hospital, Mr Green,' she replies. 'You had a nasty car crash four days ago and you've been unconscious ever since you were brought in. But don't worry about anything – you're in a great hospital and we've got the best doctor looking after you.'

'Four days, eh?' says Sidney, 'it's no wonder I'm so hungry. So bring me a hot salt beef sandwich on rye with mustard and a new green cucumber and some *latkes* on the side.'

'I'm sorry, your doctor has instructed me not to feed you with any solids,' says the nurse. 'You're being fed rectally. Do you see that large tube down there? If you follow it, you'll find it is stuck up your back passage.'

'Well then,' says Sidney, 'if this really is the best hospital with the best equipment, please bring me two more tubes tomorrow. Then I would very much like to invite you and my doctor to join me for lunch.'

* * *

The nose job
Moshe, an up-and-coming actor, has been operated on in a Harley Street clinic to 'straighten' his nose. Five days later, as the surgical cast from Moshe's nose is being removed, his surgeon looks at the results and says, 'Ah, a thing of beauty and a *goy* for ever.'

* * *

GABS
Moshe returns to Israel following a trip to China and is feeling very ill. When his doctor examines him, Moshe is rushed to hospital for tests and then placed in a private room in the isolation ward to await the results. Moshe has been there no more than a few hours when the phone by his bed rings.

'This is your doctor speaking,' says the voice on the phone. 'I now have the results of your tests and I'm sorry to have to tell you that you have an extremely contagious disease known as GABS. I can't see you in person – in fact, no one can. That's why I'm using the phone.'

'GABS?' gasps Moshe. 'What is that. What does it mean?'

'Well,' says his doctor, GABS is a disease combining gonorrhoea, AIDS, bird flu and syphilis. It can be deadly if not treated quickly.'

'*Oy veh*, Doctor,' screams Moshe, 'how are you going to treat me?'

'Well, we're going to keep you in isolation and put you on a strict diet of slices of *worsht*, fried egg, *matzo* and *kichels*,' says the doctor.

'Will they cure me?' asks Moshe.

'Not really,' replies the doctor, 'but those are the only foods we can slide under the door.'

* * *

The newcomer

Moshe is always telling jokes and thinks he could make a great stand-up comedian. So when one of his friends suggests he do a try-out, Moshe volunteers to entertain patients in one of the wards at a nearby hospital.

Moshe starts by telling the patients some jokes and finishes by singing some funny songs. Just before he leaves, he says to the patients, 'I hope you all get better.'

One elderly man replies, 'I hope you get better, too.'

Psychiatrists and Psychologists

Up in the air

Sadie goes to see her psychiatrist, Dr Myers, to get help on an issue concerning her sexual relationship with her husband Abe.

Dr Myers explains, 'OK, but I can only help you if you are open and honest with me. Is that agreed?'

'Yes,' says Sadie.

But after just 15 minutes, Dr Myers has to tell her, 'We're

getting nowhere, Sadie. You're too secretive. I'll try just once more – please reply quickly to the questions I'm going to ask you or I won't be able to help.'

'OK,' says Sadie.

'Have you ever looked directly into Abe's face while you were making love?' asks Dr Myers.

'Yes,' replies Sadie.

'We're making progress at last,' says Dr Myers. 'So tell me, Sadie, when you looked directly into Abe's face while you were making love, did you see any emotion there?'

'Yes,' replies Sadie, 'I saw great anger on his face.'

'Excellent,' continues Dr Myers, 'we're nearly there. So when you looked directly into Abe's face while you were making love and saw great anger, could you please explain to me exactly what Abe was doing at the time?'

Sadie replies, 'He was up a ladder looking at me through the bedroom window.'

* * *

Psychology
Sophia and Hannah are discussing the best ways to make their young sons finish their meals. Sophia says, 'As an Italian mother, I put on a fierce look and say to Primo, 'If you don't finish your meal, I'm going to kill you.' It works most of the time.'

'Well, as a Jewish mother, I look mine Isaac in his eyes and say, "If you don't eat the meal I've slaved over all day, I'm going to kill myself." It works every time.'

* * *

Course change

One day, Max – who is away at university – rings his mother. 'Hi Mum,' he says, 'I thought you should know that I've just switched courses and I'm now taking Psychology.'

'*Oy veh*,' says his mother, 'I suppose you'll now be analysing everyone in the family.'

'Oh no, Mum,' he replies, 'I don't take abnormal psychology until next term.'

* * *

A visit to a psychiatric hospital

During a visit to the community psychiatric hospital, Morris, a journalist from the *Jewish Chronicle*, asks the director how the hospital decides whether or not a patient should be institutionalised.

'Well,' replies the director, 'we fill up a bathtub, then we offer a teaspoon, a teacup and a bucket to the patient and we ask him or her to empty the bathtub.'

'Oh, I understand,' says Morris. 'A normal person would use the bucket because it's bigger than the spoon or the teacup.'

'Actually,' says the director, 'a normal person would just pull the plug. So tell me Morris, do you want a room with an east view or a west view?'

* * *

Confusion

Morris works in a local care home looking after the elderly. He's very good at his job. For example, during the admission procedures he always asks new arrivals if they're allergic to anything and if they are, he prints it on an allergy band, which he places on their wrist.

One day, he asks a new arrival, 'OK, Becky, I have just one more thing to ask you. Are you allergic to anything?'

'Yes I am,' replies Becky. 'I'm allergic to bananas.'

Later that morning, Becky's son comes storming angrily into the office and shouts, 'OK, who's responsible for labelling my mother "bananas"?'

* * *

Solving mother's problems

Miriam is a mother who's having serious problems with her young son, Nathan. She's in such a state that her doctor recommends she see a psychiatrist as soon as possible. He then writes out a letter for her to give to the psychiatrist.

Later that week, Miriam has her first appointment with the psychiatrist. After he spends an hour talking to her, he says, 'You seem to be far more upset and worried about Nathan than you ought to be. So, Miriam, I'm going to give you a prescription for some tranquillisers. These are the very latest on the market. Start taking them regularly from today and I'll see you again in a month's time.'

On her next visit, the psychiatrist asks, 'So, Miriam, you look much more relaxed than the last time I saw you. Have the tranquillisers I gave you calmed you down?'

'Yes, Doctor, the pills have been marvellous. I feel so carefree,' replies Miriam.

'And how is Nathan behaving?' he asks.

'Who cares?' replies Miriam, shrugging her shoulders.

* * *

I love that bike

Renee and Lawrence take their four-year-old daughter Talia to the Oy Veh Toy Store. The toy that immediately catches Talia's eye is a beautiful pink three-wheeler Barbie bike. She gets on it and rides around the store. One hour later, she's still on the bike and no matter how much Renee and

Lawrence beg her to get off, Talia refuses. The shop staff try and even Sidney the store manager tries, but to no avail. Talia won't get off the bike and begins throwing temper tantrums.

Sidney quickly decides that it can't hurt to call in Benjy Levy, the famous child psychologist, whose office is only a few minutes' walk away. He just might be able to help.

'Is that Benjy Levy?' asks Sidney.

'Yes it is,' replies Benjy, 'how can I help?'

'I'm from Oy Veh Toys and I was wondering whether you could spare a few minutes to help us with a difficult child,' asks Sidney.

'Yes, of course,' replies Benjy, 'I'm leaving the office now.'

Five minutes later, Benjy arrives and immediately goes over to Talia. He smiles, leans over and whispers something in Talia's ear. Straight away, with no arguing at all, Talia gets off the pink bike and runs over to her parents and within minutes, they have left the store to go home. Sidney and his staff rush over to Benjy to ask what words of wisdom he used to get Talia off the bike.

'Oh, it was nothing special,' said Benjy. 'I used words that anyone could have used.'

'So what were these words?' they all ask at once.

Benjy replies, 'I said to her, "Now you listen here, *tsatskelah*, if you don't get off this bike right away, I'm going to give you such a *potch* on the *toches* that you won't be able to sit down for a week!"'

* * *

Dead or alive

Ever since the *Jewish Chronicle* printed his obituary in error, Hymie just can't get it out of his mind that he really is dead. His delusion becomes such a problem that his sons finally pay for a psychiatrist to visit him to sort him out.

The psychiatrist spends many laborious sessions trying to

convince Hymie that he is, indeed, still alive, but nothing seems to work.

Finally the psychiatrist tries one last time. He takes some medical books with him to help him prove to Hymie that dead men can't bleed. After an hour of argument and book reading, it seems that he has finally succeeded.

'So, Hymie,' says the psychiatrist, 'do you now agree with the medical establishment that dead men don't bleed?'

'Yes,' replies Hymie.

'Very well then,' says the psychiatrist as he pricks Hymie's finger with a pin causing it to bleed a little, 'look at this. What does that blood tell you, Hymie?'

'*Oy veh*,' says Hymie, as he stares incredulously at his finger, 'it means that dead men really do bleed.'

* * *

The trouble with phobias
Simon has a problem. In fact he's had the problem for so long that it's beginning to worry him to death. Finally, he decides he has to do something about it and goes to see Dr Bloom, his local psychiatrist.

'*Oy*, Doctor, have I got a problem,' says Simon. 'Every night, when I get into my bed, I think there's a crazy person under it ready to do me some serious harm. I'm going *meshugga* with fear. Please help me.'

'Don't worry, Simon,' says Dr Bloom, 'I can cure you of your fears, but it will not happen overnight.'

'So how long will it take, Doctor?' asks Simon.

'Well,' replies Dr Bloom, thinking, 'come to me twice a week for three months and I'll rid you of your phobia.'

'And how much do you charge a session, Doctor?' asks Simon.

'My charges are £100 per session,' replies Dr Bloom.

'But that will cost me £2,600 in total,' says Simon. 'I'm

going to have to think about it and let you know. I can't easily afford that kind of money.'

Many months later, Simon meets Dr Bloom in Waitrose supermarket.

'So why didn't you decide to let me cure you of your fears?' asks Dr Bloom.

'Well,' replies Simon, 'as I told you then, your fees were really too high for me. And then my rabbi gave me the cure for nothing. I was so happy to have saved all that money that I went on a week's holiday to Tel Aviv.'

'So how, may I ask, did your rabbi cure you?' asks Dr Bloom.

'Easy,' replies Simon, 'he told me to cut the legs off my bed. It's now so low that nobody can possible get under it.'

Seeing and Hearing

Double trouble

Issy goes with Sarah to his local optician's to buy a new pair of glasses for himself. He chooses a pair 'off-the shelf', pays for them and leaves wearing them. As they are a bit hungry, they decide to have a coffee and a sandwich at a nearby restaurant. As he is looking through the menu, Issy says, 'Sarah, you'd better order for me. I'm seeing everything double with my new glasses. And while you're doing that, I'm going to the toilet.'

When Issy returns, Sarah notices that the front of his trousers are wet.

'*Oy veh*,' says Sarah, 'what happened, Issy? Your trousers are all wet.'

'You wouldn't believe it,' Issy replies, 'I was standing in front of the urinal and when I looked down, I saw two. So I put one back!'

* * *

The eye test
When Jacob from Poland applies for a driver's licence, he is asked to take an eyesight test. The optician points to a card on the wall with the letters C Z W I X N O S T A C Z and says to Jacob, 'Can you read this?'

'Read it?' replies Jacob. 'The man's my best friend.'

* * *

The eye and the tongue
David leaves London and makes *aliyah* to Israel. As soon as he settles down in Tel Aviv, he goes to see the local optician.

'I'm having trouble reading,' he says. 'Maybe you could check my eyes?'

The optician sits David in front of a large eye-test chart. 'Can you read the letters on the bottom line?' he asks.

'No,' replies David.

'So how about the next line up?' asks the optician.

Squinting, David replies, 'No, I still can't read them.'

'OK,' says the optician, 'let's start at the top line. Read out the letters please.'

'But I can't,' says David.

'Are you perhaps a teeny bit blind?' asks the optician.

'Certainly not,' replies David. 'It's just that I've never learned to read Hebrew.'

* * *

Are you blind?

A Mini car crashes into the back of Melvyn's Rolls-Royce as Melvyn is waiting to turn right. The Mini driver is furious. 'Why didn't you indicate?' he shouts.

'What would have been the point?' shrugs Melvyn. 'If you couldn't see my Rolls-Royce, how could you have seen my indicator?'

* * *

Golfing injury

It's Sunday and Emma and Rose are in the middle of their regular round of golf. At the 13th hole, Rose tees off and watches in horror as her ball heads directly towards the two men playing the 14th hole. The ball hits Nathan, who immediately clasps both hands to his groin and falls to the ground rolling around in agony.

Rose rushes over to Nathan and says, 'Look, I'm sorry about this, but I'm a chartered physiotherapist and I know how to relieve your pain. Do you want me to help you?'

'Oh there's no need to do anything,' Nathan says through clenched teeth. 'I'll be OK soon.'

But after two minutes pass, Nathan is still obviously in pain. He's lying on the grass in the foetal position and he's still clasping his hands to his groin. So Rose once again asks whether she can help him. This time, Nathan replies, 'Yes, oh yes. Please get rid of my pain.'

So Rose gently goes over to him, bends down and gently takes his hands away from his groin. She then loosens his belt, undoes the top of his trousers, put her hands inside, and administers special, tender and artful massage to his parts. After a while, Rose asks Nathan, 'So how does that feel?'

'It feels absolutely wonderful,' replies Nathan, 'but I still think my thumb is broken.'

* * *

The tapper

Louis has a bad attack of laryngitis and completely loses his voice. To help him communicate with his wife Becky, he devises a system of taps.

One tap means, 'Kiss me, my darling.'

Two taps means, 'Yes please.'

And 95 taps means, 'I'll do the drying up.'

* * *

Insider information

Benny has been suffering with his hearing for many years and at last decides to see a doctor. After examining Benny, the doctor tells him, 'I'm surprised you've put up with this problem for so long. All you need is a hearing aid.'

Within days, Benny is fitted with a state-of-the-art hearing aid and is asked to return in four weeks' time for a check-up.

Benny returns to the doctor a month later and after another examination, the doctor says, 'Your hearing is perfect, almost one hundred per cent. Your family must be really pleased that you can hear again.'

Benny replies, 'Oh, I haven't told my family yet. I just sit around and listen to the conversations. As a result, I've changed my will three times already.'

* * *

What did you say?

Sam's daughter says to him one day, 'Dad, as you're coming up to 80, why don't you go see Doctor Seigal and get him to give you a full medical? You haven't been yourself ever since Mum died.'

'OK,' says Sam. And sure enough, a week later, he has a full health check.

Three days afterwards, Doctor Seigal is surprised to see

Sam walking towards him in the street with a beautiful, sexy-looking lady on his arm. She looks no more than 30. When they meet, Doctor Seigal says, 'It's nice to see you, Sam. When you have a moment, why don't you call me? I have something I need to discuss with you.'

'OK, Doctor,' says Sam, 'I'll call you this afternoon.'

When Sam rings later that day, Doctor Seigal says to him, 'I see that you've decided to start seeing other women, Sam.'

'Yes doctor,' replies Sam, 'I'm doing what you suggested when you said, "Get a hot mamma and be cheerful." '

'But that's not what I said, Sam,' says Doctor Seigal, 'I told you that "You've got a heart murmur...be careful." '

* * *

Hear no evil

It's tea break at their office and Avrahom and Harry, both deaf, are talking about being out late the night before. Avrahom says, 'My wife was asleep when I got home, so I sneaked into bed and didn't get into any trouble.'

Harry says, 'Then you're very lucky. When I got back, I realised I was in *shtook* – my wife was awake and waiting for me in bed. She was *broyges* and started swearing at me for being out late.'

Avrahom asks, 'So what did you do, Harry?'

'I just turned out the light,' replies Harry.

* *.*

Wrong one

Kitty and Anna, two elderly ladies, are out having a bite to eat one day when Anna notices something odd and takes a long hard look at Kitty's right ear. 'Kitty,' she says, 'do you know that you've got a suppository sticking out of your right ear?'

'You say I have a suppository in my ear?' replies Kitty. 'So let me see, already.'

Kitty pulls it out, stares at it for a while, then says, 'Anna, I'm so glad you saw this thing. Now I think I know where my hearing aid is.'

* * *

Hear today, gone tomorrow
Now that Moshe, Gary and Abe have retired, they enjoy meeting once a week for a round of golf. They are, thank God, all healthy except for having poor hearing.

One day, during a round of golf, Moshe says, 'Windy, isn't it?'

'No,' replies Abe, 'it's Thursday.'

And Gary says, 'So am I. Let's have a beer.'

Prescription Drugs (including Viagra)

A pain in the mouth
Maurice wakes up with a terrible pain in his mouth and books an emergency appointment to see Adrian, his dentist. When Maurice gets into the chair, Adrian checks his teeth and says, 'You've got a badly decayed molar, which really needs to be extracted right away. Are you OK with injections?'

'No, I'm afraid of needles,' replies Maurice.

'How about gas?' asks Adrian.

'No, I'm allergic to gas. I come out in a terrible rash,' replies Maurice.

Adrian then says, 'I have an idea. Wait here while I get something.'

When he returns, Adrian gives Maurice a glass of water and two blue pills.

'What kind of pills are these?' Maurice asks.

'They're just ordinary Viagra pills,' replies Adrian.

'What? Will these deaden the pain?'

'No,' replies Adrian, 'they won't help your pain at all, but they will give you something to hold on to while I extract your tooth.'

* * *

A rabbi's verdict on Viagra

Q: What *brocheh* does one say before taking Viagra?

A: There is a choice of three blessings: (1) *Boruch Atah Hashem zokeif k'fuffim* – Staighten those who are bent. (2) *Boruch Atah Hashem ya'aleh v'yovo* – Arise and come. (3) *Boruch Atah Hashem Mechayei hameitim* – Raise the dead.

* * *

New drugs being developed for men

In light of the success of Viagra, Israeli chemists are developing a whole line of drugs oriented towards improving the performance of men in today's society. Here are a few of them:

DIRECTRA – a dose of this drug was given to 100 men before they went on a car trip. It caused 72 of them to stop and ask for directions when they got lost, compared to a control group of just two men.

PROJECTRA – Men given this experimental drug were far more likely than normal to finish a household repair job before starting on the next.

COMPLIMENTRA – In clinical trials, 82 out of 100 middle-aged men given this drug noticed that their wives had a new hairstyle. The drug is now being tested to see if its effects extend to noticing new clothing.

BUYAGRA – After taking this drug for only two days, married

men reported an urge to buy their wives expensive jewellery and gifts.

NEGA-SPORTAGRA – This drug has the effect of making men want to turn off TV sport and actually converse with other family members.

FLATULAGRA – This complex drug makes it more pleasant to take long car trips with certain men.

* * *

Yeshurun (the straight one)

Dear Rabbi Levy,

Is it permissible to take Viagra on *shabbes*?

Regards

Moshe

My dear Moshe,

There are two differing thoughts on this. One is that it's disallowed because it violates the law that forbids erecting a structure (*boneh*) on *shabbes*. However, I believe that one should read '*boneh*' as '*boner*' and thus it's permitted to ingest Viagra on *shabbes*.

Looking at it another way, the taking of Viagra is permitted before sundown as long as the *Kabbalat Shabbat* takes less than a half-hour to complete, the children are asleep and your wife doesn't have a headache.

Regards

Rabbi Levy

* * *

On the beach

Isaac falls asleep on a beach for several hours and gets sunburned. His legs are the worst and they are already starting to blister. In agony, Isaac goes to the local hospital and is immediately admitted after being diagnosed with second-degree burns.

Dr Cohen tells the nurse, 'This man needs continuous intravenous feeding with saline and electrolytes, a sedative, and a Viagra pill every four hours.'

The nurse is astonished by this and says, 'Dr Cohen, what good will Viagra do him?'

'It'll keep the sheets off his legs,' replies Dr Cohen.

Life (and Death)

Mishaps and Emergencies

A little change

On his way back from work one evening, Benny gets hit by a car as he crosses the street and is knocked unconscious. To the bystanders, he looks in a bad way. A priest happens to be passing and not knowing Benny's religion, administers last rites. But immediately, Benny's eyes open and he's quickly fully awake.

'What were you saying to me?' asks Benny.

The priest tells him about the last rites.

'I suppose a little bit of a different religion won't hurt,' says Benny. 'Thanks.'

Benny can't wait to tell his family about his experience. When he gets home, he says to his wife, 'Yetta, you won't believe what's just happened to me.'

But she tells him, 'Later, Benny, later. I don't have time. I'm late for my supervision meeting. I've left your dinner in the oven. See you later.'

So Benny goes up to his daughter's room and says, 'Leah, you won't believe what's just happened to me.'

But she says, 'Sorry, Dad, I'm on the phone planning my weekend. Could you please come back later, and close the door behind you, will you?'

He then goes to look for his son, whom he finds driving the car out of the garage.

'Maurice, you won't believe what's just happened to me.'

But his son says, 'Dad, I'm late for a date. I need the car and some money. Can you lend me £100 please? I'll talk to you tomorrow.'

So Benny goes back into his house, shakes his head and says, 'I've only been a Gentile for two hours and already I hate three Jews.'

* * *

Good news and bad
Leah phones her husband at work. 'Issy, do you have time for a chat?'

'Sorry, darling, this is not a good time – I'm about to go into a board meeting.'

'But this won't take long,' Leah says, 'I just want to tell you some good news and some bad news.'

'I really haven't the time,' says Issy, 'so just quickly tell me the good news.'

'Oh all right, then. The air bag on your new Lexus works very well.'

* * *

Last rites
Sean, a Catholic, is struck by a bus on a busy street. He's lying near death on the pavement and a crowd begins to gather. Suddenly, in a painful voice, Sean shouts, 'A priest. Please somebody, get me a priest!'

Minutes drag by but no priest appears. Then a policeman yells out, 'A priest! Please! Isn't there a priest here to give this man his last rites?'

Finally, out of the crowd steps 80-year-old Abe.

'Mister policeman,' says Abe, 'I'm not a priest – I'm not even a Christian. But for 50 years now I'm living behind a Catholic church and every night I'm overhearing their services. I can recall a lot of it and maybe I can be of some comfort to this poor man.'

The policeman agrees and clears the crowd so Abe can get

through to where Sean lies. Abe kneels down, leans over the prostrate Sean and says in a solemn voice, 'B-4. I-19. N-38. G-54. O-72....'

* * *

The accident
Unfortunately, there has been a terrible accident at the nuclear energy plant and three leading nuclear physicists are very badly contaminated. After a specialist has seen them, he declares that they are all dying and none is likely to survive the night. Each is quickly asked for their dying wish.

'What would you like, Pierre?'

Pierre replies, 'I would like to meet the President and be awarded the Legion of Honour for my contribution to new energy sources.'

'What would you like, John?'

John replies, 'I would like to meet the Queen and be knighted for my services to cheap UK energy.'

'And what would you like, Moshe?'

Moshe replies, 'I would like a second opinion.'

* * *

His new ears
One day, there's an explosion at the oil refinery where Moshe works and although he doesn't lose his life, he does lose his ears – both are blown off in the blast. So he goes to see Dr Myers, a Harley Street specialist. After examining him, Dr Myers says, 'Well Moshe, I can reconstruct your ears without too much of a problem.'

'That's great news, Doctor,' says Moshe, 'but how will you do it?'

'I use one of three types of material for reconstructing ears,' says Dr Myers. 'I can rebuild using plastic, cow's ears or pig's ears. Here's some samples to help you choose.'

Moshe carefully feels each sample in turn. He thinks the plastic too hard and the cow's ears too soft. But the pig's ears feel very natural and though he isn't happy using non-kosher materials, Moshe decides to go for them.

Three weeks after the operation, Moshe goes back to Harley Street for a check up. Dr Myers is pleased with the appearance of Moshe's new ears and asks him whether his hearing is impaired in any way.

'No doctor,' replies Moshe, 'but I do get some crackling from time to time.'

* * *

Men from the JVFC
One evening, a fire starts inside Shmatta Ltd, the leading clothing factory, and within minutes it becomes a fierce blaze.

As soon as the first fire engine arrives on the scene, Jacob goes over to the firemen and says, 'Please. I'm the chief executive of this factory. All our next season's designs are in my office in the centre of the building. They must be saved. I'll give you £25,000 if you can save them.'

Even though the thought of the money encourages the men to take risks, the strong, hot flames keep them from going inside. When two more fire engines arrive, Jacob shouts out that the offer is now £50,000 to the team who saves the design files.

Then, a single siren is heard and a fourth fire engine comes rushing up the hill towards the fire. From the initials on the front, JVFC, everyone knows it's from the Jewish Volunteer Fire Company, whose members are all over 65. But how can they possibly help? To everyone's amazement, the old-fashioned JVFC fire engine doesn't stop outside the building but drives straight into the middle of the fire.

As everyone watches, the elderly Jewish firemen jump down from their engine and begin fighting the fire with unbelievable energy and commitment. Five minutes later, the men from JVFC have extinguished the fire and save the secret designs. Jacob keeps to his bargain and writes out a cheque to JVFC for £50,000. He then personally thanks each one of the elderly fire fighters and in particular Moshe, the 75-year-old head of the team.

Jacob asks him, 'What are you going to do with all that money?'

'Vell,' says Moshe, 'the first thing ve are going to do is fix the brakes on our run-down fire engine.'

* * *

Saved in Bournemouth

Moshe is on holiday in Bournemouth to celebrate his 70th birthday. It is a nice day, so he decides to go for a swim. But he has only been out for five minutes when a huge wave comes from nowhere and sweeps him out to sea.

'*Oy veh*,' cries Moshe, 'Help! Help me someone, please. I'm drowning.'

Fortunately, a lifeguard hears his cries and swims out to him. He grips Moshe tightly and swims back to the shore with him. As soon as he gets Moshe on to dry land, the lifeguard gives him mouth-to-mouth resuscitation. Five minutes later, Moshe sits up – he is saved.

The lifeguard helps Moshe to his feet and says, 'If I were you, sir, I'd take it easy for the rest of the day. Why don't you go back to your hotel and put your feet up?'

As the lifeguard turns to walk away, Moshe whispers to a lady next to him, 'Excuse me, but could you help me please. How much does one tip for a thing like that?'

* * *

He's missing

Sadie's husband Bernie doesn't come home from work one day. She is a bit worried because she has not received any calls from him to say he'd be late. She rings Bernie's office, but there is no reply and she rings Bernie's mobile, but it is switched off. By 9pm, she is very worried. She rings all the people who might know where he is, but nobody knows. At 10pm, she decides to go to the police station to report him missing.

When she gets there, she tells the duty officer, 'I don't know what to do. My husband Bernie didn't come home from work today. I can't live without him. Please help me.'

'OK, madam,' he replies, 'calm down. I just need you to answer a few simple questions.'

'Ask away,' she replies.

'First of all, can you describe him for me? I need this so we can put out a search for him.'

'Well, Officer, he's 52 with brown eyes and dark brown hair – what's left of it. He's well built – well that's not strictly true, he's quite fat really, and he sweats a lot. He's also got what I call an aggressively loud voice. He's got two missing front teeth…he wears thick old-fashioned glasses…and he's…wait a minute, Officer, I've had second thoughts, maybe you shouldn't bother looking for him.'

Big Business

The business competitors

Benjy and Issy were in conversation. Benjy says, 'Did you know our *shul* has not one but two podiatrists as members?'

'Yes,' replies Issy, 'and did you know that they have both just opened new clinics in the same street?'

'Well, that doesn't really surprise me,' says Benjy with a gleam in his eye, 'after all, they were arch enemies.'

* * *

Reductions

Moshe's haberdashery business is doing very badly and he decides he has to reduce his staffing level by two if he wants to survive. So two have to go. But it doesn't help for long and he soon has to let another two go, and then soon after that, another two. Moshe dies not long afterwards. All who knew him said that the terrible strain of running his business contributed to his death.

Later, as they're carrying Moshe's body to his grave, Moshe suddenly pushes off the lid, sits up in his coffin and asks, 'How many men are carrying me?'

'Eight,' comes the reply.

'Better lay off two,' says Moshe, lying down again.

* * *

Unexpected marketing

Sharon has reached the age of 18 and is regarded by many as, well, a stunner. One day, she goes to buy a new dress.

'Can I please try on that dress in the window?' she asks Benjamin, the boutique owner.

'Go ahead,' Benjamin replies with a shrug, 'maybe it'll attract some business.'

* * *

Business lesson number 1

Some company executives meet at a school reunion. One of them, Moshe, arrives in a chauffer-driven Rolls-Royce. Moshe has with him a beautiful young woman and she is dressed in very expensive clothes. All evening Moshe donates and spends money as if there were no tomorrow. His friends quickly realise that he is very rich and so they ask him how he has managed to become so wealthy.

'Moshe, don't be offended but we never thought you would be successful. How did you do it? Please tell us.'

'I don't mind telling you,' replies Moshe. 'I'm in manufacturing and I've got a successful product which costs me just £1 to make. I sell all I can produce for £5 and you'd be surprised how quickly five per cent adds up.'

* * *

Business lesson number 2

Hyman emigrates to England and sets up Kosher Tailors Ltd. He starts with making alterations and then moves into bespoke suits. Over time, his three sons join him and the company grows and prospers. Soon, the company is exceedingly profitable and his sons want to float KTL on the Stock Exchange.

'Dad,' they say, 'we need to establish a financial basis for KTL. How should we determine costs and assets? How do we establish value?'

Hyman thinks for a while, then replies, 'Go down to the basement and bring me the box behind the old boiler. You should find some flat irons inside the box. Then go upstairs and bring down the old tailor's dummy behind the door. You will also find an old treadle sewing machine upstairs together with an ironing board. Bring these also to me.'

The sons do as they are told.

Hyman looks at the old instruments and says, 'These are what I started with. Everything else is profit.'

* * *

The threatening letters

Moshe is a kosher butcher. He's not doing very well and to make matters worse, his wholesaler keeps on writing him threatening letters to pay his outstanding invoices. After the fifth such letter, Moshe looses his patience and replies to his wholesaler as follows:

Dear Sir

I object to your recent threatening letters and I think I need to explain to you how I do business. Every month, my accountant calculates how much money I can afford to pay out. Then I place all my creditors' invoices in a hat and get my secretary to draw out as many invoices from the hat as I have money to pay. If you persist in sending out these threatening letters, I won't even put your invoices in the hat.

* * *

Classical advice

Hymie and Sadie are on holiday in Italy and on one of the duller days decide to go on a coach tour of Rome. They are having a nice, relaxed time when their guide points out the Colosseum to them.

'Well Sadie,' says Hymie, 'isn't that a perfect example of what I've been telling everyone for ages? If you don't have sufficient capital, you mustn't begin to build.'

* * *

The order
Moshe's business was struggling. So he was very dismayed to receive this letter from his supplier:

Dear Moshe
We regret that we won't be able to fill your recent order for 3,000 dark-brown men's suits until full payment has been received for your last order. Please advise.

Moshe wrote back:

Dear supplier
Please cancel my recent order for 3,000 dark-brown men's suits. I cannot wait that long.

* * *

The herring seller
Daniel is walking down the street when he sees his old friend Victor sitting outside Bank Leumi. Daniel hasn't seen Victor for many years and so is looking forward to meeting him again. As Daniel comes up to Victor, he is surprised to see that Victor is not just sitting there doing nothing – he's actually selling *shmaltz herrings* from a barrel – and he appears to be doing good business. Daniel goes up to Victor and within seconds they are both hugging each other.

Daniel asks, 'So how are you getting on, Victor?'

'I'm OK,' replies Victor, 'I'm making a living.'

'Well then,' says Daniel, 'maybe you could lend me £20. I'm not doing so well these days.'

'I'm sorry,' replies Victor, 'I just can't do that. It's not allowed.'

'What do you mean it's not allowed?' asks Daniel.

'Well, in order to get Bank Leumi to allow me this pitch outside their bank, I made a deal with them. They promised not to sell *shmaltz herring* and I promised not to lend money.'

* * *

Big business

Abe is just starting out in business, but he has to start small and decides to open up a lemonade stand outside Ben's Bagels. He puts up a sign that says: ALL YOU CAN DRINK FOR 25p

It's a hot day and almost immediately some children arrive and pay him 25p. One boy quickly drinks the lemonade he's given, goes over to Abe with the empty cup and says, 'Could you please refill my cup?'

Abe replies, 'OK, but that will be another 25p.'

'How come?' says the boy. 'The sign clearly says, "All you can drink for 25p."'

'*Nu?*' says Abe. 'You had a glass of lemonade, didn't you?'

'Yes.'

'Well,' says Abe, 'that's all you can drink for 25p.'

* * *

How to sell a shirt

Sam, who is learning the tailor's trade by working in his father's shop, has been attending to a customer for almost 30 minutes when he goes over to his father and whispers, 'Dad, my customer wants to buy a shirt and has tried on our top-of-the-range Baleboss shirt, you know, the un-shrinkable silk and cashmere version. He wants to know whether the shirt will shrink. What shall I tell him?'

'So *nu*, does it fit him?' says his father.

'No,' replies Sam, 'between you and me, it's a bit too large for him.'

'So go tell him it will shrink.'

* * *

Taken from the Shmatters R Us Annual Report and Accounts

'This year, business is so bad that not only are customers staying away in vast numbers but also the dress manufacturers are firing their sons-in-law.'

* * *

Customer relations

Tony owns a local car repair garage. One day, Martin, one of his customers, arrives to pick up his car. Tony goes over to him, shakes his hand and says, 'I'd just like to say thanks for your patronage. I wish I had 10 customers like you.'

'Wow! It's nice to hear you say that,' says Martin, 'but why are you thanking me? You know I always argue with your prices and I always complain about the work you do on my car.'

'I know,' says Tony, 'but I'd still like 10 customers like you – the trouble is, I have at least 50 like you.'

* * *

My son the businessman

Freda and her friend Ruth were having a chat about their sons. 'So Ruth,' asks Freda, 'I hear that your Paul has just been made a director of Shmultz PLC. Is he a good businessman, then?'

'Is he a good businessman?' replies Ruth. '*Oy!* He's a brilliant businessman, Freda. In fact mine Paul is so dedicated to his company that every night he takes his secretary to bed with him – just in case he comes up with a brilliant idea.'

* * *

Business trouble

Aaron and Jonathan, two businessmen both in their eighties, meet one day while out shopping. Aaron asks, 'So *nu*, Jonathan, what's new?'

'Vat's new, you ask me? Trouble, that's vat's new,' replies Jonathan. 'Mine secretary is suing me for breach of promise.'

'But I don't understand,' says Aaron. 'At your age, what could you promise her?'

* * *

Now that's *chutzpah*

Ethel, a little old lady with a lovely smile, makes a living selling roses on a street corner for £1 a rose. Maurice, on the other hand, works for a bank in the same street and is doing very well for himself.

Maurice has always felt sorry for Ethel and whenever he leaves his office for lunch and passes Ethel, he always gives her £1. But Maurice never takes a rose from her and although this has been going on for two years, the two of them have never spoken to each other.

One day, as Maurice passes Ethel and leaves his usual £1, Ethel speaks to him for the first time. 'I appreciate your business, sir. You really are my best customer, but I must point out to you that the price of a rose has now gone up to £1.50.'

* * *

The telephone call

Daniel, a single 40-year-old, has just returned from a business trip to New York and is telling his friend Sam about a telephone conversation he had while there.

'What an embarrassing conversion it was,' Daniel says.

'In what way was it embarrassing?' asks Sam.

'Well,' replies Daniel, 'Whenever I go on a business trip, I always pick up one of the cards left in various places that advertise girls willing to help men relax – you know what I mean, don't you, Sam, massage and all that?'

'Yes, of course I know what "all that" means,' replies Sam, with a wide smile on his face.

Daniel continues, 'So as soon as I had checked into my hotel, I took out the card I found in my airport taxi. It was from a girl called "SEXYLEGS" and believe me, Sam, the photo on the card was of a long-legged beauty with great curves and a gorgeous smile, kneeling on a bed. You know the kind, don't you, Sam?'

'I sure do,' replies Sam.

'So I'm in my room and I call her,' continues Daniel. '"Hello," the lady says to me, and *oy veh*, did she sound sexy! I couldn't wait to meet her so I said, "Hello, I understand that you give a wonderful massage and I'd like you to come to my room and give me one. But I also want more. Let me be honest with you – I've just arrived from London and I'm feeling horny. What I need badly is some sex. And I want it for the whole night. You name it, we'll do it, so bring all of your lotions, potions and toys with you and we'll have an all-night session to remember. You can even cover me with strawberries and cream. How does that grab you, darling?"'

'Wow,' says Sam, 'so what did she say to that?'

'She said, "That sounds pretty fantastic to me, but for an outside line you need to dial 9 first."'

* * *

What a day

Harry comes home from work one day and says to his wife, 'Kitty, just for once, please, don't start telling me about all the troubles you encountered today. Instead, why don't you ask what happened to me today?'

Kitty remains silent.

'So ask already,' says Harry, 'what kind of day did I have? Go on, just ask will you.'

Kitty relents. 'OK Harry, so what happened?'

At this, Harry buries his head in his hands, moans and says, 'What happened? *Oy veh*, Kitty, better you shouldn't ask.'

Benevolence

The benefactor

Issy the millionaire goes to *shul* one *shabbes* and at the end of the service stops to shake Rabbi Levy's hand.

'Rabbi,' says Issy, 'that was a God-damned fine sermon you gave today.'

Rabbi Levy replies, 'Why thank you Issy, but I'd rather you didn't use that kind of language in the Lord's House.'

But Issy continues, 'In fact I was so God-damned impressed with your sermon that I've decided to send you £10,000 for the synagogue rebuilding fund.'

Rabbi Levy replies, 'No shit?'

* * *

The fund-raisers

Four ladies from their synagogue's fund-raising committee are driving home one Sunday afternoon when they are involved in a terrible car crash. Unfortunately, none of them survive. When they arrive at the Pearly Gates, they are kept waiting to get into heaven because the angel at the gates can't find them listed in the book of heavenly new arrivals. 'I'm sorry,' he says to them, 'but I can't find you in the book.'

So he has no choice but to send them down to hell.

A week later, God visits the Pearly Gates and says to the

angel, 'Where are those nice Jewish ladies who were supposed to be here by now?'

'You mean the fund-raisers? I didn't see them listed, so I sent them to hell,' replies the angel.

'You did what?' God says, 'I wanted them here. If you don't want to join them, you'd better call Satan and get them transferred back here right away.'

So the angel phones Satan and says, 'Satan, you know those Jewish ladies I sent you last week? Well we really need them up here. Could you please send them back?

'Sorry, I can't oblige,' Satan replies, 'they've been down here only a week and already they've raised £100,000 for an air-conditioning system.'

* * *

The beggar

Moshe is strolling down the street one afternoon when he sees a beggar sitting on the pavement outside a department store with a placard around his neck saying, 'PLEASE CAN YOU HELP A POOR MAN'.

Moshe notices that the beggar is always smiling and whenever passers-by put money in his hat, the beggar thanks them personally. So Moshe goes over to the beggar and puts a £5 note in his hat.

'Why thank you very much sir,' says the beggar, 'you are very generous.'

'Tell me,' asks Moshe, 'don't you have a family?'

'Oh yes,' replies the beggar, 'I have a lovely family.'

'Do you have any children?' asks Moshe.

'I have two handsome boys and two beautiful girls,' replies the beggar, 'and all four are very happily married.'

'Well I think it's disgraceful that they won't support you,' says Moshe.

'But they would support me if I let them,' says the beggar.

'So why don't you let them?' asks Moshe.

'What, and lose my hard-won independence?' replies the beggar.

* * *

Inflation?

As Sam is walking down the street, he's accosted by a *shnorrer*. 'Please can you give me £1?' says the *shnorrer*.

'Why should I?' asks Sam.

'Because I need to buy a cup of tea,' replies the *shnorrer*.

'But a cup of tea is only 50p,' says Sam.

'I know,' says the *shnorrer*, 'but I'm a big tipper.'

* * *

It will be a *mitzvah*!

One day, as Judith is reaching inside her fridge for something for dinner, she notices a plastic-wrapped chicken right at the back, on the bottom shelf. She removes it from the fridge and she's not happy with what she sees. This is a chicken she bought many weeks ago and has forgotten about. It's looking very ragged and unappetising – even a bit smelly. But just as she's about to throw it in the bin, her husband Harry stops her.

'Don't do that,' says Harry. 'Our neighbour Bernie has been out of work for months and he and his family probably haven't had a roast chicken meal for ages. I think you should give him the chicken.'

'But it's no good, it's probably gone off,' says Judith.

'It doesn't matter,' says Harry, 'just do it. It will be a *mitzvah*!'

So Judith gives the chicken to her next-door neighbour. But then, two days later, they learn that Bernie is terribly sick and has been taken to the local hospital.

'We must go to the hospital right away', says Harry, 'and pay Bernie a visit – it will be a *mitzvah*!'

The day following their visit, they learn that Bernie has died.

'*Oy gevalt*,' cries Judith, 'what on earth shall we do, Harry?'

'What shall we do?' Harry replies. 'We shall go to Bernie's *levoyah*, that's what. It will be a *mitzvah*!'

Two days after attending Bernie's *levoyah*, Harry says, 'Judith, we've got to pay a visit to Bernie's family while they're sitting *shivah*. It will be a *mitzvah*!'

So Judith and Bernie go next door to join the family in prayers for the loss of their husband and father. By the time they return home, Judith is crying. 'Harry,' she sobs, 'don't you think it was wrong of us to give Bernie that old chicken?'

'You must be joking, Judith,' replies Harry. 'From that one old chicken, we got ourselves four *mitzvahs*!'

Education

Elephant papers

There is a story told of an Oxford University professor who decided to ask his students to write a paper on the elephant. This is what he got back from them.

- The British student wrote about 'The human rights of the elephant'.
- The French student wrote about 'The elephant and his love life'.
- The Japanese student wrote about 'The elephant and its place in IT'.
- The American student wrote about 'Elephants and the war machine'.
- The Israeli student wrote about 'The elephant and the Jewish problem'.

* * *

Did I hear right?

Sadie is sitting on a bus when it stops and two Italian men get on. They sit down in front of her and begin to chat. At first, Sadie ignores them but suddenly she hears things she would rather not hear in public. One Italian says to the other,

'Emma come first. Den I come. Den two asses come together. I come once-a-more. Two asses, they come together again. I come again and pee twice. Then I come one lasta time.'

'I think you two are disgusting,' shouts Sadie. 'I think you're both sex maniacs and I've a good mind to call the police. Over here in England, we don't speak aloud in public places about our sex lives....'

'Hey, coola down lady,' says one of the men, 'who talkin' abouta sexa? I'm a justa tellin' my frienda how to spella "Mississippi".'

* * *

What's the difference?

Young Sam asks his father, 'Dad, what's the difference between potentially and realistically?'

His father ponders for a while, then replies, 'I suggest you first ask your mother if she would sleep with Robert Redford for £1 million. Then ask your sister if she would sleep with Brad Pitt for £1 million. Then come back and tell me what you learned.'

'OK, Dad,' says Sam.

Sam finds his mother and asks, 'Mum, would you sleep with Robert Redford for £1 million?'

She replies, 'Absolutely, Sam, how could I miss such an opportunity?'

Sam then goes to his older sister and asks, 'Sis, would you sleep with Brad Pitt for £1 million?'

His sister replies dreamily, 'Oh Sam, of course I would, just give me the chance, that's all I ask.'

Over the next few days, Sam thinks a lot about what his mother and sister have said. Then he goes back to his father.

'So Sam,' asks his father, 'did you find out the difference between potentially and realistically?'

Sam replies, 'Yes dad, I learned that potentially we're sitting on £2 million pounds, but realistically we're living with two *kurveh*.'

'That's my boy,' says his father.

* * *

On the job
Abe goes into his local bookshop and asks the saleswoman, 'Excuse me, but where is the self-help section?'

She replies, 'If I told you, sir, it would defeat the purpose.'

* * *

Seminars for Jewish men, given by women lecturers
- Combating stupidity
- You, too, can do housework
- PMS – learn when to keep your mouth shut
- Parenting – no, it doesn't end with conception
- Get a life – learn to cook
- How not to act like a moron when you're obviously wrong
- You – the weaker sex
- Reasons to give flowers
- How to stay awake after sex

* * *

The ape experiments

Sidney attends a lecture on the subject of 'Hunger or Sex, which instinct is the stronger?'.

The lecturer describes to the audience a series of tests he has conducted to find a scientific answer. 'For my tests,' he says, 'I used one healthy male and one healthy female chimpanzee. Before each test, I kept them apart so they could not see or hear each other. I also starved the male of both food and sex for a week.

'For my first test, I put a bowl of food in the middle of my lab and then placed the male in one corner and the female in the opposite corner. The male looked at the female, then looked at the food, then rushed to the bowl of food and devoured it. So, ladies and gentlemen, it looked like hunger prevailed over the sexual instincts of the male.

'But as a true scientist, I did a second test to see whether the earth's magnetic field had influenced the outcome. Again I kept the apes separate, starved the male and put the bowl of food in the middle of the lab. Then I put the male in the southwest corner and the female facing him in the northeast corner. The male immediately looked at the female, then at the food, then rushed to the bowl of food and devoured it. So once again the male preferred food to sex.

'But I wanted to be absolutely sure of the results so I carried out a third test, this time placing the male much closer to the female than to the food. The result was the same. The male looked at the female, then at the food, then rushed to the bowl of food and devoured it.

'So, ladies and gentlemen, I can say with some confidence that hunger is a much stronger drive than sexual instincts in the male animal. Thank you.'

After the applause has died down, Sidney stands up and says aloud, 'I have a question for you, mister lecturer. Have you tried doing the experiments with a different female ape?'

* * *

Mathematics of a Jewish relationship
Wise man + Wise woman = Romance
Wise man + Dumb woman = Affair
Dumb man + Wise woman = Marriage
Dumb man + Dumb woman = Pregnancy

* * *

Reading the results
Ten-year-old Sam comes home from school with his end-of-term exam results and gives his report to his father Sidney. Sidney reads through Sam's results and sees:

English 46%
French 35%
Mathematics 43%
Computing 49%
History 40%
Geography 25%
Technical Drawing 51%
Singing 88%

As soon as he finishes reading, Sidney walks over to Sam and gives him a *klop* on the head.

Taken by surprise, Sam cries out, 'Ouch! What did you do that for, Dad? Didn't I get a high mark for my singing?'

'With marks like these,' replies Sidney, 'and you still felt like singing?'

Occupations

Time off for a happy event

Issy went to see his personnel manager. 'Could I please have this Friday off so that I can have a long weekend?'

'Why?'

'Because my wife is expecting a baby,' Issy replied.

'But of course you can, Issy,' came the reply. 'Why didn't you say so in the first place? When is the event due?'

'About nine months after I get home.'

* * *

What's your position?

Jacob is out sailing in his expensive yacht when he gets into difficulties and has to call out the lifeboat. Because the coastguard needs an accurate fix on the yacht's location, he calls the yacht on the radio.

'What is your position? Repeat, what is your position?'

Jacob replies, 'My position? It's very good. I'm marketing director of a medium-sized firm of solicitors in London.'

* * *

The job seeker

Stan is nearly 60 and for many years now, he's been regularly going to his local job centre every Tuesday. Every time he goes, he picks up his jobseeker's allowance – he's never been known to actually look for a job.

It's Tuesday again. Stan walks up to the desk and says to the clerk, 'Good morning. What job do you have for me? As you know, I never like claiming any benefits or allowances – I'm not a sponger. I think it's far better to look for a good job.'

The clerk is surprised to hear this, but replies, 'You're really in luck today, Stan. We've just received instructions from a very wealthy man who wants a bodyguard/chauffeur for his nymphomaniac daughter. It says here that the hours are very long, but in return, you'll get to wear smart suits, shirts, ties and shoes, all of which will be provided free of charge. Meals will also be provided. You will get to drive a big Lexus when you're not working and you'll have to escort the young lady on her many overseas trips. The salary package is £100,000 a year plus expenses.'

Stan says, 'You're pulling my leg, aren't you?'

The clerk replies, 'Yes, of course, but you started it.'

* * *

The watch tower

In the middle of a forest is a small town. It was built far from the main roads and the Jews living there were afraid that when the Messiah comes, he would not know they were there and would pass them by. So they build a tower on the edge of town and appoint the town beggar as watchman. If the Messiah should come, the watchman would give him directions to the town.

One day a stranger visits the tower and as instructed, the watchman comes down to greet him.

'What are you doing here in the middle of nowhere?' asks the stranger.

'My job is to sit on top of this tower and wait for the Messiah,' answers the watchman.

'So how do you like your job?' the stranger asks. 'It can't pay you much.'

'I know,' replies the watchman, 'but at least it's steady work.'

* * *

The big escape
Sarah, Rebecca and Sadie work in the same accounts office
and every day they notice their tough and demanding boss
Kitty leaving work early. So they decide that when Kitty next
leaves early, they will leave right after her. After all, she
never phones them or returns to work later on, so how would
she know they left early? That afternoon, Kitty leaves early
again and within five minutes, so do Sarah, Rebecca and
Sadie.

Sarah is thrilled to get home early. She does some
gardening, plays with her son and goes to bed early.

Rebecca is elated to be able to get in a quick workout at the
gym before going out on a dinner date.

Sadie is happy to get home early because she wants to
surprise her husband. But when she gets to her bedroom
door, she hears muffled noises from inside. She opens the
door quietly and is shocked to see her husband in bed with
her boss, Kitty. Gently, Sadie closes the door and creeps out
of the house.

Next day, during their coffee break, Sarah and Rebecca
agree to leave early again and ask Sadie if she is going to
leave with them.

'No way,' says Sadie, 'I almost got caught by Kitty
yesterday and I don't want to take another chance.'

* * *

A retirement riddle
Q: What do you call someone who enjoys work and refuses
to retire?
A: A *meshugganah*.

* * *

Captain Judith

Moshe is on a trip to London. As the El Al Jumbo airliner pushes back from the gate, the flight attendant gives the passengers the usual information regarding seat belts, etc. Finally, she announces, 'Now sit back and enjoy your trip while your captain, Judith Levy, and her crew take you safely to your destination.'

When the flight attendant arrives with the drinks trolley, Moshe asks her, 'Did I understand you correctly? Is this big plane really being flown by a woman?'

'Yes sir' replies the attendant. 'In fact the plane's entire crew is female.'

'*Oy veh*,' says Moshe, 'I'd better have two gin and tonics. I don't know what to think of being on a plane with only women controlling it. Do you think you can arrange for me to go up to the cockpit to see for myself?'

'Yes of course sir,' says the attendant, 'but that's another thing you might like to know – we no longer call it the cockpit.'

* * *

Sadie knows she works for a Jewish company because:

- When she knocks her mug of coffee on the floor and the mug shatters, her office friends shout out, in unison, '*Mazeltov*'.
- Her manager knows how many times per week she ordered in lunch; from whom she ordered it; what exactly she's ordered; and how much it cost her.
- She can leave her wallet on her desk unattended and never have it stolen, but she can't do the same for her unattended lunch.
- At least seven people in her office are related to each other.
- No two employees have exactly the same benefits package.
- Half the senior managers have Masters degrees in Jewish

Education, Jewish History or Jewish Humour.
- One manager has a degree in Business Studies but no one listens to him because he does not have *smicha*.
- All the men employed by her company are considered professional staff, while all the women employed by her company are considered support staff but actually run the company while the men run back and forth having meetings and looking busy.
- She can't make use of Microsoft Spellcheck because most of the words used in office memos are only vaguely reminiscent of English.
- Her job description (in fact every job description she sees) is at least 10 years out of date.
- If any employee pays income tax, it's regarded as a dismissible offence.
- She gets only one day's notice to prepare her department's annual budget (which is eventually approved six months into the new financial year).
- Everyone in her office gets paid on the basis of how much money they need, or say they need, or want.
- She has off Jewish holidays, Legal holidays, Christian holidays, African holidays, Canadian holidays, Calendar holidays....
- She attends many lengthy meetings where no decisions are ever reached.
- Every elderly person she speaks to mentions that they have a grandson who's single.
- Telephone callers to her company listen to Israeli music while on hold.
- Friday afternoon is eerily quiet after 1pm.
- All office events are catered by the same kosher restaurant over and over again, until she never wants to eat, smell, or think about their food again.

* * *

Windows of opportunity

Bill Gates decides to organise an enormous session of recruitment for a chairman for Microsoft Europe. The 5,000 candidates are all assembled in a large room. One of the candidates is Maurice Cohe. Bill Gates thanks all the candidates for coming and asks that all those who do not know the programming language JAVA PLUS to rise and leave. Two thousand people rise and leave the room.

But Maurice Cohen says to himself, 'I don't know this language, but vat haff I got to lose if I stay? I'll give it a try.'

Bill Gates then asks all remaining candidates who have never had experience of team management of more than 100 people to rise and leave. Two thousand people rise and leave the room.

But Maurice Cohen says to himself, 'Oy, I never managed anyvun but myself, but vat haff I got to lose if I stay? What can happen to me?' So he stays.

Bill Gates then asks all remaining candidates who don't have degrees in People Management to rise and leave. Five hundred people rise and leave the room.

But Maurice Cohen says to himself, 'Oy veh, I left school at 15 so I never vent to university, but vat haff I got to lose if I stay?' So he stays in the room.

Bill Gates finally asks all the remaining candidates who don't speak Serbo-Croat to rise and leave; 498 people rise and leave the room.

But Maurice Cohen says to himself, '*Oy veh zmir*, I don't speak Serbo-Croat, but vat the hell! Haff I got anything to lose?' So he stays in the room and finds himself alone with one other candidate – everyone else has gone.

Bill Gates joins them and says, 'Apparently you are the only two candidates who speak Serbo-Croat, so I'd now like to hear you both have a little conversation in that language.' Calmly, Maurice Cohen turns to the other candidate and says to him, '*Ma nishtana halaila hazeh mikol halelot.*'

The other candidate answers, '*Shebechol halelot anu ochlin hamatz umatza.*'

Eating and Dining Out

A lunchtime riddle
Q: What does a Jewish Princess make for lunch?
A: Reservations.

* * *

The limping waiter
Benny is in a restaurant, calls over the waiter and asks, 'Oy, do you have *matzoh* balls?'

'No,' replies the waiter, 'I always walk like this.'

* * *

The joker
One evening, Moshe and his partner Abe are having dinner together to celebrate a recent business deal. They are having a great time when suddenly Moshe begins to find it hard to breathe. He says, 'Abe, help me, I tink I hev svallowed a bone.'

'Are you choking, Moshe?' asks Abe.

'No, dem it – I'm being serious.'

* * *

A supper-time riddle
Q: How do Jewish wives prepare their children for supper?
A: They put them in the car.

* * *

Kreplachaphobia

Miriam has a problem with her young son Ben – he goes into a total panic every time she serves up the family's favourite dish of *kreplach*. Every effort she and her husband make to explain to Ben how nice *kreplach* tastes fails miserably. So she takes Ben to see Dr Lewis, an eminent psychiatrist.

Dr Lewis listens to the problem, then says, 'I think this situation is easy to resolve. All you have done so far is talk – you've told Ben how nice *kreplach* are but you haven't yet shown him how nice they are. So take him home and let him watch you prepare the *kreplach*. First of all, let him see the ingredients that go inside a *kreplach*. Then show him how a *kreplach* is made. Once he sees there's nothing to be scared of, he will grow to like them.'

When they return home, Miriam follows Dr Lewis's advice. She takes Ben into her kitchen and sits him down to watch her prepare a *kreplach*. She puts in front of him a small mound of dough and a plate of chopped meat she had prepared earlier. 'See Ben,' she says, 'is there anything here to be worried about?'

'No Mum,' smiles Ben.

Miriam then puts some minced meat in the centre of the dough and folds over one corner. She looks at Ben and sees he's still smiling. 'Maybe this will actually work,' she thinks.

She folds over the second corner (Ben is still smiling) and then the third. All is going better than she has dared hope. Then she folds over the last corner – and immediately Ben starts to get into a state and shouts, '*Oy veh, kreplach.*'

* * *

Follow my leader

Little Emma is watching her mother preparing their Shabbat dinner – this week it's salt beef. Emma watches her mother slice off both ends of the joint and place it in a saucepan ready for cooking. So Emma asks, 'Why did you cut both ends off, Mum?'

Her mother pauses for a few seconds, then replies, 'That's a good question, Emma. It's what my mother always did when she made salt beef and I just do the same. But I've no idea why. Let's phone *Bubbeh* and ask her.'

So they phone *Bubbeh* and ask why she always sliced the ends off the salt beef before cooking.

Bubbeh replies, 'You know, I'm not sure why – that was the way I always saw my mother make salt beef.'

Because they are now very curious, they visit Emma's great-grandmother in the nursing home and say to her, 'You know when we make salt beef, why do we always slice off the ends before cooking it?'

'I don't know why you do it,' says the great-grandmother, 'but I never had a saucepan that was large enough!'

* * *

The sandwich

Every time someone goes into a delicatessen and orders a pastrami sandwich on white bread, somewhere a Jew dies.

* * *

All's fair in love and war

Kitty and Freda are having lunch together. They know how big the portions are so they order only one dish of 'fried fish pieces', which they intend to share. They also ask for an extra plate. When the order arrives, the plate contains one big piece of fish and one little piece of fish. Kitty and Freda politely look at each other.

Kitty says, 'Please, you choose first.'

'No,' replies Freda, 'you can choose first.'

Kitty says, 'OK, I'll take first,' and puts the big piece of fish on the empty plate.

Freda is surprised. 'Why did you take the big piece? That's not very polite.'

'So which piece would you have taken, then?' asks Kitty.

'I would have taken the small piece,' replies Freda.

'So what's the problem, Freda?' says Kitty. 'That's what you've got.'

* * *

Conversation in a restaurant

Maurice and Sadie are out eating in the 'Bubbeh-Myseh' restaurant. While Maurice is eating his grilled steak and chips, the waiter comes over to him and asks, 'Is everything OK, sir?'

'Well,' replies Maurice, 'I asked for my steak to be rare, and it was well done.'

'Thank you sir,' says the waiter, 'we always aim to please.'

* * *

The Creation – alternative version

And on the seventh day, God said, 'Let there be Danish.'

* * *

Calendar statistics

According to the Jewish calendar, the year is 5769. According to the Chinese calendar, the year is 4703. This means that the Jews went without Chinese food for 1,066 years. This period was known as the Dark Ages.

* * *

A marketing decision

Mordechai and his wife Ruth go to Peeler's Kosher Restaurant and order steak and chips. They are served with fantastically tasty, giant sirloin steaks, which they think are the best they've had for years. They are so excited about their meal that they tell their friends Abe and Rifka about it.

Abe doesn't believe any meal could be that good, so all four decide to go to Peeler's next weekend to check it out. When they get there, they all order sirloin steak and chips. However, much to their disappointment, the waiter brings them very small steaks. Mordechai asks to see the manager.

'I'm very upset with our meals,' he says to the manager. 'My wife and I were in this restaurant only last week and you served us big juicy steaks. Today, however, just when I've bought my best friends with us, you serve us such small ones.'

'Yes, sir, I know,' replies the manager. 'But last week you were sitting by the window.'

* * *

Eating on his own

Issy's wife is unwell and that's why Issy is sitting in a restaurant on his own for a change. He spends a good deal of time looking at the menu and even when the waiter returns to take his order, Issy is still poring over the menu. The waiter clears his throat and asks, 'Ahem, excuse me for asking, sir, but is there a problem with the menu?'

'No there isn't,' Issy replies. 'It's just that my wife Betty usually tells me what I am allowed to eat, and she's not here.'

'That's no problem,' says the waiter. 'The soup of the day is chicken soup with *lokshen* and to make it real tasty we add *giblets* and chicken fat. But I'm sure your wife would want you to have the tomato juice.'

The waiter then continues. 'Today's special is potted *flanken* nosh-up. This is made with especially fatty meat to which we add potatoes and carrots and leave the whole caboodle in the oven for almost eight hours. We then serve it with home-made *challah* bread for dipping into the gravy. But I'm sure your wife would want you to have the boiled chicken wings and rice.'

On hearing this, Issy puts down the menu and says, 'Nag nag, nag. That's all Betty ever does. I'm tired of her telling me what to do. I'll have the chicken soup and *flanken* nosh-up.'

* * *

A pensioner's riddle
Q: What do pensioners call a long lunch?
A: Normal.

* * *

Guide to good cooking
Q: What's the first sentence you'll find in a Jewish cook book?
A: 'Before you start, please take a few deep breaths and CALM DOWN.'

* * *

The celebratory Chinese meal
Yitzhak and Hannah decide to eat out to celebrate their 50th wedding anniversary and after some deliberation, they choose the Kosher Moshe Chinese restaurant. When they arrive, they discuss the menu with the waiter and agree to share the chef's special 'Chicken Surprise'. After a short wait, the waiter brings over their meal, which is served inside a lidded cast-iron pot, and departs without removing the lid.

Hannah is ready to start eating but before she can reach over to the pot, the lid suddenly rises by 1 cm all by itself.

Hannah looks closely at the pot and briefly sees two beady little eyes looking at her. Then the lid slams back down again.

Hannah is worried. 'Did you see that?' she asks Yitzhak.

'No, darling, I didn't,' replies Yitzhak.

'So look in the pot already,' she tells Yitzhak.

As he reaches for the lid, it again rises up by 1 cm all by itself. Yitzhak looks closely and sees two beady little eyes looking at him. Then the lid firmly slams back down again.

Hannah starts to panic and shouts at Yitzhak, 'Call the manager over, CALL THE MANAGER OVER!'

So Yitzhak gets the manager and they tell him what they saw and demand an explanation.

'Well sir, I think I can explain,' says the manager. 'What did you order?'

'We both chose the same,' Yitzhak replies, 'the Chicken Surprise.'

'Oh I do apologise,' says the manager, 'the waiter brought you the 'Peking Duck' by mistake.'

* * *

Which is which?

Jeremy and Isaac are out having a celebratory meal at Minky's Kosher Cafe. At the end of the meal, the waiter comes over and asks, 'OK, gentlemen, will it be tea or coffee for you?'

'I'll have a glass of lemon tea,' replies Jeremy.

'Me too,' says Isaac, 'and make sure the glass is clean.'

Five minutes later, the waiter returns with two lemon teas on his tray. As he's about to hand them out, he asks, 'Who asked for the clean glass?'

* * *

Improving productivity

Freda and Kitty hear about a very new and advanced restaurant called Modern Minky's, which has just opened, and decide to try it out. When the waiter arrives to take their order, Kitty notices that he has a spoon sticking out of his shirt pocket – in fact, she notices that all the waiters have spoons sticking out of their shirt pockets. She thinks this very odd and after they give their order, she mentions it to Freda. Freda says, 'Why not ask the waiter about the spoon when he returns?'

The waiter arrives with their chicken soup and Kitty says, 'Excuse me for asking, but why the spoon?'

'Well,' he explains, 'when the restaurant first opened, Mr Minky hired Baleboss Consulting to ensure that our productivity was at its highest level. After a full analysis, they told us that every time a spoon is dropped, it takes time to pick it up, take it to the kitchen and return with a new one. Baleboss said that if the waiters were better prepared, we could reduce these unnecessary kitchen trips and the restaurant would save 40 man hours per week. So we all carry a spoon now.'

Freda and Kitty thank him for the explanation and he leaves them to enjoy the soup. But then, guess what? Freda accidentally drops her spoon while halfway through her soup. Almost immediately their waiter appears and quickly replaces the dropped spoon with the spare one from his pocket. 'I'll get another spoon next time I go to the kitchen,' he says, 'it'll save me having to make an extra trip to get it right now.'

Kitty is impressed but then notices a small piece of string hanging out of the waiter's fly. Looking around, she sees that all the waiters have pieces of string hanging from their flies. So before he can walk away, she points to the string and says, 'Excuse me, but what's with the string?'

'It's simple, madam,' he quietly replies. 'Baleboss also discovered that we waiters can save time when we have to visit the toilet. By tying string to the tip of our...you know what, we can pull it out without touching it and thus eliminate the need to wash our hands afterwards. This reduces the time we spend in the toilet.'

'But after you get it out,' asks Kitty giggling, 'how do you put it back?'

'Well,' he whispers, 'I don't know about the others, but I use the spoon.'

Memory/Senior Moments

Dangerous driver

Sharon and her friend Kitty, two little elderly ladies, are out for a drive in a large Mercedes with Kitty driving and Sharon in the front passenger seat. After a few minutes, they come to some traffic lights but although the lights are clearly red, the car just continues across the intersection.

Sharon says to herself, 'I must be losing it. I could have sworn we just went through a red light.'

A few minutes later, they come to another set of lights and again they go through red, this time narrowly missing a car driving across them. Although Sharon is sure the light was red, she is still convinced she is losing it. She is now getting very nervous.

At the next intersection, the light is again showing red and as before, the car goes across without slowing.

So Sharon turns to Kitty and says, 'Hey, did you know that you just passed three red lights in a row? What on earth are you doing – are you trying to kill us?'

Kitty turns to Sharon and replies, '*Oy veh!* Am I driving?'

* * *

Back to front

Eighty-year-old Rachel is very upset indeed when she calls the police on her mobile phone. She cries, 'Help me please. My car's been broken into. The thief has stolen the CD player, the steering wheel, the gearshift lever and the pedals. *Oy veh*, what will I do?'

The dispatcher says to her, 'Stay calm, madam, I'll ask a police officer to get to you as quickly as possible.'

Ten minutes later, the police control centre gets the following message from the police officer, 'Please disregard the distress call. The lady got in the back seat of her car by mistake.'

* * *

A night out

Issy decides to go out for the evening. He might be nearly 90 years of age, but Issy still thinks of himself as one of God's gifts to the ladies. He gets himself ready in the usual manner and then looks at himself in the mirror. What does he see? He sees a handsome, mature, smartly dressed gentleman in a great-looking modern suit, a carnation in his lapel, well-groomed hair and sparkling eyes. Issy is pleased with the vision. He finishes by spraying on his favourite Eau Savage cologne and then makes his way to the Park Lane Hilton.

Seated at the Hilton bar is Becky, in her mid-eighties. Issy walks over, sits besides her, and orders a drink. When it arrives, he takes a sip, turns to Becky and says, 'So tell me, do I come here often?'

* * *

Memories
Bernie and Shlomo, both in their eighties, are taking their weekly ZFT (Zimmer Frame Totter) in the park.

'So, Shlomo, how are you?' asks Bernie.

'*Oy veh*, I'm getting worse and worse,' replies Shlomo. 'All of a sudden, my memory's decided to play me tricks. I can't even remember whether it was you or my brother who died last month.'

* * *

What money can't buy
During their business lives, Joel, Mordechai and Emanuel did so well that they became millionaires. Now, in retirement, they meet up in one of the most expensive hotels in the world, the Mazuma Mit Mazel Hotel, no less. During their conversation, it soon becomes clear that they all have problems with deteriorating body parts.

'It's unfair,' says Joel. 'Now that I have money and I'm a widower, I could go with any of the beautiful women who come here looking for a husband. But because of my poor eyesight, I'm unable to see who's beautiful and who's not.'

'I know what you mean,' says Mordechai. 'Now that I have money, I could order anything from the seven-star Michelin restaurant here – lobster, caviar, even the most expensive champagne they sell, Krug's Clos du Mesnil, but my doctor tells me that I must stick to things such as sardines, water biscuits, spinach and milk. With me it's my bad stomach.'

'I too have a problem,' says Emanuel. 'Take last night, for example. I'm in bed and feeling frisky so I ask mine Sarah to roll over onto her back. But she says to me, "Oh no, not again, you can't be serious – we just made love for the third time only 10 minutes ago." So you see, guys, with me it's my memory.'

* * *

The best friends
Charlotte and Linda have been friends for over 50 years and in this time, they have shared all kinds of activities and visited many parts of the world together. Now, in the latter part of their lives, their activities are limited to meeting twice a week to play cards. Today is one of those card days.

While Charlotte is dealing out the cards, Linda looks at her and says, 'Now don't get mad at me. I know we've been friends for a long time, but I just can't think of your name. I've tried for five minutes but I just can't remember it. Please, please tell me your name.'

Charlotte stares at Linda for some time before replying, 'How soon do you need to know?'

* * *

Mr Grumpy
Moshe and Sadie, both in their seventies, are driving to Birchington-on-Sea when they decide to stop at a nice country pub for a bite to eat. After finishing their meal, they get back into their car and continue on their journey. But 15 minutes after leaving, Sadie suddenly says, 'Moshe, you've got to turn around and go back to the pub. I've left my glasses on the table there.'

'I don't believe it,' Moshe shouts angrily at her. 'You silly moo, you'll forget your head one day.'

Moshe turns the car around and starts driving back to the pub. All the way there, he's grumpy and makes many snide comments like, 'Your memory is getting really bad,' and 'Because of you, we won't now be able to get to Birchington in time to see the sunset.' The more he rebukes Sadie, the more agitated he becomes, and he doesn't let up for the entire 15-minute drive back to the pub.

To Sadie's relief, they arrive back at the pub. As she gets out of the car and hurries inside to retrieve her glasses,

Moshe yells to her, 'And while you're in there, Sadie, you might as well get my hat. I left it in the cloakroom.'

* * *

Endearing terms

It's Daniel and Rivkah's 50th wedding anniversary and to celebrate, their son Aaron invites the close family to a golden wedding dinner at his house. During the evening, Aaron gets very emotional every time he hears his dad call his mum by such endearing terms as 'darling', 'petal', 'sweetheart' and 'my lover'. It's clear to Aaron that his parents are still very much in love. While Rivkah is out the room, Aaron goes over to his father, kisses him and quietly says, 'Dad, I'm so pleased for you both. I think it's fantastic that after 50 years you're still calling Mum by those loving pet names.'

But Daniel, looking very embarrassed, says, 'Things are not always what they seem to be, son. I must tell you the truth – I forgot your mother's name about five years ago.'

Growing Old

A light bulb riddle

Q: How many pensioners does it take to change a light bulb?
A: Only one, but it might take all day.

* * *

Elderly privileges

Hetty, an elderly lady, has been driving around a shopping centre's car park for some time looking for a place to park when at last she finds one and stops to pull into it. Suddenly, a youngster drives his car around her and parks his smart silver Audi in her space.

Hetty is so upset that she gets out of her car and says to the young driver, 'I was going to park there!'

As he walks away, the man just laughs and says, 'That's what you can do when you're young and quick.'

Well, this really infuriates Hetty. She gets back into her car, backs it up and then drives it at speed straight into his Audi. The youngster runs back to his damaged car and asks, 'What did you do that for?'

Hetty smiles and replies, 'That's what you can do when you're old and rich.'

* * *

A story for the chronologically challenged

It's Fay's 80th birthday and she decides to celebrate it on her own at the Savoy Hotel because they make good drinks there. As soon as she arrives, Fay goes into the bar and orders a whisky with two drops of water.

As the barman gives her the drink, Fay tells him, 'I'm 80 years old today, you know.'

The barman says, 'As it's your birthday, this drink is on me.'

'Thank you,' says Fay, and she quickly finishes her drink.

Then a woman next to her says, 'I'd like to buy you a drink, too.'

'Why thanks,' says Fay. 'Barman, a whisky with two drops of water, please.'

'Coming right up,' says the barman. Fay again knocks back her drink.

Then a man next to her says, '*Mazeltov*, madam, may I too buy you a drink?'

'Why yes,' says Fay. 'Barman, a whisky with two drops of water please.'

As he hands her the drink, the barman says, 'Excuse me for asking but why the whisky with only two drops of water? I'm dying to know.'

Fay replies, 'It's simple – when you're my age, you know how to hold your liquor, but take it from me, water is something altogether different!'

* * *

Growing old
At age 4 success is.........not peeing in your pants.
At age 12 success is........having friends.
At age 17 success is........having a driver's licence.
At age 20 success is........having sex.
At age 35 success is........having money.
At age 50 success is........having money.
At age 60 success is........having sex.
At age 70 success is........having a driver's licence.
At age 75 success is........having friends.
At age 80 success is........not peeing in your pants.

* * *

A woman's lament
Becky says out loud, '*Oy veh.*'

'What's wrong, Becky?' her friend Shlomo asks.

'I was thinking about myself this morning and I couldn't believe just how things have got worse now that I'm getting chronologically challenged. I'm living with osteoporosis and my kidneys are so bad that I have to have weekly dialysis. I have terrible circulation in my feet and can't feel my toes. I've survived a triple heart bypass operation and had both my hips replaced. I'm loosing the sight in my right eye and my hearing is terrible. I've got a new left knee and the other one is deteriorating.'

'You are in a bad way,' says Shlomo.

'And that's not all, Shlomo,' says Becky. 'I'm sure I'm suffering from senile dementia – I can't remember whether

I'm 73 or 79. I'm also suffering from senile dementia – I can't remember whether I'm 73 or 79.'

'*Oy veh*,' says Shlomo.

'But I continue to survive, Shlomo – at a price!' says Becky. 'As a result of the 50 daily medications I take to live from one day to the next, I suffer from diarrhoea, wind, dizziness and sometimes even blackouts. But, my dear Shlomo, thank God I still have my driver's licence.'

* * *

A dressing-up riddle
Q: Among pensioners, what is considered 'formal attire'?
A: Tied-up shoes.

* * *

Morning joy
Renee and Daniel have been married for over 50 years. One morning, they both awake from a good night's sleep. As usual, Daniel reaches over and takes her hand in his.

'Don't touch me,' says Renee.

'Why not, my dear?' replies a shocked Daniel.

'Because', says Renee, 'I'm dead.'

'What on earth are you talking about?' says Daniel. 'We're both lying here in bed together and we're talking to one another. How can you be dead?'

'But I am, Daniel,' says Renee. 'I'm definitely dead. I'm sure of it.'

'So what makes you think you're dead?' asks Daniel.

'Because I woke up this morning and nothing hurts.'

* * *

Thought for the day
There is more money being spent on breast implants and Viagra today than on Alzheimer's research. This means that by 2040, there should be a large elderly population with perky boobs and huge erections and absolutely no recollection of what to do with them.

* * *

Signs of ageing (men)
First you forget names.
Then you forget faces.
Then you forget to pull up your zip.
Then (even worse) you forget to pull it down.

* * *

The honest interview reply
Reporters from the *Jewish Chronicle* are interviewing Sadie, who is celebrating her 108th birthday.

'Sadie, dear, can you please tell us what you think is the best thing about being 108? I'm sure our readers would love to know,' one of the reporters asks.

Sadie replies, 'There's no peer pressure.'

* * *

Advice for seniors before making love
• Put on your glasses – then check that your partner is in bed with you.
• Set the timer for two minutes – in case you doze off in the middle.
• Set the mood with the proper lighting effect – turn them all off.
• Before you begin – make sure you've got 999 in your telephone's speed dial.

- In case you forget – write your partner's name on the back of your hand.
- Keep extra polygrip close by – to ensure your teeth won't end up on the floor by the bed.
- Make all the noise you want – after all, your neighbours are deaf too.
- If it works – call everyone you know with the good news (WARNING: Don't even think about trying it twice).

* * *

A few seconds of thought
Esther, 85 years old, is walking around the lounge in Becky's Nursing Home. As she walks past each male resident, she flips up the hem of her nightgown and says, 'Supersex!'

As she reaches wheelchair-bound Cyril, she flips up her gown at him and says, 'Supersex!'

Cyril sits silently for a few seconds and then says, 'I'll take the soup, please.'

* * *

The difference between girls at various ages
At 8: You take her to bed and tell her a story.
At 18: You tell her a story and take her to bed.
At 28: You don't need to tell her a story to take her to bed.
At 38: She tells you a story and takes you to bed.
At 48: You tell her a story to avoid going to bed.
At 58; You stay in bed to avoid her story.
At 68: If you take her to bed, that'll be a story.
At 78: If you can get out of bed, that's another story.

* * *

A good sex life

Isaac is 80 years old and goes to see Dr Myers for a full health check. After completing his tests, Dr Myers says to Isaac, 'Well, for someone your age, everything seems very normal to me. But I'd like to ask you just one more question, Isaac. How is your sex life?'

'Well,' replies Isaac, 'it's not really too bad, Doctor. My wife isn't really interested in sex any more, so I just drive around the streets of London once or twice a week. I'm really quite successful at finding one-night stands. For example, last week I picked up and made love to two young women.'

'*Oy*, and at your age too,' says Dr Myers. 'I do hope, Isaac, that you took some precautions.'

'Oh yes, Doctor,' replies Isaac. 'I may be old, but I'm not senile yet. I gave both of them a phoney name.'

* * *

Morning activity

Bernie awakes and, as he's been doing now for over 35 years, he immediately goes into the bathroom to get ready to go to work. But 15 minutes later, he's still in the bathroom and it's no surprise that his wife Renee finally hammers on the door and shouts out, 'What on earth are you doing in there, Bernie? Why are you taking so long?'

'It's simple, Renee,' Bernie shouts back. 'As I get balder and balder, it's taking me longer and longer to wash my face.'

* * *

A senior riddle

Q: Why do pensioners enjoy being called 'seniors'?
A: Because the term comes with a 10 per cent discount.

* * *

Reminiscing

Ruth, Hetty and Naomi, all three in their eighties, are sitting together in their retirement home reminiscing about the good old days. Ruth says, 'I remember when I used to be able to buy lovely big cucumbers at the greengrocers for no more than 1p each. They were giants (she demonstrates their length and thickness with her hands as she talks), not like the little cucumbers on sale today.'

Hetty then says, 'Well I remember the giant onions I used to be able to buy for 2p each. Every week, I always bought two of them (and she demonstrates the size of the two onions with her hands as she talks) for my chicken soup.'

Naomi, who has been sitting quietly listening to Ruth and Hetty, then says, 'I couldn't hear a word either of you were saying, but I remember the guy you were talking about.'

* * *

A bedtime riddle

Q: When does a pensioner go to bed?
A: Three hours after he falls asleep on the couch.

* * *

Not quite 'Weakest Link'

Freda is 75 years old and lives in a retirement home. One day, she bursts into the games room where a number of men are playing tiddlywinks and draughts, holds her clenched left fist in the air and announces, 'If anyone here can guess what's in my hand, they can make love to me tonight in my room.'

An elderly gentleman stops what he's doing and replies, 'Is it a plate of salt beef and *latkes*?'

Freda thinks for a few seconds and says, 'Yes, that's close enough.'

* * *

For the wine lovers among you
You will all know that Pinot Noir is one of the oldest grape varieties to be cultivated for the purpose of making wine. It is recognised worldwide as a great wine grape and is grown in many countries of the world. Now the Israelis have come on to the scene. They are marketing a new wine developed especially for elderly drinkers based on a new hybrid anti-diuretic wine grape. They are calling this wine 'Pinot More'.

* * *

A lofty riddle
Q: Why are pensioners so loath to clean out their loft?
A: Because whenever they do, one of their adult children stores stuff there.

* * *

Retirement activities
Arnold is out doing some shopping when he meets Lionel. They haven't seen each other for many years.

'So what are you doing with yourself these days, Lionel?' asks Arnold.

'Well,' replies Lionel, 'I used to work for Rothschild's Bank but I retired last year.'

'Lucky old you,' says Arnold, 'so what do you do with yourself all day?'

'I get up late each morning,' replies Lionel, 'have my breakfast and then lie down on my veranda and relax. At midday, I go inside for some lunch. Then I go outside and lie on my veranda again. At the end of the day, I have dinner and drink only the finest of wines. Then I light up a good cigar. Later on, I go lie on my veranda again.'

'Wow,' says Arnold, 'that sounds fantastic to me. I envy

you. Please God I should make enough money to retire soon.'

When Arnold gets home, he tells his wife Naomi all about his conversation with Lionel. After hearing Arnold's story, Naomi asks, 'Did he tell you his wife's name?'

'I'm not sure,' replies Arnold, 'but I think it's Veranda.'

Shoppers

Directions

Avrahom has just been shopping and is walking home down the high street when a man comes up to him and says, 'Excuse me. Do you know where I can find Levy's Bagel Bakery?'

Avrahom hands over the parcels he is carrying to the stranger, spreads his arms out as wide as he can, shrugs and replies, 'How should I know? I don't live here.'

* * *

A trip to the bakers – 1

'How much are the bagels?'
'Forty pence for two.'
'How much for one?'
'Twenty-five pence.'
'Then I'll take the other one.'

* * *

A trip to the bakers – 2

Q: How do you prevent your bagels being stolen?
A: Put lox on them.

* * *

Which way to face?
Q: What is a Princess's favourite position?
A: Facing a department store.

* * *

You're driving me crazy
Jacob meets his friend Max in the delicatessen. 'So Max, how's your wife Kitty?'

'*Oy veh*,' replies Max, 'she's driving me absolutely crazy. Every night she dreams that she's married to a millionaire.'

'That's nothing,' says Jacob, 'my Sadie dreams she's married to a millionaire during the day.'

* * *

Search party
Sixty-year-old Yitzhak and 65-year-old Hyman are pushing their shopping trolleys around the supermarket one day when they collide. Hyman immediately says, 'Sorry. I was looking for my wife Sadie and I wasn't really paying attention to where I was going. I hope I didn't hurt you.'

'No problem,' says Yitzhak, 'but what a coincidence. I'm also looking for my wife. I just can't find my Judith anywhere and I'm getting a little worried.'

'So let's help each other,' suggests Hyman. 'What does your Judith look like?'

Yitzhak replies, 'Well, she's a young 35-year-old. She's got long legs, she's slim and she has...how shall I say this...prominent breasts. She has blonde hair, green eyes and is wearing blue shorts. What does your Sadie look like?'

'It doesn't matter,' replies Hyman, 'let's just look for your Judith.'

* * *

And the winner is...

Whenever Freda goes shopping, she carefully scrutinises everything she buys and always battles to get the best deals. Today is the turn of the local delicatessen. As soon as she enters the shop, she looks around and puts a few items in her trolley. Then she goes over to the cash desk and says to the owner, 'I don't like the look of this whitefish of yours.'

'Lady,' says the owner, 'if you're buying for looks, then don't buy whitefish. Buy goldfish instead.'

'Clever doesn't suit you,' she replies sarcastically, 'but I'll take it.'

Then pointing to the chicken in her basket, she says, 'And what about this here chicken? It has a broken leg!'

'Look lady,' says the owner, 'do you want to eat it or dance with it?'

'Ha ha, very funny you're not,' says Freda. 'OK. But before you weigh the chicken, I want you to take out the bones.'

'Listen lady,' says the owner, 'because I buy with bones, you'll buy with bones.'

'But I never pay for chicken with bones,' says Freda.

'OK,' says the owner, 'no bones, then,' as he starts removing the bones.

'Thank you,' says Freda smiling, 'you're a *mensh*. Now put the bones in a separate bag for soup. Oh...and never mind the flesh – I don't like your chicken anyway.'

* * *

What extravagance!

Jeremy and Lisa are arguing again. 'You know, darling, you must be the most extravagant spender of all time,' says Jeremy.

'How on earth can you say that about me? It's not true.'

'But it is, Lisa. If only you would look at all the items on our bank statements.'

'Statements, schmatements,' says Lisa, 'it's just not true.'

This goes on for some time – 'Yes it is.' 'No it's not.'

Then suddenly, Lisa says, 'OK, all right, already. So what if I enjoy spending money? But I bet you can't name any other extravagance of mine.'

* * *

The sexual couch

Morris goes into Harrods furniture department and says to one of the salesmen, 'Good morning. I'd be grateful if you could show me where I can find a sexual couch.'

Trying very hard to conceal a smile, the salesman replies, 'Does sir mean a sectional couch?'

'No,' replies Morris, 'I really do mean a sexual couch. You see, mine wife Sarah says she wants an occasional piece in the living room.'

* * *

The delivery

The new postman is delivering a registered parcel and needs a signature so he rings the doorbell. Sadie sticks her head out of the bedroom window and says, '*Nu*, what is it?'

'I have a registered parcel for Mrs Levy,' he replies.

'Is it wrapped in fancy gift paper or just plain brown paper?' Sadie asks.

'Ordinary brown paper, madam,' he replies.

'So who is it from?' Sadie asks.

'It's from John Lewis department store, madam,' he replies.

'Does it say from which branch?' Sadie asks.

'Yes, madam,' he replies, 'it's from Oxford Street.'

'Does it say what's in it?' Sadie asks.

'It says it's from their Writing Instruments department,' he replies. 'Will you now come down and sign for it, please?'

'Sorry,' replies Sadie, 'I can't do that.'

'Why not?' he asks.

'Because,' Sadie replies, 'I'm Sadie Cohen. Mrs Levy lives next door.'

Travel and Tourism

Some stupid questions asked by cruise passengers

Moshe: How many feet are we above sea level?

Hetty: Do all the crew sleep on board?

Judith: Do you use salt water or fresh water in the toilets?

Jacob: Does this ship generate its own electricity?

Issy: Which of the lifts will take us right to the front of the ship?

Sadie: What time does the ship's midnight buffet start?

Hannah: Is this lovely tropical island completely surrounded by water?

* * *

Visit to a hotel

Sadie is a very successful businesswoman and loves all the nice things in life money brings her. One day, she decides that she and her husband Moshe should spend a week's holiday at the Gelt Plaza, a six-star hotel, and she decides to drive there in her new top-of-the range Aston Martin saloon.

Two hours later, she's pleased to see the looks of awe on the faces of the staff as she pulls up outside the hotel's front door. Three porters come out to greet her as she steps out of the car. She immediately says to one of them, in a commanding voice, 'Carry my luggage into the hotel, my good man.' Then she says to the two other porters, 'And could you two please carry my husband into the hotel.'

They're surprised by this request but nevertheless carry Moshe into the lobby and place him in an armchair by reception.

Then the hotel manager, who sees all of this, comes over to Sadie and says, 'Mrs Bloom, welcome to our hotel. I'm sorry to see that your husband is too ill even to walk.'

'What do you mean he can't walk?' replies Sadie. 'Of course he can walk. But thank God I'm now wealthy enough that my Moshe doesn't have to walk.'

* * *

The procession in Marbella

Benny and Leah are on holiday in Marbella and decide to go to a bullfight. While they are watching the grand procession that takes place before the bullfight commences, Leah starts asking a lot of questions. Fortunately, Benny has been to a bullfight some years earlier during a business trip and is able to answer them.

'Benny, who's that leading the procession?' asks Leah.

'That's the toreador, Leah.'

'So who's that behind the toreador?'

'That's the matador, Leah.'

'And who's that man behind the matador, Benny?'

'That's the picador, Leah,' says Benny, a little fed up with all the questions now.

'And who's the little man behind the picador?' asks Leah.

'That's Isadore, the kosher butcher.'

* * *

The company to work for

Benny is on his way to Tenerife for a two-week holiday. As he's waiting in the departure lounge at Heathrow airport, a gorgeous woman walks over and sits down next to him. Benny is convinced that she must be an airline stewardess. However, because she's not in uniform, he doesn't know which airline. So he attempts to find out without asking her directly.

He turns to her and chants aloud the Delta Airlines slogan, 'Love to fly and it shows'? She just stares at him in a confused kind of way, so he's sure she doesn't work for Delta Airlines.

He turns to her again and this time chants aloud the Singapore Airlines slogan, 'Something special in the air'? Once again she gives him the same confused look, so he's sure she doesn't work for Singapore Airlines.

Benny then turns to her for a third time and chants aloud the Thai Airways slogan, 'Smooth as Silk'? At this, the woman gets very, very angry. With a snarl on her face she turns to Benny and shouts, 'What the hell do you want?'

Suddenly, all is clear to Benny – he knows who she works for. He slumps back in his chair and says, 'Ah, so you work for El Al.'

* * *

Why didn't you ask?

Fact: The children of Israel roamed the desert for 40 years.
Conclusion: Even in those days, a man would never ask for directions.

* * *

The three Jews

Three Eastern European Jews named Berel, Cherel and Shmerel are talking about moving to the USA.

Berel says, 'When I emigrate to New York, I'm going to have to change my name. They won't call me Berel anymore, they'll call me Buck.'

Cherel says, 'When I emigrate to New York, I'll also have to change my name. They'll call me Chuck.'

Then Shmerel says, 'Well I'm not going anywhere.'

* * *

The false teeth

Moshe has been living in Poland all his life, but just before World War II, he sees big trouble coming. So he sells all his assets, converts them into gold and then melts down the gold to have five sets of false teeth made for himself. He flees Poland and after much travelling, arrives at Ellis Island, New York, where he is interrogated by an immigration official who also goes through the contents of his battered suitcase.

When the official sees the five sets of false teeth, he asks Moshe why he has so many. Moshe replies, 'As you might know, we Orthodox Jews have two separate sets of dishes, one for meat and one for dairy products. However, I'm so kosher and religious that I also need to have separate sets of teeth.'

The official is confused. 'Well that accounts for two sets of teeth. What are the other three for?'

'Well,' Moshe replies, 'we ultra-Orthodox Jews also use separate dishes for Passover and I'm so observant that I need two sets of Passover teeth to go with the dishes, one for meat and one for dairy food.'

The official is still confused. 'You've convinced me that you're a highly religious man and I accept that you therefore need four sets of teeth. But what about the fifth set?'

'Well, to tell you the truth, mister official,' replies Moshe, 'every once in a while I like to eat a ham-and-cheese sandwich.'

* * *

Well, I never

Yitzhak and Fay are travelling by car to Scotland. It is now quite late in the evening and after many hours on the road they are too tired to continue. So they decide to find somewhere to sleep for six hours and then get back on the road. They find a nice hotel and book a room.

Later, when they check out, the receptionist hands them a bill for £250.

Yitzhak is angry because the charge is so high and he tells the receptionist that the rooms aren't worth anywhere near £250. He asks to speak the manager.

The manager listens to Yitzhak and explains that the hotel has an Olympic-sized pool and a conference centre that were available for Yitzhak and Fay to use.

'But we didn't use them,' Yitzhak complains.

'Well, they are here and you could have,' explains the manager.

The manager then explains they could have taken in the variety show for which the hotel is famous. 'The best entertainers in the UK perform here,' he says.

'But we didn't go to any of those shows,' complains Yitzhak again.

'Well, we have them and you could have,' the manager replies.

Yitzhak gives up, writes out a cheque and gives it to the manager.

'But sir,' the manager says, 'this cheque is only made out for £75.'

'That's right,' says Yitzhak. 'I charged you £175 for sleeping with my wife Fay.'

'But I didn't,' exclaims the manager.

'Well,' Yitzhak replies, 'she was here and you could have.'

* * *

The same person

Issy and Jacob have finally left Russia and are on their way to London. On the way, they stop off in Paris for some sight-seeing. As they near the Arc De Triomphe, they see their old friend Moshe walking towards them. They are keen to talk to him and so they both shout out his name.

The shouting embarrasses Moshe and his face goes bright red. When they meet, Moshe quietly asks them, 'Please, my friends, here I am no longer Moshe *Pisher* but Maurice de la Fontaine.'

* * *

Clever answer

Hannah works for El Al and is stationed at the departure gate to check tickets. A man approaches and as she extends her hand for the ticket, he opens his overcoat and 'flashes' her. Without blinking, Hannah says, 'Sir, I need to see your ticket, not your stub.'

* * *

The anniversary cruise

Bernie and Faye, a wealthy couple, are coming up to their ruby wedding anniversary and Faye has been thinking for some months about how they should celebrate. Then she comes to a decision. 'Bernie,' she says, 'I'm going to book us a wonderful six-week cruise. I know you don't like ships because you got seasick last time, but trust me, this one will be perfect for us. It's called *Bubbeh of the Sea*, an intimate seven-star luxury liner with everything kosher we could ever want to eat made available. Let's give it a go.'

Bernie certainly isn't pleased with Faye's decision, but who is he to argue – he could never win. So he says, 'OK dear.'

On the day of the cruise, Bernie and Faye drive up to the quay in their Bugatti Veyron 16.4. Captain Cohen is on the bridge as they pass by and calls in the purser. 'Find out who they are and invite them to dine at my table tonight.'

Later, the purser knocks on the door of the Royal State Room. When Faye answers the door, the purser says, 'Compliments of Captain Cohen, madam. He would very much like you both to dine with him this evening.'

Bernie comes to the door and says, 'Who is it Faye, is there a problem?'

'This man says that Captain Cohen wants us to eat with him this evening,' replies Faye.

'I told you we shouldn't have come,' says Bernie. 'Seven-star or no seven-star, we have only been on this boat half an hour and already we have to eat with the crew.'

* * *

Sinai tourist

Peter, a tourist wondering through the Sinai desert, gets lost and very soon is very tired and desperate for some water. Then, just when he had given up hope, he sees in the distance a tiny oasis, consisting of a few palm trees. When he arrives, he sees a sign saying MOSHE'S TIE WAREHOUSE and there, sitting under one of the trees in the shade, is Moshe himself.

Moshe is reading the *Jerusalem Post*. Next to him is a table displaying dozens of different kinds of patterned, coloured ties. So Peter goes over to Moshe and asks for some water.

Moshe says, 'I'm sorry, but I don't have any water. However, since you're here, would you like to buy a tie?'

Peter is angry. 'What good is a tie to me in my condition? Can't you see that all I need is some water? You know where you can stuff your fancy ties.'

Moshe says, 'It's no good being rude to me. If you don't want a tie, then don't buy a tie. Whether you do or not is up to you. But the fact of the matter is that I still don't have any water for you.'

As Peter begins to walk away, Moshe calls him back and, pointing, says, 'OK, I'll tell you where you can get some water. If you walk in that direction for about 30 minutes, you'll come to a restaurant. It's owned by my brother Max and there you'll be able to get plenty of food and water. So Peter starts walking and soon disappears over the sand dunes. Moshe just continues to read his paper.

Two hours later Peter returns to Moshe's Tie Warehouse, crawling on his hands and knees. He is now extremely desperate for water and practically on his last breath. Moshe asks, 'So what happened? Didn't you find Max's restaurant?'

'Oh, I found the restaurant all right,' gasps Peter, 'but Max wouldn't let me in without a tie.'

* * *

Do you want the good news or bad news?
Nathan and Hannah are celebrating Nathan's 50th birthday on a cruise ship. Suddenly, on the evening of the fourth day, while they are standing at the back of the ship watching the moon, a storm develops from out of nowhere and a wave comes up and washes Hannah over the side. She can't swim and although they search for her all day, they can't find her. At their next port of call, the captain sends Nathan ashore and promises that he will call him should they find something.

Three weeks go by when finally Nathan gets a fax from the captain. It reads:

FAX from the captain to Nathan:

I'm sorry to have to inform you that when our deep-sea divers went looking for your wife, they found her dead at the bottom of the ocean. But there's some good news. When we hauled her up to the deck, attached to her *toches* was an oyster and in it was a large pearl, which I have had valued at £30,000. Please advise.

Immediately, Nathan sends the following fax back to the captain:

FAX from Nathan to the captain:

Please send me the pearl and re-bait the trap.

* * *

A question of flight
Q: Why do seagulls fly over the sea?
A: If they flew over the bay, they'd be 'bagels'.

* * *

Groan!
Motze is a well-respected 70-year-old Israeli tour guide who still works every day. He does most of his business with American tourists who have travelled with him before. They all seem to love him because if you ask any of them, they would reply, 'Motze's tour ya sure oughtta see.'

* * *

Visit to a hotel
Rifka and Benjy, a 70-year-old married couple, are on a long drive and decide to stop off for a night's rest before continuing with their journey. So when they reach Minky's Hotel, they go up to the desk and ask the clerk for a room.

'I'm sorry,' he tells them, 'all our normal rooms are taken.

But don't worry, I've got the ideal room for a nice couple like you – the bridal suite.'

'Don't be stupid,' says Benjy, 'we've been married for over 40 years. Why do you think we need the bridal suite?'

'Well,' replies the clerk, 'if I gave you the ballroom, would you have to dance?'

* * *

The trip to Israel – 1

A voice is heard over the intercom at the start of an El Al flight to Israel.

'Welcome on board. Your stewardesses today are Naomi Jacobs, Miriam Goldberg and myself, Judith Kosiner. And we mustn't forget, of course, my son Paul, the pilot.'

* * *

The cheap taxi ride

Mordechai, his wife and their three children have just finished their shopping trip and decide to get a taxi back home. So he hails a cab and says to the driver, 'If you turn off the meter, how much will you charge to drive us to north London?'

'For you and your wife, I'll charge just £12,' says the taxi driver, 'and I'll take the three children for free. Is that OK?'

Mordechai turns to his children and says, 'Jump into the taxi, children, this nice man will take you home. Your mother and I will take the bus.'

* * *

Sarah's cruise diary

DEAR DIARY – DAY 1

The taxi has arrived to take me to the port for the start of my Mediterranean cruise. I'm really excited, even though my

Moshe is not able to join me on this trip. I've packed all my Gucci outfits, my breakfast wear, my sportswear, my lounge wear, my evening wear and my seductive negligees. And I only needed seven suitcases.

DEAR DIARY – DAY 2

We spent the entire day at sea. It was beautiful and I saw some whales and dolphins. What a wonderful holiday this has started to be. I met the captain today – he seems like a very nice man.

DEAR DIARY – DAY 3

Today I spent some time in the ship's swimming pool. I also played bridge with some ladies in the piano bar and did some aerobics. The captain invited me to join him at his table for dinner. I felt honoured and had a wonderful time. He's a very attractive and attentive gentleman.

DEAR DIARY – DAY 4

I spent the morning in the ship's casino and won £95. The captain invited me to have dinner with him, this time in his state room. He somehow knew I was Jewish and so our menu was *knaidelach* soup followed by hot salt beef, roast potatoes and *latkes*, plus some new green cucumbers and hot peppers, followed by a *lockshen* pudding. The champagne he chose was very nice. Afterwards, he asked me to stay the night with him but I declined – I told him there was no way I could be unfaithful to my Moshe. The captain seemed upset after all the thought he had put into the meal.

DEAR DIARY – DAY 5

I went back to the top-side swimming pool today and got a little sunburned so decided to spend the rest of the day in the piano bar. The captain saw me there and bought me a couple of drinks. He really is a charming man. He again asked me to spend the night with him. But when I again declined, he got angry and told me that if I didn't stay the night with him tomorrow, he would sink the ship. I was obviously horrified and very worried.

DEAR DIARY – DAY 6

I saved 1,600 lives today – twice!

* * *

A cry for help

Abe is travelling on a bus. It's a hot day and everyone on board is quiet and subdued. Suddenly, Abe hears what seems to him to be a cry for help from the back of the bus. He looks to find out who is making the noise and sees that it's an elderly *bubbeh*.

'*Oy*, am I thirsty,' she cries out. '*Oy*, am I thirsty.'

This is repeated over and over again every few minutes. '*Oy*, am I thirsty. *Oy*, am I thirsty,' and each time, there is more and more pain to the *bubbeh's* voice.

This quickly begins to get on Abe's nerves, so he gets the bus driver to stop at the next corner and he goes to get the *kvetcher* a drink already. When he returns, he goes straight to the *bubbeh* with a bottle of mineral water and says, 'Here grandma, drink up. And then be quiet, will you?'

The *bubbeh* drinks the water, Abe goes back to his seat and the bus continues on its journey. Some passengers begin to nod off again, others start reading their newspapers and the rest are just relieved that the old *bubbeh* is quiet.

All of a sudden they hear from the back of the bus, 'Oy, vas I thirsty…. *Oy*, vas I thirsty.'

* * *

A message from the pilot
'Ladies, gentlemen and children. *Sholem Aleichem* to you all. This is your pilot, Captain Daniel Himmelfarb, speaking. On behalf of El Al airways, my crew and I welcome you on board this flight to Tel Aviv. We will do all we can, God willing, to make sure you have a great flight with us this afternoon. But if, God forbid, by some remote eventuality, we run into some trouble, please keep calm and don't panic. You'll find your life jacket under your seat and if you need to put it on, please wear it in the best of health. Thank you.'

* * *

An up-to-date visitor
Eighteen-year-old Daniel, an up-and-coming Jewish rapper, is visiting the USA for the first time. When he gets to his hotel room, he picks up the phone and says to the operator, 'I'd like the number for Rachel Cohen in Brooklyn, New York, please.'

After a short pause the operator says to Daniel, 'I have eighteen listings for a Rachel Cohen in Brooklyn. Do you have a street name?'

Daniel thinks for a second, then replies, 'Well, most of my friends call me "Danny the *pisher*".'

* * *

The coach journey
Thirty very senior citizens from a Jewish care home in Golders Green are travelling by coach to Waddesdon Manor to see, what else, the Rothschild antiques collection.

They have been travelling for only 30 minutes when 80-year-old Hetty walks up to the driver from the back of the coach and tells him, '*Oy*, mister, there's a pervert onboard.' She then returns to her seat.

One minute later, 82-year-old Ethel walks up to the driver from the back of the coach and tells him, '*Oy veh*, mister driver, there's a pervert on this coach.' Then she too returns to her seat.

The driver feels he must check it out because there have been two similar complaints within minutes of each other. So he stops the coach and walks to the back. There he finds Cyril, a very frail, elderly bald-headed man, crawling around under the seats on his hands and knees. The driver immediately asks Cyril, 'What on earth do you think you are doing down there?'

Cyril looks up at the driver and says, 'I've lost my toupee and I'm looking for it down here. Twice in the last five minutes I thought I had found it, but mine is parted on the side.'

* * *

Designs for senior citizens
Miriam has never been on a cruise before. One day, she meets her friend Leah and they stop for a chat.

'So where are you and Simon going for your holidays this year?' asks Leah.

'I'd like to try out a cruise, Leah,' replies Miriam, 'but I'm not sure whether Simon and I would enjoy ourselves. We're almost 70 now and Simon thinks cruising is for younger people.'

'No, you're wrong in thinking that, Miriam,' replies Leah. 'Most cruise ships have special design features just for senior citizens.'

'So give me an example, already,' says Miriam.

'Well…OK,' replies Leah. 'They have bifocal portholes.'

* * *

Zip problems

Naomi is waiting for a bus to take her to the shopping centre. When it arrives she tries to get on, but because she's wearing a very tight mini skirt, she can't get her leg up onto the first step of the bus. So she reaches behind her, undoes her zipper a little and tries again to get on the bus. But she can't – her skirt is still very tight. So she again reaches behind her and undoes the zipper a little bit more. But she still can't lift her leg.

She's getting a bit anxious now because there are people behind her waiting to get on. So she reaches behind her a third time and yanks the zip all the way down. But she can't believe it – she still can't lift her leg.

Just then, the man directly behind her picks her up and drops her into the bus. Instead of thanking him, Naomi turns to him and says angrily, 'How dare you? Only a close friend would dare do such a thing.'

The man smiles at her and says, 'Please forgive me. After the expert way you dealt with my zipper, I really thought we were friends.'

* * *

Hold on

Rifka and Sam are Londoners on their first driving holiday in the USA. Everything is going well until, driving through a remote part of Arizona, their car breaks down. Luckily, an Indian on horseback sees their predicament, rides up to them and offers to take one of them to a nearby town to get help.

Sam says to Rifka, 'Darling, I think it best that you go with him to this town while I stay here to protect our car and its contents. When you get there, find someone who can fix the car. Be careful and I'll see you soon.'

So Rifka climbs up behind the Indian and off they ride.

They have been going for only a few minutes when the

Indian suddenly lets out an ear piercing, 'Y-e-e-e-e-e-h-a-a-a,' and he repeats this scream every five minutes or so until they arrive in town. He rides over to the local garage, helps her down, and then rides off with one final screeching, 'Y-e-e-e-e-e-e-h-a-a-a-a-a-a-a-a!'

'Wow,' says the garage owner, 'how did you get that Indian so excited?'

'I didn't do anything, honest,' replies Rifka, 'All I did was sit behind him on his horse, with my arms around his waist and holding onto the saddle horn to keep me from falling. That's all.'

'Lady,' says the garage owner laughing, 'Indians never use saddles.'

Housework

The strict Princess
Q: There once was a Princess who wouldn't allow certain four-letter words to be spoken in her house. What were those words?
A: 'Iron', 'dust', 'cook' and 'wash'.

* * *

What a day
One afternoon Max comes home from work to find total mayhem. His two young children are in the front garden, naked, soaking wet and playing with the garden hose. There is food all over the lawn, rubbish spilled everywhere and some of their plants have been pulled up and are lying on the path.

The front door to their house is wide open and there's no sign of their dog. As Max enters his house, he finds an even bigger mess. The nest of tables are lying on their sides, all the vases have been knocked over and wet flowers are on the floor, the armchair cushions are lying where they were thrown and one of the children has been sick over the carpet. The TV is blaring out and the children's room is strewn inches deep with toys and various items of clothing.

Max goes into the kitchen and finds the sink full of unwashed dishes from the morning's breakfast, none of the food has been cleared up, the fridge door is wide open and there's dog food on the floor.

He's quite worried by now and heads up the stairs to look for his wife Fay. He has to step over yet more toys and piles of clothes. He's worried Fay might be ill, or even worse.

As Max passes the bathroom, water is trickling under the door and into the hall. So he peers inside and sees wet towels, spilt bath oils, his shaver lying on the floor and toothpaste smeared everywhere. He turns off the bath tap and rushes to his bedroom. There he finds Fay.

She's curled up in bed, still in her pyjamas and reading a book. She smiles at him and says, 'How did your day go, darling?'

Max looks at her bewildered and asks, 'What happened here today, Fay?'

She again smiles, 'You know every day when you come home from work and you ask me what in the world did I do today?'

'Yes,' he replies.

'Well,' says Fay, 'today I didn't do it.'

* * *

News story: good in bed

Really, it's true. A recent survey says that men who help out with the dusting are better in bed. It seems that nine out of 10 women who received two or more hours of assistance per week from their partners said that they enjoyed very good sex lives. This should lead men to ask the question, 'Where can I enrol in an advanced course on house-cleaning skills?'

* * *

A housework riddle
Q. How do you know when it's time to wash the dishes and clean the house?
A. Look inside your pants – if you've got a *putz*, it's not time.

Glamour

The Dior dress
One day, just as Rebecca is walking past Yiddishe Mumma Exclusive Fashions, she sees them putting a new dress in their window. It stops her in her tracks – it's a pale-green Dior evening dress and she's totally entranced by this brilliant creation. She's convinced it's *bashayrt* – it was meant for her. But it's priced at £3,500 and she has to think of a good way to persuade her Hymie to buy it for her. Then she has an idea. She can't wait to get home.

'Hymie, darling?'
'Yes, what is it, Rebecca?'
'Last night I had a lovely dream, Hymie,' she says.
'So what kind of a dream was it, Rebecca?' he asks.
'I dreamed that we passed by Yiddishe Mumma, and in the window was this gorgeous Dior dress at only £3,500. And do you know what you did, Hymie?'
'*Nu*, so what did I do?' he asks.
'You went into the shop and bought it for me, darling.'
'Did I really?' Hymie says. 'That really was a wonderful dream. Please God, in all your future dreams, you should wear it in good health.'

* * *

The coughing fit

Moshe and Sadie are in *shul* one *shabbes* when in the middle of the service Sadie suddenly develops a coughing and sneezing fit. It lasts nearly two minutes. Later, at the end of the service, as Moshe is waiting outside for Sadie to come down from the ladies' gallery, a friend comes up to him and says, 'I feel really sorry for your Sadie. That must have been a very embarrassing few minutes for her, the way she was coughing and sneezing. I noticed most of the congregation was looking at her.'

'Really?' says Moshe. 'Then she'll be pleased when I tell her that – she was wearing her new hat.'

* * *

The alternative solution

Sharon is very despondent about her ageing looks and makes an appointment to see a plastic surgeon. After he examines her, he recommends she undergo a full face lift.

'Doctor,' she says, 'what will the operation to give me a full face lift cost?'

'For you,' says the doctor, 'I would estimate £25,000.'

'*Oy veh*, that's far too much, Doctor,' she says. 'Isn't there something less expensive?'

'Well,' replies the doctor, 'you could try wearing a veil.'

* * *

A pretty smart riddle

Q: Why would the average Jewish woman rather be pretty than smart?

A: Because the average Jewish man can see better than he can think.

* * *

Purity in motion

Naomi is shopping in Harrods and is looking for a new dress. She sees something she likes and calls over a salesman. 'See that pale-blue-and-grey designer dress on that dummy over there?' she says.

'Yes, I see it,' he replies.

'Well, how much is it?' Naomi asks.

'Madam, that dress over there is £599,' he replies.

'*Oy veh*,' says Naomi, 'I could get the same dress locally at Minky's Shmatters for only £50.'

'But madam,' says the salesman, 'our dress is 100% pure English virgin wool, whereas I'm sure you'll discover that the dress at Minky's is made from recycled wool.'

'So,' replies Naomi, 'for £549 extra, I should be caring what the lambs do at night?'

* * *

The pair of trousers

Jeremy orders a pair of trousers from Levine Bros Tailors. Frank takes the order and tells Jeremy that they will be ready in a week's time.

But when Jeremy returns a week later, he's disappointed to learn that the trousers are not yet ready and that he has to come back in another week's time.

When Jeremy returns again the following week, he's disappointed to learn that the trousers are still not ready and that he has to come back in another week's time

This goes on for two months until finally, on Jeremy's ninth visit, the trousers are ready for him. Frank proudly displays them not only to Jeremy but also to everyone in his shop.

'Thanks for the trousers, Mr Levine,' says Jeremy, 'but I need to ask you a question. How come God was able to create the world in only six days, yet it took you 60 days to make just one pair of trousers?'

'Ah, it's simple,' replies Frank. 'Just look at the condition of the world and then take a look at this gorgeous pair of trousers I've made for you.'

* * *

How to get out of it
Miriam meets her friend Leah out shopping and says, 'So what's wrong with your hair, Leah? It looks just like a wig.'

'You know something, Miriam,' replies Leah, 'it is a wig.'

'Well what do you know?' says Miriam, 'you would never notice it.'

* * *

A nymphomaniac riddle
Q: What is a Jewish nymphomaniac?
A: A wife who does her hair and sleeps with her husband on the same day.

Weight Watching

Fast calories
Moshe is talking to his friend. 'Did you know, Abe, that during sex, an average man loses about 250 calories whereas the average Israeli loses 1,250 calories?'

'So how do you explain that?' asks Abe.

'Well,' replies Moshe, 'the Israeli also uses up 250 calories during sex but he then uses a further 1,000 calories while he's running around telling all his friends.'

* * *

How to lose weight

Abe is just a bit overweight (well a lot, really) and goes to see a dietician.

'For the first two weeks,' says the dietician, 'I want you to eat normally for five days, then skip one day and start all over again. If you do this, I guarantee you will lose at least 14 pounds in the first two weeks.'

Two weeks pass and Abe goes back to the dietician and gets on to the scales. The dietician is stunned. 'Abe, you've lost 20 pounds. This is unbelievable. Did you follow my instructions?'

'Yes I did,' replies Abe, 'I followed your instructions explicitly, even though I nearly died on day six.'

'Do you mean die, as in hunger?' asks the dietician.

'No,' replies Abe, 'I mean die, as in all the skipping.'

With One Foot in the Grave

The special cookies

As 80-year-old Benny lies dying in his bedroom, he suddenly smells the aroma of freshly cooked chocolate chip cookies wafting up the stairs. They are his favourite. So he gathers his remaining strength, lifts himself from his bed and, leaning against the wall, slowly makes his way out of the bedroom. Then, with great effort, he makes his way down the stairs, gripping the rail with both hands. Finally, breathing hard, he leans against the kitchen doorframe and stares in.

'I'm already in heaven,' he thinks, as there, spread out in front of him, are hundreds of his favourite chocolate chip cookies.

'Am I really in heaven,' has asks himself, 'or is it an act of devotion from mine darling Rebecca to ensure that I exit from this world a happy man?'

Then with one final effort, Benny propels himself towards the cookies, but ends up on his knees near the table. His aged hand trembles as it makes its way to the cookie nearest the table edge, his mind already beginning to think about the wondrous taste that he will soon experience.

All of a sudden, Rebecca smacks his hand with her wooden spoon.

'Please don't touch them,' she says, 'they're for the *Shiva*.'

* * *

Planning a will

Issy is seriously ill and decides to write a will. He calls his brother Jacob, who is a solicitor, to help him. When Jacob arrives at Issy's bedside, Issy says, 'Please write this down, Jacob. I give to my son David £250,000. I give to each of my three daughters, Leah, Rose and Freda £100,000. And I give to my only grandchild Henry £50,000.'

'Hold on, Issy,' says Jacob. 'You told me recently that your entire estate doesn't come to more than £50,000.'

'*Nu*?' replies Issy. 'So let them work for it like I did.'

* * *

The end is near

Maurice is in hospital and knows he is dying. As he lies in bed in his private room, struggling to breathe, his family and children around him, he starts to talk very quietly.

'Freda,' he whispers.

'Yes dear, what is it?' Freda says.

'I want you should know something before I die. Harry the butcher owes me £100, Levine the pharmacist owes me £400, and our next-door neighbour Moshe owes me £600 and the return of my lawnmower. Don't let them off, will you?'

'Of course I won't, darling,' Freda replies.

Freda turns to her children and says, '*Oy*, what a wonderful man your father is. Let this be a lesson to you all – even though he's dying, he still knows who owes him money. What a *mensh* he is.'

Then Maurice finds some strength to say a bit more. 'Freda, I want you also to know that I still owe Bernard, my cousin, £1,700 of the £5,000 he lent me three years ago.'

'*Oy veh*,' cries Freda, 'it's nearly the end for my Maurice – he's getting delirious.'

* * *

The confession

Hyman is dying and his wife Faye is at his bedside in hospital. She's holding his fragile hand and with tears running down her face starts to pray. But her praying awakens Hyman. He looks up at her and with pale lips hardly moving whispers, 'Is that you, Faye?'

'Yes, darling, it's me,' she replies, 'but don't talk. You need to rest.'

But Hyman wants to get something off his chest. 'Faye,' he whispers, 'I have a confession to make.'

'It's OK, darling,' she weeps, 'there's nothing to confess, really. Everything's fine. Now go to sleep.'

'No, Faye, I must die in peace. I slept with your sister and I slept with your best friend. There, I've got it off my chest.'

'I know, darling,' says Faye, 'now be quiet and let the poison work.'

* * *

Our friend Hymie

Jeremy and Nathan meet in the Post Office while they queue for their pensions. Nathan says, 'Did you hear what happened to Hymie Himmelfarb?'

'You mean Hymie Himmelfarb with the smoker's cough?' asks Jeremy.

'Yes, that's the one,' replies Nathan.

'Hymie Himmelfarb with the gout and double hernia?' asks Jeremy.

'Yes, that's him, Jeremy,' replies Nathan.

'Hymie Himmelfarb with the blotchy skin and who's always fainting?' asks Jeremy.

'Yes, him, but all right with the questions already,' replies Nathan.

'No, I didn't hear about Hymie Himmelfarb,' says Jeremy. 'So what happened to Hymie?'

'He died yesterday,' replies Nathan.

'*Oy veh*! And he was such a healthy man,' says Jeremy.

* * *

How to handle bad news
Sadie isn't feeling too well and goes to see Dr Myers. He gives her a full examination, sighs and says, 'I've got bad news for you. You have cancer and I'd advise you to put your affairs in order ASAP.'

Sadie is shocked, but manages to compose herself and walk out into the waiting room, where her daughter Shoula is waiting.

'So how did it go, Mum?' asks Shoula.

'Well Shoula, we women celebrate when things are good, and we celebrate when things are not so good. Unfortunately, in this case, things aren't so good. I've cancer. Let's go to my golf club and have a drink.'

Later, after several martinis, the two are feeling a little less sombre. They have some laughs and then some more martinis. But after a while they're approached by two of Sadie's club mates, who are curious as to what they are celebrating. Sadie tells them that they're drinking to her impending death. 'I've been diagnosed with AIDS,' she tells them.

'*Oy veh*,' they say, and give Sadie their condolences. Then they all have a couple of martinis.

After Sadie's friends leave, Shoula leans over and whispers, 'Mum, I thought you said you were dying of cancer? You've just told your friends that you're dying of AIDS. I'm confused, Mum.'

Sadie replies, 'I told them that because I don't want any of those *kurveh* sleeping with your father after I'm gone.'

* * *

Family help
After a short illness, little Jeremy dies. He was only nine years old. At his funeral, his family and friends weep at his grave. Rayne, his mother, is inconsolable and is crying heavily as the gravediggers start to cover his coffin with earth.

'Oh my poor darling Jeremy. Why did you leave me at such a young age? You didn't even get a chance to become a doctor. So *bubbeleh*, when you get to heaven, don't forget to tell God how terribly miserable all those you left behind are, especially your mother. And while you're talking to him, please ask him to help your dear father find a good job so that he can properly support me and your brothers and sisters. And Jeremy, *bubbeleh*, you must tell God about my back problems and my flatulence and ask him to cure me. And Jeremy, my darling baby, maybe if you told him also of your uncle's in-growing toenail, maybe he could find time to cure him also. And, *bubbeleh*, don't forget to tell God that your elder sister Sarah is already 24 years old and still hasn't found a husband – maybe he can make her less fussy and help her find a nice property developer to marry? Oh, and Jeremy, my sweet child, ask...'

One of the gravediggers has heard enough. He turns to Rayne and says, 'With all the problems you and your family have, Mrs Levy, you shouldn't send a young boy to sort them out, you should go and sort things out in person.'

* * *

The funeral discussion

Friends and family are at Finchley cemetery for Moshe's funeral. Just before the funeral service commences, Rabbi Zeller goes over to Ruth, a very elderly widow, and asks, 'So how old was Moshe?'

'He was 99, *kin-a-hora*,' replies Ruth, 'two years older than me.'

'So you must be 97,' says Rabbi Zeller.

Ruth replies, 'Yes. Hardly worth going back home, is it?'

* * *

Clever, or what?

Moshe, Reilly, Sean and Rowan have been best of friends for over 10 years when, unfortunately, Rowan is killed in a car crash. The next day, the three remaining friends are looking at Rowan's body in his coffin.

Reilly says, 'You know, Rowan was such a great guy and friend to me that I don't want him to go empty handed. I'm going to give him £500.'

With that, he takes out £500 in notes and throws them into the coffin.

Then Sean says, 'I agree with you. I'll match your gift.'

And Sean throws £500 in notes into the coffin.

Moshe says, 'I liked him more than you two, so I'm going to give him £1,000.'

With that, Moshe writes out a cheque for £2,000, throws it into the coffin and takes out £1,000 change.

* * *

Déjà vu

Abe is on holiday in Israel with his wife, children and mother-in-law. Sadly, while they are visiting Jerusalem, Abe's mother-in-law dies. Abe goes to the British Embassy with her death certificate in his hand to make arrangements to send her body back to the UK for burial. As soon as the Embassy official realises that it's Abe's mother-in-law who has died, he tells Abe that it's very expensive to send a body back to the UK.

'It could cost as much as £2,000,' he says, 'so in most cases, the family decide to bury the body here in Israel because this only costs £100.'

But Abe gets agitated. 'I don't care how much it costs to send her body back to the UK, that's what I want to do. OK?'

'OK,' says the official, 'calm down. We'll do it. You must have loved your mother-in-law a lot, considering the price difference.'

'No, that's not the reason,' says Abe, 'it's just that I know of a case of someone who was buried here in Jerusalem many, many years ago and on the third day he arose from the dead. I just don't want to take that chance.'

* * *

Duplication not required

Rebecca's husband has died and the funeral is almost over. Rabbi Bloom goes up to her and says, 'I don't think you'll ever find another man like your late husband Morris.'

Rebecca replies, 'So who's looking for one?'

* * *

The funeral procession

One morning, as Sarah is leaving Starbucks with her usual take-away coffee, she notices an unusual funeral procession coming along the road towards her. At the front is a large black hearse and 20 yards behind this is a second black hearse. A solitary woman is walking behind the second hearse with an Alsatian on a lead. Behind the woman are 50 other women walking single file.

Sarah is very curious and goes over to the woman with the dog and says, 'I'm sorry about your loss.'

'Thank you,' says the woman, 'you're very kind.'

'I know it's a bad time to ask,' says Sarah, 'but whose funeral is this?'

'It's my husband's funeral,' replies the woman.

'So what happened to him?' asks Sarah.

The woman replies, 'My dog attacked and killed him.'

'And who is in the second hearse?' asks Sarah.

The woman answers, 'My mother-in-law. She was trying to help my husband when the dog turned on her.'

A poignant and thoughtful moment of silence passes between the two women.

'Can I borrow the dog?' asks Sarah.

'Go to the back of the line,' replies the woman.

* * *

Funeral arrangements

Aaron is over 90 years old and is close to death. Nevertheless, he is surprised to overhear his two sons discussing his funeral arrangements. 'Let's order two dozen bottles of whisky and kosher red wine, plus 10 plates each of smoked salmon bagels, egg and onion rolls, *shmaltz herring*, fish balls, mixed olives, rye bread and cakes, and invite all the mourners back to Mum's house afterwards,' says Joshua.

'Are you crazy?' says Mervyn, 'That would cost too much. Better we give everyone just a cup of tea and a piece of cake.'

'OK,' says Joshua, 'but I think we should hire 10 Rolls-Royces to take family and mourners to and from the cemetery.'

'Are you *meshugga*?' says Mervyn. 'That's much too extravagant. All we need do to save money is hire just one large Ford for you, me and Mum. The rest can find their own means of transport.'

Just then, Joshua and Mervyn hear Aaron's faint voice from upstairs. 'Mervyn, will you please fetch me a nice clean pair of trousers.'

'But Dad, you know what the doctor told you,' says Mervyn, 'you must stay quietly in bed and not overexert yourself.'

'Yes, I know, Mervyn,' says his father, 'but I've decided to walk to the cemetery. It will save you having to hire a hearse.'

* * *

The miser

Jonathan has worked hard all his life and has saved most of his earnings. He's a real miser when it comes to his money, which he loves more than just about anything. So before he dies, Jonathan says to his wife, 'Now listen, Sarah, when I die, I want you to take all my money and place it in the coffin with me. Please do this because I want to take my money with me to the afterlife. Promise me.'

She promises she will.

Finally the day comes when Jonathan dies. At his funeral, Sarah is with her best friend Rebecca. After they've buried him, Rebecca says to Sarah, 'I hope you weren't stupid to put all that money in there with Jonathan.'

Sarah replies, 'Well, I promised him – I'm a good Jew and I can't lie. I promised him that I would put that money in with him.'

'You mean to tell me', says Rebecca, 'you put every penny of his money in the coffin with him?'

'I sure did,' says Sarah. 'I got it all together, put it into my bank account and wrote him out a cheque.'

* * *

Kind wishes
Henry says to Alan, 'You should live, please God, to 120 years plus three months.'

'Thank you, Henry,' says Alan, 'but why the three months?'

'Because', replies Henry, 'I wouldn't want you to die suddenly.'

Dead and Buried

The afterlife
Moshe and Rebecca make a vow that whoever dies first will come back and inform the other of the afterlife. Their fear is that there is no afterlife.

Many, many years later, Moshe dies and true to his word, he makes contact.

'Rebecca…Rebecca,' he says, 'can you hear me?'

'Is that you, Moshe?' asks Rebecca.

'Yes, Becky,' he replies. 'I've come back, just as we agreed.'

'So what's it like, Moshe?' asks Rebecca.

'Well Becky, it's like this,' replies Moshe. 'Every morning, I get up and have sex. I have breakfast and then off to the golf course where I have sex. I sunbathe and then have sex twice. I have lunch, another romp around the golf course, then sex all afternoon. After dinner, it's the golf course again, then I have sex until late. It's like this every day.'

'Oh Moshe,' says Rebecca, 'you really must be in heaven.'

'Not exactly, Becky,' says Moshe. 'I'm a rabbit on the local golf course.'

* * *

The special
Hetty is enjoying a good game of bridge with her friends when she suddenly shouts out, '*Oy veh,* look at the time. I must get home quickly and fix dinner for mine Moshe. He's always so angry if it's not ready on time.'

When she gets home, she quickly realises that she hasn't done her weekly shopping and all she has in the fridge is a hard-boiled egg, some parsley and a tin of cat food. But our Hetty is quite resourceful – she scrapes out the cat food onto a plate, adds some slices of egg, puts parsley around the food, adds a dollop of tomato sauce and puts the plate on the table, just as Moshe arrives home.

She meets him at the front door with a kiss, leads him to the table and then watches anxiously as he sits down to eat. To her great relief, Moshe enjoys her concoction. 'Hetty, this new dish is the best meal you've made in a long, long time. Please make it for me regularly.'

After that, Hetty makes Moshe his 'special' every bridge night. And then…she tells her bridge group her secret.

'But my dear Hetty, you can't let him eat it – apart from not being kosher, it's likely to kill him in due course,' says one. And six weeks later, he does indeed die.

When her bridge friends come around to pay their respects, one of them says 'You killed him, Hetty. We told you he would die if he kept on eating cat food.'

But Hetty answers, 'For what it's worth, I definitely did not kill mine Moshe. He fell off the piano while he was licking himself.'

* * *

A sharp practice

Joshua has been an active member of the Union of Newspaper Typesetters for over 40 years. Then, just before his retirement, he suddenly dies. When his union hears the sad news, they check first that it's OK for a *goy* to attend Joshua's funeral. Then they choose Brother Peter Smith to represent them.

After the funeral, the Union's General Secretary phones Peter Smith for a report on how the funeral went.

'Well,' says Peter, 'sometimes I think Jews can be as crazy as the rest of us. When I got there, this little man with a beard came up to me and asked if I was a brother. When I said I was, he took out a penknife and started cutting up my suit.'

* * *

Furniture moves

Rivkah gets in to work late one Monday morning and goes to see her boss to apologise. 'I'm sorry I'm late, but I had to move some furniture this morning before I came in to work. In fact my back is killing me after my efforts.'

'So why didn't you wait until your husband gets home tonight?' asks her boss.

'I could have,' says Rivkah, 'but the couch is easier to move if he's not on it.'

* * *

Customer service

Joshua works for Levine's Tailors and is a successful salesman. He's always polite to his customers and as a result is nearly always able to sell a suit to anyone who walks into the shop. So it's a surprise when, after 10 successful years, he resigns to join the police force.

His father can't understand why his son should give up a good job to become a policeman. So at the end of Joshua's first week, he rings Joshua and asks how he likes his new job.

'Well, Dad,' Joshua replies, 'It's nice of you to ask. The salary is just about OK, the hours aren't as bad as I thought they would be and my colleagues are a great bunch. But what I like best is that the customer is always wrong.'

People and Professions

Boasters

The breadwinner

One day, Becky meets her old friend Rachel. She asks, 'So how is your son the solicitor?'

'David's fine, thanks. Please God every solicitor should be as busy as he is – he's even having to turn away new business.'

'And how's your daughter Hannah?'

'She's doing really fine. She's now playing her violin in almost every major concert hall around the world and we hardly see her these days.'

'And what about your youngest son?'

'Oh Issy? He's doing OK, I suppose. He's currently selling cheap clothing to all the street markets in central London. Mind you, if it wasn't for Issy, we would all be starving.'

* * *

Love match

Esther meets Rebecca while she's out shopping. They haven't seen each other for years and immediately start talking about their favourite subject – their children.

'So how's your lovely little boy Lawrence?' asks Esther. 'Is he still giving you much *naches*?'

'He's not so little any more – he's nearly 20 years old,' replies Rebecca, 'and to tell you the truth, we were *broyges* with him last year.'

'Why, what did he do?' asks Esther.

'He hadn't been at Oxford University more than a fortnight when he rang to tell us he'd "come out",' replies Rebecca.

'*Oy gevalt*!' says Esther. 'I bet you were both *farmisht*.'

'Well, we were at first,' says Rebecca, 'but then we found out he's going out with a nice Jewish doctor.'

* * *

Walking away from dinner
Yetta and Sarah, both well-known braggers, meet one Sunday out shopping. 'I held a fantastic dinner party last night,' says Yetta, 'My guests had so much good food and wine available to them that when they left to walk over to their cars, they were all doubled-over.'

Without missing a beat, Sarah replies, 'From your house they could walk?'

Builders and Decorators

It's a bit fishy
Isaac has just had a beautiful swimming pool built in his garden. But his joy is short lived when a council inspector knocks on his door and asks to see the pool.

'Mr Levy,' says the inspector, 'we've checked our records and we can't find any evidence that you obtained council approval to build this pool. Is this correct?'

'Yes,' answers Isaac, 'but I didn't know I needed permission to build in my own back garden. Is permission really required?'

'Oh yes,' replies the inspector, 'indeed it's required. A swimming pool must get official sanction before it's built. Only if it were an ornamental fish pond, say, would permission not be necessary.'

'OK,' says Isaac, 'what you see in front of you is really an ornamental pond.'

'I'm not stupid,' says the inspector. 'A 40-metre-long pool such as yours cannot be described as a pond, Mr Levy.'

'But it is a pond,' argues Isaac, 'indeed it is.'

Then the inspector spots a filtration plant at the end of the garden. 'So why is there a filter?'

'Because,' replies Isaac, 'it's a *gefilte fish* pond.'

* * *

The handywoman

Rivkah, a beautiful blonde, is fed up being typecast by men as silly, useless and starry-eyed. 'I'm as good as most men I meet,' she says to herself and makes a decision to prove it – she will earn some decent money by hiring herself out as a handyman.

First thing next morning, Rivkah begins canvassing her wealthy neighbourhood and starts by ringing the bell of the first house in the first road she comes to. This happens to be Moshe and Leah's house. When Moshe opens his door, Rivkah asks him if he has any jobs for her to do.

'Well, my porch needs painting. How much will you charge me?'

Rivkah thinks for a while, then replies, 'Forty pounds.'

'OK,' says Moshe, 'you're hired. You'll find the paint, paintbrushes, primers, scrapers and other such tools in my garage. It's not locked.'

When Rivka goes into the garage, Leah says to Moshe, 'Do you think the girl realises that we have a very large porch?'

'That's up to her to have found out,' replies Moshe, 'let's leave her to it.'

Thirty minutes later, Rivkah knocks on the door to collect her money.

'You're finished already?' asks Moshe.

'Yes,' replies Rivkah, 'and as I had paint left over, I gave it an extra coat.'

Impressed, Moshe reaches into his pocket for his wallet. But before he could pull it out, Rivkah says, 'And by the way, it's not a Porch, it's a Ferrari.'

* * *

The telephone call

Issy is a very wealthy man and for his mother's birthday he goes to a Sotheby's sale and buys her a very expensive painting. When he gets back home, he can't wait to phone to tell her what he's bought for her. 'Hi, Mum, it's me, Issy, your number one son, your *boychik*.'

'Oh (pause) is everything all right, *bubbeleh*?' she asks.

'Yes, Mum,' replies Issy, 'everything is fine. I'm ringing to tell you that for your birthday, I've just bought you a Rubens.'

'Rubin?' she says, 'Do you mean Rubin the accountant?'

'No, mum, Rubens is a great painter,' explains Issy, laughing.

'Oh, this I didn't know,' she says. 'Listen, *bubbeleh*, ask him how much he'll charge to paint my kitchen.'

* * *

Extraordinary decorating

Kitty has decided to have her house re-decorated. When the decorator arrives to give her a quote, he asks her to describe how she wants her house done.

Kitty says, 'I'm going to leave the choice of colours, material and design entirely to you. I only ask that whatever you choose, it must be extraordinary.'

'What do you mean by that?' asks the decorator.

'I want it done in such a way that when my best friend, Mrs Josephs, comes in to see the work you've carried out, she should instantly have a heart attack with jealousy and drop down dead.'

The Legal Side of Life

It's not my fault

Jacob is in court facing the judge. The judge says to him, 'It has been brought to my attention that you are now four months behind with your alimony. Do you realise that this is a serious omission?'

'Yes, your honour, but let me explain,' replies Jacob. 'It's all because my second wife Judith isn't very well at the moment and she can't work too hard.'

* * *

What female Jewish judges might say

- 'I have a question for the blonde juror in the red at the end. Can I ask you if you are married? You're not – *oy*, do I have a son for you.'
- 'Stop already with this discussion of oral sex. It's dirty, dirty, dirty!'
- 'Look at that face! How can a nice boy like him be guilty?'
- 'Enough with the objections already! And stand up straight – your mother would die if she saw you like this. Not that she ever sees much of you any more, I'll bet.'
- 'Objection, schmobjection. You and the DA, come back to my chambers and we'll talk this out over a nice hot cup of tea.'
- 'I've just awarded you £1 million and you can't even thank me? I take it back!'
- 'Fine, go have your little conference with your client and leave me here, sitting alone, up on the bench.'
- 'If you don't try the chicken soup, it's five days in jail for contempt.'
- 'Evidence, shmevidence. He just looks guilty.'
- 'Oh, you want to object, do you? You don't think I can do my job? Well, how about you come up and take this gavel,

Mr Smarty Pants? Here, I'll put it on the desk – right next to my heart. No, go ahead, take it. You're right, I'm just a senile old woman and should probably be sent off to some sort of home. Your Aunt Myra really likes her room, why don't you give her a call? But really, I shouldn't have to remind you to call your Aunt Myra. I guess you just don't love her any more, either. I should have expected it, you being a big-shot lawyer now. Would it kill you to just believe me once instead of always having to argue? Overruled.'

* * *

Community warning

Watch out! We have reason to believe that there's a one-fingered Jewish pickpocket operating in your area. He specialises in stealing bagels.

* * *

Jury service

Did you hear about the typical Jewish mother?

Once, when she was on jury service, they sent her home. She insisted SHE was guilty.

* * *

The lawyer's lament

Moshe the lawyer arrives home at 10pm and opens his front door. He's shattered after a day of trying to get a stay of execution for William Rite. This client of Moshe's is due to be executed for murder at midnight and his last-minute plea for clemency has failed. So as he enters his house, Moshe is understandably feeling very tired and depressed.

But when Moshe walks in, there is his Hetty waiting for

him. 'So what time of night do you call this?' she shouts at him. 'Where have you been?'

Too weary to play his usual role in this familiar ritual, Moshe walks past her, goes into the front room, pours himself a large whisky, downs it in one go, then heads upstairs for a relaxing hot bath – all the time pursued by the predictable sarcastic remarks.

The phone rings while Moshe's in the bath and when Hetty answers it, she is told that Moshe's client has been granted his stay of execution after all. Quickly realising what a day Moshe must have had, she feels sorry for him and goes upstairs to give him the good news. As Hetty opens the bathroom door, all she sees of Moshe is his naked rear view as he's bending over drying his feet. 'They're not hanging Rite tonight,' she says to Moshe.

Immediately, Moshe whirls around and screams hysterically, 'For crying out loud, Hetty, don't you ever stop?'

* * *

Not enough
Sadie is arrested for shoplifting. During her trial, which her husband Sidney attends, the judge asks her, 'How old are you?'

'I'm 60, your Honour,' replies Sadie.

'And what did you steal?' he asks.

Sadie replies, 'A tin of peaches, your Honour.'

'Why did you steal this tin?' asks the judge.

'Because I was hungry,' replies Sadie.

The judge then asks, 'And how many peaches were in the tin?'

'Five,' replies Sadie.

The judge then says, 'OK, I think five days in jail would be appropriate.'

But before the judge can pronounce sentence, Sidney

suddenly stands up and asks him, 'Is it OK to give the court some more information?'

The judge replies, 'Yes, I suppose so, if you're brief. What is it?'

Sidney replies, 'She also stole a can of peas.'

* * *

How clever is that?

Morris is in court as one of the witnesses to a burglary. Because he's an elderly person, they're treating him gently. 'So you say you saw my client commit this burglary?' the defence lawyer asks Morris.

'Yes,' replies Morris, 'I saw him take the goods as clear as can be.'

'But Morris,' says the defence lawyer, 'this burglary took place at night. Are you really sure you saw my client commit this crime?'

'Yes,' says Morris, 'I definitely saw him do it.'

'Listen, Morris,' continues the defence lawyer, 'you're 80 years old and your eyes are probably not as good as they once were. Just how far can you see at night?'

'I can see the moon, how far is that?' replies Morris.

* * *

The car accident

One day, as Isaac Levy is driving home, a lorry crashes into his car. He's very lucky and suffers only moderate injuries. Nevertheless, he's off work for two months. As a result, he contacts a personal injury lawyer who, after hearing the details, recommends that Isaac take the lorry driver to court for dangerous driving. Isaac agrees.

A few weeks later, Isaac arrives in court and soon he's in the witness box answering questions thrown at him by the lorry driver's very aggressive defence lawyer.

'Mr Levy,' asks the lawyer, 'did you or did you not say, at the scene of the accident, that you were fine?'

'Vell, I'll tell you exactly vot happened at the scene of the accident,' replies Isaac. 'I had only just put my dog Cindy into the –'

'Mr Levy,' interrupts the lawyer, 'I didn't ask you for any details. All I need from you is a simple answer to my question – did you or did you not say, at the scene of the accident, "I'm fine, thank you, I'm fine"?'

'Vell,' replies Isaac, 'as I vas saying, I just got mine Cindy into my car and vas driving down the road ven –'

'Mr Levy!' Once again the lawyer interrupts Isaac. This time, the lawyer turns to the judge and says, 'Your Honour, I'm trying to establish an important fact. This man told the police officer at the scene of the accident that he was just fine. Now he's trying to sue my client. I believe, your Honour, that Mr Levy is a liar. Please tell him to simply answer my question.'

But the judge is now interested in Isaac's reply and says to the lawyer, 'I'd like to hear what Mr Levy has to say about his dog Cindy.'

On hearing this, Isaac continues, 'Vell, like I vas saying, your Lordship, I put mine Cindy, mine vunderful, friendly Cindy, into the car and drove off. But within minutes, a large lorry vent across a red light and crashed into my car. I vas trapped by mine legs and vas in pain. Den I heard mine Cindy moaning and whimpering. *Oy*, it vas the vorst sound I haf ever heard and I knew she vas seriously hurt. Then the police arrived. Vun of them heard mine lovely Cindy whimpering so he vent over to her, saw vat terrible condition she vas in, took out his gun and shoots mine Cindy dead. Den the policeman walks over to me in my car and I see he's still holding his gun. He looks at me and says, 'How are you feeling?' So *nu*, your Lordship, vat vould you haf said?'

* * *

Open-and-shut case

Nathan is talking to his solicitor. 'Here's the deal, Abe. If you're absolutely sure I'll win the case, I'll give you the business.'

'OK,' replies Abe, 'but before I can give you my opinion, I obviously need to know the facts.'

So Nathan goes into great detail about his failed partnership and ends up saying, 'So now you've heard everything, do you think I can sue my partner and get my money back?'

'Well,' replies Abe, 'from what I've just heard, it's clear to me that you will win. It's rare to have such an open-and-shut case.'

Nathan goes very white when he hears this.

'What's the matter?' asks Abe.

'I told you my partner's side of the case,' replies Nathan.

* * *

Conversion procedures

Bernard Levinsky wants to become a British citizen, so he changes his name to Benny Levy and applies for citizenship. After many months of waiting, he's asked to attend court, answer some questions and become, at last, a full British citizen.

Benny stands up to face Judge Hodge. 'Mr Levy,' says Judge Hodge, 'before I can grant you citizenship, I must ask you a few questions to confirm for myself that you really are interested in the UK, its government and its rulers. Do you understand?'

'Yes,' replies Benny.

'All right, who are the UK's leading political parties?' asks Judge Hodge.

'I'm a diamond merchant,' replies Benny, 'do I have time to worry about political parties?'

'Then who is our current prime minister?' asks Judge Hodge.

'That's simple,' replies Benny, 'doesn't everyone know the answer?'

'Mr Levy,' says Judge Hodge, 'are you always in a habit of answering questions in such an ambiguous manner?'

'Why shouldn't I?' replies Benny.

Judge Hodge is now getting angry. 'Mr Levy,' he shouts, 'are you willing to swear your allegiance to our Queen, to our future King Charles and to everyone else in the Royal Family?'

'Your honour,' replies Benny, 'do you really want me to swear in court?'

'Mr Levy,' shouts Judge Hodge, 'please stop answering all my questions with a question. Do you promise to support the prime minister and his government?'

'Isn't it enough that I support mine Sarah and my three darling *kinder*?' replies Benny. 'You want my blood as well?'

* * *

Proof of the pudding

Cyril goes to see his solicitor and says, 'My neighbour owes me £750 but he won't pay up. He says he owes me nothing. What do you suggest I do?'

'Do you have any proof that he owes you the money?' asks the solicitor.

'No, I'm afraid I don't,' replies Cyril.

'OK then,' says the solicitor, 'here's what you should do. Write him a formal letter asking him to pay the £1,000 he owes you.'

'But he only owes me £750,' says Cyril.

'Exactly right,' says the solicitor, 'That's what he will say in his reply to you and then we will then have the proof we need to pursue your claim.'

* * *

The final request

As Morris nears his 60th birthday, he decides to prepare his will and goes to see Patrick, his solicitor. They spend a couple of hours putting together the details. Just before Morris leaves, he says to Patrick, 'I have two final requests to make. Firstly, I want to be cremated, and secondly, I want my ashes scattered over the biggest department store in town.'

'Why?' asks Patrick.

'Because then I'll be sure my wife will visit me twice a week,' replies Morris.

The Media and Publicity

The advert

Bernie has been ill for some months and then suddenly dies. As is the custom, his wife Sadie puts an advert in the 'deaths' section of the *Jewish Chronicle*, but this advert is slightly unusual – it states that Bernie died of gonorrhoea. Immediately, a close friend of Bernie rings Sadie to complain.

'Sadie,' he says, 'you know full well that Bernie died of diarrhoea, not gonorrhoea. So why did you word the advert incorrectly?'

'I looked after Bernie day and night for over three months,' replies Sadie, 'so of course I know he died of diarrhoea. But I thought it would be best for people to remember Bernie as a great lover rather than the big shit he was.'

* * *

Two personal adverts in a Jewish magazine

- Israeli lady age 28. Serves behind the falafel counter in Moshe's Deli. Looking for nice Jewish guy with a good sense of humus.

- I'm looking for the girl I met last week at the *kiddush* after *shul* service. You went to get some *chrayn* for your *gefilte fish* but you never came back. I was the man with the wine and *cholent* stains on my tie.

* * *

Escorted off the bus

Leah is eight months pregnant and gets on a bus to go to her local shopping centre. Morris is already on the bus and watches her sit down opposite him. Leah looks up and notices that Morris is smiling at her, so she immediately moves to another seat. This time Morris's smile turns into a grin and she moves seats again. Morris is now more amused than ever and after Leah moves for the fourth time, he bursts out laughing and can't stop.

So Leah goes over to the driver and complains. One thing leads to another and soon Morris is escorted off the bus by an inspector.

As the bus moves off, the inspector asks Morris, 'OK sir, what have you got to say for yourself?'

Morris replies, 'Well it was like this. When the woman got on the bus, I couldn't help notice that she was heavily pregnant. So when she sat under an ice cream advert that said THE PEACH TWINS ARE COMING. I couldn't help smiling.

'Then she moved and sat under an advert that said MINKY'S EMBROCATION WILL REDUCE THE SWELLING and I had to grin.

'Then she moved again and sat under a deodorant advert that said HARRY'S BIG STICK DID THE TRICK.

'I could hardly contain myself. But when she moved for the fourth time and sat under an advert that said GOODYEAR RUBBER COULD HAVE PREVENTED THIS ACCIDENT, I just lost it.'

* * *

How to get a man

Ruth is Naomi's only child. Unfortunately, Ruth is a rather plain girl and as a result is still single at 30 – she doesn't even have a boyfriend. So naturally, Naomi is getting worried and sees her chance of becoming a *bubbeh* fading fast. So one day Naomi decides to have a heart-to-heart talk with Ruth.

'Darling,' she says, 'I'm your mother and I love you, so please don't get angry with me when you hear what I have to say. I'm getting worried about you because you won't find a nice man by staying at home, night after night, doing nothing but looking sad and watching TV. Believe me, darling, the best thing to do is to advertise yourself in the *Jewish Chronicle* dating section.'

'Oh Mum,' says Ruth, embarrassed, 'I just couldn't do that.'

'But you could, darling,' says Naomi. 'You don't give your name, you just put in a box number where suitors send their details about themselves. And we won't tell a soul we're doing it, not even your dad.'

After another 10 minutes of serious discussion, Naomi gets her way and next day they place the following advert in the paper: CHARMING JEWISH GIRL WITH GSOH, SLIM BUT SHAPELY, POLITE, EXCELLENT EDUCATION, COOKS GREAT MEALS, LOOKING TO MEET KIND, EDUCATED, INTELLIGENT JEWISH MAN WITH VIEW TO MARRIAGE.

WRITE TO BOX 13.

Then the waiting starts. One week later, a reply drops through the letterbox. Ruth picks it up and shouts, 'Mum, I've got a reply.'

Ruth opens the letter, starts to read then suddenly gasps and bursts out crying.

'What's the matter, darling?' asks Naomi.

'It's from Dad,' replies Ruth.

* * *

How to do marketing

Issy and his friend Benny meet in town for their regular fortnightly chat over coffee. '*Oy veh*, Benny,' says Issy, 'I just can't seem to sell my car. I've been advertising it in the *Jewish Chronicle* for nearly two months and I haven't had even one enquiry.'

'Really?' replies Benny, 'So how did you word the advert?'

'It went something like this,' replies Issy: 1985 FORD CORTINA 1300 FOR SALE: ONE REAR BRAKE LIGHT MISSING, BONNET DENTED IN TWO PLACES, NO AIR CONDITIONING, NO RADIO, SIDE WINDOW CRACKED, NEEDS RE-SPRAY. £500 OR NEAR OFFER.

Benny thinks for a moment and says, '*Oy*, no wonder no one called. Take out your notebook and write down this better advert. You'll sell your car very quickly.' He then dictates: VINTAGE CAR FOR SALE: UNIQUE, LOTS OF CHARACTER, OWNED BY NON-SMOKER, GOOD RUNNER, LIGHT ON PETROL, OPEN SPACE PLAN, EASY TO MAINTAIN, ONE OR TWO THINGS TO PUT RIGHT BUT IDEAL FOR THE IMAGINATIVE EXECUTIVE WHO'S GOING PLACES.

When they meet up again a few weeks later, Benny asks Issy, '*Nu*? So did you sell the car already?'

'Are you *meshugga*?' replies Issy. 'Why should I sell such a wonderful car like that?'

* * *

Dating advert in *Jewish Chronicle*
Professional Jewish athlete, winner of Davis Cup, America
Cup and Stanley Cup. Seeking non-Jewish woman. Goyishe
Cup. Reply to Box 13.

* * *

We're not stupid
Moshe loses his rare and valuable dog and advertises in the
Jewish Chronicle offering a very generous £15,000 reward
for its return. After a few days of no replies, he goes to the
JC for some information.

He says to the receptionist, 'I'd like to see Jacob, the
advertising manager, please.'

'I'm sorry sir, but he's out,' says the receptionist.

'OK, so how about his secretary?'

'She's out too, sir. In fact everyone from his department is
out.'

'*Oy veh*,' says Moshe, 'where is everybody?'

'They're all out looking for your dog.'

* * *

I've already thought of it
Lawrence and Monty are in the jewellery business but they
are not doing at all well. So much so that one day, Lawrence
says, 'We're going into a new *gesheft* and we're going to
make a fortune.'

'What new *gesheft*?' asks Monty.

'We're going into washing powders,' replies Lawrence.

'Washing powders?' says Monty, looking very puzzled,
'What do we know of washing powders?'

'Listen, you *shmuck*,' says Lawrence, 'it's easy. We buy
crates and crates of the powder from a wholesaler for next to
gornisht and put it into little cardboard boxes. Then we sell

the boxes for £1.99 each and soon we'll be rich.'

'No, you listen to me, *potts*,' says Monty. 'We'll need to advertise the boxes and that will cost us a fortune.'

'OK, so let's advertise. What's the problem? I've already though of it. We can even advertise on TV,' says Lawrence.

'*Meshugganah*,' says Monty. 'We'll also need to hire a well-known publicity agent and he'll cost us a lot of *gelt* to come up with a suitable product name.'

'But I've already thought of a good name,' says Lawrence.

'OK clever clogs,' says Monty, 'what name do you have?'

'We'll call it FEKS WASHING POWDER,' replies Lawrence.

'What rubbish,' says Monty. 'How can anyone come up with a slogan for a product with the name of FEKS WASHING POWDER?'

'But I've already thought of a slogan,' says Lawrence.

'OK wise guy,' says Monty, 'let's hear your slogan.'

'Right,' says Lawrence. 'IF OMO DOESN'T WASH YOUR WHITES WHITER, AND PERSIL DOESN'T MAKE YOUR COLOURS BRIGHTER, THEN FEK IT.'

* * *

Shul announcement

Moshe loses his wallet and decides to place the following advert in his *shul's* weekly newsletter:

LOST OR STOLEN: Near or in the Brent Cross Shopping Centre. A brown full-length leather wallet containing my driving licence, my passport, some irreplaceable family photos and approximately £500 in £20 notes. Finder can keep the documents and the photos but should return the money, to which I am attached for sentimental reasons.

* * *

Sign in the window of Levy's Carpet Store
USE OUR EASY CREDIT PLAN. 100% DOWN. NOTHING TO
PAY EACH MONTH.

* * *

Signs and wonders
Abe owns a thriving menswear shop, but his prosperity starts
to weaken when a competitor opens a shop next door to his
on his left. Then, a month later, things get even worse when
another competitor opens a shop next door to his on his right.

'*Oy veh*,' he says to himself, 'three menswear shops in a
row is nothing but bad news.'

But then, two months later, things start to look up. The
competitor on his left has put up a sign in his window saying:
SALE. MUST CLOSE. QUALITY CLOTHING. LOWEST PRICES.

Then, a week later, the competitor on his right puts up a
sign saying: BANKRUPT. CLOSING DOWN SALE. EVERY-
THING LESS THAN COST.

So Abe immediately puts up a big sign over the front door
to his shop: MAIN ENTRANCE TO THE BIG SALE.

* * *

Snow warnings
Issy is married to Becky, a beautiful blonde. One very cold
winter morning, they hear the following local radio
announcement: 'We're expecting up to three inches of snow
today. To help the gritting lorries get through, please park
your car on the even-numbered side of your street.'

Becky goes out and moves her car. The following morning,
they hear another snow warning on the radio: 'We're
expecting another four inches of snow today. To help the
gritting lorries get through, please park your car on the odd-
numbered side of your street.'

Becky goes out and moves her car again. The next morning, they hear yet another snow warning on the radio: 'We're expecting a blizzard today – at least another six inches of snow. You must park...' when suddenly there is a power cut and the radio goes dead.

Becky says, 'Issy darling, now I don't know what to do. What do you think I should do?'

Issy replies, 'Why not just leave your car in our heated garage this time?'

Money and Investments

The customer is always right

Fred is in his usual nasty mood as he goes into a bank and says to the women cashier behind the window, 'I want to open a bloody deposit account.'

The astonished woman replies, 'I do beg your pardon, but I must have misheard you. What did you say?'

'So listen carefully this time, you stupid moo,' shouts Fred, angrily. 'I said I want to open a bloody deposit account and right now.'

'I'm very sorry sir, but I won't tolerate that kind of language,' and with that she leaves her window and goes to see Abe, the bank manager.

Abe agrees with her that she certainly shouldn't have to listen to foul language. They both return to her window and Abe says to Fred, 'What seems to be the problem, sir?'

'There is no damn problem,' Fred says. 'I've just won £10 million on the lottery and all I want to do is open a bloody deposit account in this bloody awful bank!'

'Oh, I see,' says Abe, 'and is this woman giving you a hard time?'

* * *

Who knows?
Sarah and Issy are out celebrating their 20th wedding anniversary. During the evening, Sarah broaches the subject of life insurance (his) – an issue she has been raising with him for at least 10 years, without success.

'Issy,' she says, with tears in her eyes, 'I don't think you love me.'

'Why do you think that?' he asks.

'Because if you really love me, you would ensure that if anything happened to you, God forbid, I would be properly provided for.'

'Sarah,' he says angrily, 'I need life insurance like I need a hole in the head.'

'I know your views,' says Sarah, 'but I've spoken to two of my friends recently and they tell me that their husbands have life insurance – and they're not as rich as you. If it's good enough for them, why isn't it good enough for you?'

'I'll tell you why,' replies Issy. 'It's because they've been paying high premiums month after month and what have they got so far in return? Nothing, *gornisht.*'

'So what if their husbands have been paying for nothing?' says Sarah. 'You've always told me I'm luckier than my friends – who knows, maybe this time I'll strike it rich.'

* * *

Appreciation
Gary, a financial advisor, is talking to one of his elderly lady clients about her recent purchase of £100,000 worth of Marks & Spencer shares.

'Rivkah, do you remember your recent investment in Marks & Spencer? Well, I've just heard that they are going to split.'

'*Oy veh*, vat a pity,' she replies sadly, 'I'm really very upset to hear about it – especially as they've been together for such a long time.'

* * *

Honest talking

Shlomo, regarded as one of the best-paid insurance salesman around, is talking to a prospect. 'How much life insurance do you have?'

'Fifteen thousand pounds,' comes the reply.

'So how long do you think you can stay dead on that kind of *gelt*?' asks Shlomo.

* * *

Spend, spend, spend

Freda comes back from her trip to the shops and tells her Moshe that she's just bought another new designer dress.

'What? You must be joking,' Moshe shouts at her. 'That's the third one you've bought this week. Where on earth do you think I'm going to find the money to pay for them?'

'I may be many things, darling,' Freda replies, 'but inquisitive I'm not.'

* * *

I can't wait

Naomi is out shopping in the supermarket. As she goes down the aisles putting things into her trolley, she hums and sings to herself. She is still singing as she reaches the checkout desk.

'My, you seem to be happy today,' says the cashier.

'Yes I am,' replies Naomi, 'and I have every reason to be. I've got a beautiful house, I've three handsome sons, all doctors, my bank account is extremely healthy and my husband Abe's life is insured for £5 million.'

'I'm glad to hear it,' says the cashier.

'Yes, and that's not all,' says Naomi. 'My Abe is not in the best of health.'

* * *

Reconciliation

Abe is very fussy with his money and always, regular as clockwork, goes through his wife Sadie's chequebook each month to see where their money is going. He always wants to see everything balance to the exact penny. This month, as in previous months, Sadie's figures are hard to reconcile and, tired of having to spend so much time on her inaccuracies, Abe makes her agree to spend some time putting her figures into shape before he devotes any more time on them.

After spending hours poring over her paperwork, Sadie looks up and says, 'Well, Abe, you should be proud of me. I've done it – I've made it balance.'

So Abe goes over to take a look. 'OK, let's see what you've done.'

On her worksheet he sees a long list of items starting with: Mortgage £1,550.00; Electricity £70.50; Gas £150.75; Telephones £350.22; Private Medical Insurance £5,900.50; Kosher butcher £350.99; and ending with ESP £109.01. Puzzled by the last entry, Abe says, 'What on earth is ESP, Sadie?'

'That's easy,' replies Sadie. 'It stands for, Error Some Place!'

* * *

Age matters

Avrahom is a lively 75-year-old widower. He is also very rich. One day, he turns up at the Kosher K restaurant to meet some of his friends and he has a gorgeous young redhead on his arm. She has sex appeal in abundance and listens to Avrahom's every word with great attention. All his friends think she is as sexy a lady as they have seen for years.

When she excuses herself to go to the Ladies, Avrahom's friends rush over to him. 'Avrahom, how did you manage to get such a lovely girlfriend?' they ask.

'Girlfriend?' says Avrahom looking upset, 'What do you mean girlfriend? Naomi is my wife.'

They were shocked. 'So how did you persuade Naomi to marry you?'

'I lied about my age,' Avrahom replies.

'Don't tell us that you told Naomi that you were only 50?'

'Of course not,' smiles Avrahom. 'I told her I was 90.'

* * *

Naomi's turn

It started when Faye and Naomi were friends at school. Faye seemed to spend her entire time trying to get one over on Naomi and never missed an opportunity to belittle her. Whatever Naomi had or did, Faye would better it.

Then they left school to go their own ways. Thirty years later, by chance, Faye and Naomi meet again while they're out shopping. And guess what? Nothing has changed. Within minutes, Faye is boasting about her life and whenever Naomi says something, Faye dismisses it with contempt. After 15 minutes of this, Faye looks at her watch and says, 'I must go pick up my diamonds. My husband Lou is so wealthy that once a month he sends them to Hatton Garden for cleaning. We're going to the Royal Opera tonight, it's *Madame Butterfly*, and we have the best seats. So I need my diamonds.'

'Oh,' replies Naomi with a smile on her face, 'do you clean your diamonds? My husband David is so rich that he throws my diamonds away when they get dirty and buys me new ones.'

* * *

A financial riddle – 1

Q: Who was the greatest male financier in the Bible?

A: Noah – he was floating his stock while everyone else was in liquidation.

* * *

A financial riddle – 2

Q: Who was the greatest female financier in the Bible?

A: Pharaoh's daughter – she went down to the bank of the Nile and drew out a little prophet.

* * *

How sad

Moshe meets his friend in town one day. 'Hi Abe, how are things with you?'

'OK, I suppose,' replies Abe, rather gloomily.

'So why the long face?' asks Moshe.

'Because I just found a full pay packet in the gutter, that's why,' answers Abe.

'Well surely that's no reason to be miserable?' says Moshe.

'It is – when you see how much the Inland Revenue has taxed me,' replies Abe.

* * *

The system

Bernard and Issy are having a serious chat about women. Bernard says, 'Whenever I see a woman, Issy, I give her a rating of between one and 10.'

'So what?' says Issy. 'I do the same.'

'But my system is different,' says Bernard. 'I score Jewish women differently to non-Jewish women.'

'That's new to me,' says Issy. 'So in your system, what's a Jewish 10?'

'That's a woman who I would normally rate a four but who has £1,000,000.'

* * *

Life saver
One day, it was so hot in Miami that Becky almost died on the beach. It was just lucky that a lifeguard opened her mink coat in time.

* * *

Expensive treatment
Issy is not well and goes to see Dr Myers. After examining him, Dr Myers says, 'Well, I can help you, but it will require many sessions.'

'OK,' says Issy, 'how much is this going to cost me?'

'The 12 sessions plus drugs will cost you £1,000,' replies Dr Myers.

'*Oy*,' says Issy, 'I'm not a wealthy man, Doctor. Couldn't you make it less?'

'Well…I could do it for £850,' replies Dr Myers.

'It's still more than I can afford, Doctor,' says Issy. 'I've three children and a Jewish wife to support.'

'OK,' says Dr Myers, 'how about £700?'

'It's still too high, Doctor,' says Issy. 'My business is doing terribly and my wife has told her mother that she can live with us.'

'All right already,' says Dr Myers, 'I'll do it for £600 and not a penny less.'

'Thanks doctor, I can accept that,' says Issy.

'Good,' says Dr Myers, 'but tell me – why did you come to me to seek treatment when you know I'm the most expensive doctor in this area?'

'Well,' replies Issy, 'you've got a marvellous reputation and when it comes to my health, money is no object!'

* * *

Jewish blood

Although Sean, a wealthy businessman, is only 40, he needs a heart transplant. But as he has a very rare blood group, he has to wait until his doctors can find a suitable blood donor. Fortunately, Sean doesn't have to wait too long – Benny has the same blood type and is willing to donate some of his blood to help out. After the surgery, Sean shows his appreciation by sending Benny a thank-you card and a cheque for £10,000. Benny is very surprised to receive this – after all, he didn't agree to donate his blood for any reward. Sean's priest also writes to Benny saying that it's so good to see such co-operation between the faiths.

Ten years later, Sean needs another operation and his doctors immediately contact Benny to see whether he's willing to donate his blood again. Once more, Benny agrees. After the surgery, Sean shows his appreciation by sending Benny a thank-you card and £250 worth of Marks & Spencer gift tokens. Benny is once again appreciative, as he didn't agree to donate his blood for any reward.

Sean's wife, however, is not at all happy that her husband hasn't rewarded Benny in the same generous manner as before. So she asks him why.

'*Bubbeleh*,' replies Sean, 'don't be such a *shmo*. My new blood has given me some *saychel* and it's obvious to me why I can't reward Benny as I did before. Our beautiful daughter Jane, *kin-a-hora*, is getting married next year to a wonderful *mensh* and because I don't want to be seen as a *shnorrer*, I've got to find a lot of *gelt* to pay for the *simcha*.'

* * *

The insurance policies

Old Emanuel dies. All of his life he'd been dealing in second-hand cufflinks and never got rich as a result. But one month after Emanuel's death, his widow Leah gets a shock, and surprise, when three cheques arrive in the morning's post – one cheque for each of the three life assurance policies Emanuel had taken out without her knowing. She adds up the three cheques and, *oy veh*, she's rich – they total more than £175,000. She immediately phones her daughter.

'Suzy,' she says, 'your dear father, God bless his soul, worked long and hard all his life to provide for us. We lived poor but contented. But now, just when we get some real money, Emanuel is not around to enjoy any of it.'

* * *

The alternative name

Although Abe and Hetty, both in their sixties, have lived in New York all their lives, they decide to move to London. Within six months of their move, they're lucky enough to win £10 million on the lottery. They are naturally over the moon and use most of their winnings to buy a small mansion in one of the smartest parts of town. They also decide to employ a chauffeur for their new Lexus, an au pair, a gardener to care for their half-acre back garden and a butler to serve all their meals. Soon after moving into their new home, they invite their London friends Max and Hannah over for dinner.

During the meal, Max says to the butler, 'My good man, so what is your name, what shall we call you?'

The butler replies, in perfect Queen's English, 'Well sir, my master calls me shipwreck.'

As soon as the butler leaves the room, Max asks, 'So what kind of a name is "Shipwreck", Abe?'

In his usual thick New York accent, Abe replies, 'Vats mit shipwreck? He's de voist butler in da voild, so ve call him *shtick dreck*.'

* * *

The sea rescue

Jacob is pulled from the sea at Birchington by a lifeguard. When his wife Judith sees all the commotion, and then realises that it's her Jacob who is lying flat out on the sands, she goes running over, sobbing all the way. When she gets to him, she shouts, '*Oy veh*, Jacob, Jacob, vat's happened to you?'

The lifeguard tells her to calm down. 'Lady,' he says, 'please don't get too hysterical – I'm looking after your husband. I'm now going to give him some artificial respiration and I'm sure he'll then be fine.'

'Vat do you mean artificial respiration?' Judith says to the lifeguard. 'Mine Jacob gets either real respiration or he gets notting at all.'

* * *

The big diamond

Max and Hyman are having a chat about what it would be like to own the richest things money can buy. 'So what about owning the biggest diamond in the world?' says Max. 'Now that's something I wouldn't mind having in my display case. Real cool.'

'Yes, I agree,' says Hyman. 'By the way, Max, what's the name of this world's biggest diamond?'

'Koh-i-noor,' replies Max.

'I might have guessed it would be a Jewish diamond,' says Hyman.

* * *

A motor-vating riddle

Q: What's the best thing a man can do to impress a Jewish Princess?

A: Do pull-ups. By that, I mean pull up in a Lexus…pull up in a Mercedes…pull up in a Bentley convertible.

Selling

Hungry salesman

Benny the salesman has been driving all day and now it is getting dark, so he stops for the night at a small hotel. He goes to reception and a lady comes to the desk. There doesn't seem to be anyone at the hotel – the place is deserted.

'Can I help you?' she asks.

'A room please and something to eat,' Benny says. 'I'm dying of hunger.'

She looks at him and doesn't like what she sees. He is sweaty, tired-looking, with bags under his red eyes and his suit is badly creased. It doesn't look like he could afford a meal.

So she says, 'I'm sorry, sir, but we're right out of food.'

Benny looks straight at her and says, 'In that case, I'm going to have to do what my father did.'

Immediately she grows frightened. 'What did your father do?' she asked.

'My father,' Benny replies, 'did what he had to do.'

She becomes even more frightened when she hears this. Who knows what kind of father this madman had? Maybe his father was a thief or a rapist even. And she is alone with him. So maybe she should keep him happy.

'Hold on, sir,' she says and returns with a plate full of roast beef, potatoes, hot peppers and slices of rye bread.

She watchs in amazement as Benny eats it all in quick time. When he has emptied his plate, he say, 'That was great, the best meal I've had in weeks.'

Seeing that he is now relaxed, she asks the question that has been worrying her for the last hour. 'Could you please tell me what it was that your father did?'

'Oh yes, my father,' says Benny. 'Whenever my father couldn't get anything to eat…he went to bed hungry.'

* * *

Salty story

Aaron is out shopping when he remembers that he has guests coming over for tea and needs to buy some tea bags. He goes into Moshe the Grocer and starts looking for tea bags. As he walks down the first aisle, he can't help but notice that all the shelves are packed with bags of salt. Shelf after shelf, in aisle after aisle, all packed with bags of salt. So he calls for the manager.

'Can I help you?' says Moshe.

'Yes you can,' replies Aaron. 'I've come in here to buy some tea bags and all I can find is salt. What kind of grocer do you call yourself? It's a bit pointless, isn't it, just selling salt? I just don't believe you can sell all this salt.'

'I couldn't agree with you more,' says Moshe. 'I personally can't sell much salt, but *oy veh*, the sales rep who sold me the salt – can he sell salt!'

* * *

The sales pitch

Monty is looking for a new job that would best make use of his skills, so one day he tries his hand selling second-hand cars at Levy's Motors. Although he has no experience in this field, he's confident that he can succeed.

On his first day, he tries to sell cars using the traditional approach, by using phrases such as, 'This car has only been driven by little old Kitty Cohen to go to the local shops once a week,' and, 'This car is almost brand new, just like my mum's *Rosh Hashanah* hat.' Monty uses this approach on every prospective buyer but none believe him and he doesn't sell a car all day.

Next day, he changes his sales pitch and sells three cars. His manager is so pleased that he calls Monty into his office and says, 'Well done! What did you do to make these sales?'

'Well,' replies Monty, smiling, 'because the previous day's

customers didn't believe my little old lady story, today I told them the car was previously owned by Rebecca Lovegod, a nymphomaniac who only used the back seat.'

* * *

Moshe the salesman – 1

Moshe applies for a job at Vot-Lovely Menswear. During his interview, Benjamin the personnel manager asks him, 'Where did you last work?'

'Shmatters R Us,' replies Moshe, proudly.

'And how long did you work for them?' asks Benjamin.

'A long time – 40 years, in fact,' replies Moshe.

Benjamin is a bit startled by this response and says to Moshe, 'Forty years, eh? So how old did you say you were?'

'I'm 51 years old, *kin-a-hora*,' replies Moshe.

'I don't understand,' says Benjamin. 'If you're 51, how come you say you worked for them for 40 years?'

Quick as a flash, Moshe replies, 'I put in a lot of overtime.'

* * *

Moshe the salesman – 2

Morris is passing by Vot-Lovely Menswear when he sees a sign in their window: JACKETS – SPECIAL PRICE – £250. So he goes inside. Moshe, the assistant on duty, goes over to Morris and says, 'Can I be of help, sir?'

'Yes you can,' replies Morris. 'I'd like you to make me a Beatles jacket.'

'A Beatles jacket? I don't know what that is exactly,' says Moshe. 'Can you describe it to me?'

'Of course,' says Morris.

So Moshe takes out his notebook and starts to make notes.

'It's like an ordinary jacket,' says Morris, 'but this one has no collar. Neither does it have a lining…or buttons…or button holes. It doesn't even have lapels.'

'Is that it?' asks Moshe.

'Yes,' replies Morris. 'So *nu*? How much will such a jacket cost?'

'For you,' replies Moshe, 'such a jacket will cost £350.'

'But your sign outside says, JACKETS – SPECIAL PRICE – £250,' says Morris.

'I know it does,' says Moshe, 'but with all the extras you've asked for….'

Fools and Idiots (*Shmucks*)

Forest drive

Avrahom is walking down the high street one day when a smart Lexus saloon draws up next to him. Who should be in it but his friend Yitzhak.

Avrahom asks Yitzhak, 'Where did you get such a nice car, Yitzhak?'

'My girlfriend Sarah gave it to me.'

'*Mazeltov*! I knew Sarah has been telling everyone that she's in love with you, but…to give you such a car?'

'Well, even I admit it was very strange,' says Yitzhak. 'We were out driving in Sarah's car in Epping Forest when she suddenly drove into a small covered area hidden from the road. She then got out of the car, took off all her clothes and said to me, "Yitzhak, take whatever you want." So I took the car.'

'Yitzhak,' says Avrahom, 'you are one smart cookie. Her clothes would never have fitted you.'

* * *

Helping out

Sidney has never been known to help out with any of the household chores, but after a serious argument with his wife Hannah on this subject, he agrees to try to get more involved. The next day, Hannah is shocked – Sidney has decided to wash his favourite sweatshirt!

She watches him put his sweatshirt into the washing machine and then just stand there with a puzzled look on his face. After a few minutes, he turns to Hannah and says, 'OK, I give in. So what setting do I use for washing a red, long-sleeved, 90% cotton, 10% polyester sweatshirt?'

'It all depends,' replies Hannah. 'What does it say on your sweatshirt?'

'*Yeshiva* University,' he replies.

* * *

The hoax

Sadie sends the following email to all her women friends: 'Dear All, I hate hoax warnings, but this one is important! Please send this warning to all the women friends in your email address book. If a man comes to your front door saying he is conducting a survey and asks you to take off your clothes, don't do it. It's a scam. He only wants to see you naked.

'PS: I wish I had got this yesterday. I feel so stupid and cheap now.'

* * *

Marriage advice

Melvyn says to Howard, 'My father is always advising me to find a girl who has the same belief as the family, and then marry her.'

'That advice wouldn't work for me,' says Howard. 'Why would I want to marry a girl who thinks I'm a *shmuck*?'

* * *

Shipwrecked

At the end of a hard year's work, Moshe decides to take a holiday right away and he books himself on a Caribbean cruise. The first few days of the cruise are perfect, but then calamity – the ship sinks and Moshe ends up on a small, uncharted island. He looks around and sees that there is nothing nearby except bananas and coconuts. Still, these are better than starving to death.

Ten weeks later, as he is sitting in the shade, to his surprise a small boat lands on the beach and the most beautiful woman he has ever seen gets out, walks over to him and says, 'Hi.'

He can't believe his luck. He replies, 'Hi to you too. Where on earth have you come from? How did you get here? What's your name?'

'Hold on,' she says, 'one question at a time. I landed on the other side of this island about 10 weeks ago when my cruise liner sank. I've just rowed here from the other side. Oh, and my name is Hannah.'

'That's amazing, Hannah,' he says. 'My name is Moshe. You were lucky to have a rowboat wash up with you.'

'Oh, this?' replies Hannah. 'I made it myself out of raw materials I found on the island. The oars are made from pine tree branches, I wove the bottom from palm branches and the sides came from a eucalyptus tree.'

'But where did you get the tools from?' he asks.

'Oh, I made the tools myself,' replies Hannah. 'I found an unusual stratum of exposed alluvial rock, which I heated in my kiln. It melted into a soft iron-like material, which I used to make the tools, which in turn I used to make the boat.'

Moshe is silent. He can't believe her skills.

'If it's OK with you, why don't I now row you to my place?' she says.

Moshe just nods his acceptance.

It takes Hannah just 10 minutes to row to her place. As they near the shore, Moshe is surprised to see a stone walkway leading up to a very smart sky-blue bungalow.

Hannah ties up her boat at a small jetty using a hand-made flaxen rope, and they enter the bungalow.

'It's not really much,' says Hannah, 'but to me, Moshe, it's home. Please sit down and I'll get you a drink.'

'No thanks,' Moshe replies, 'I just couldn't drink any more coconut juice.'

'But you don't have to have coconut juice,' says Hannah. 'How about a piña colada? I've made a still.'

As they sit on her hand-made couch drinking their piña coladas, Moshe looks around and is amazed at what Hannah has achieved in such a short time. After a while, Hannah gets up and says, 'I'm going to slip into something more comfortable. While you're waiting, why don't you take a shower and then have a shave? You'll find a razor in the bathroom cabinet.'

Moshe goes into the bathroom and runs his bath. It even has hot water from a kind of thermal heating device Hannah has rigged up. After his bath, he goes to the wooden cabinet and finds a razor made of shells roped together inside a swivel mechanism. While he's having an excellent shave, Moshe thinks, 'Hannah is unbelievable, truly amazing – whatever will I discover next? She can do anything.'

When he returns, Hannah greets him wearing only a few carefully placed vine leaves and smelling of honeysuckle – she looks utterly fantastic. Hannah beckons Moshe to sit next to her, which he does. Hannah smiles at Moshe in a seductive manner and slithers up closer to him.

'Moshe,' she says, staring into his eyes, 'we've both been out here for 10 weeks. Now you've found me, is there something you really feel like doing right now, something you've been longing to do for all these weeks. You know....'

Moshe can't believe it. 'You mean...I can check my email from here?'

* * *

Is that you?

Becky is making love to her toy boy when she hears her Bernie's car coming up the drive. 'Hurry,' she says to him, 'stand in the corner, my husband's here.' Becky quickly rubs baby oil all over him and dusts him with a thick layer of talcum powder. 'Don't move until I tell you to,' she whispers to him, 'pretend you're a statue.'

'What's this, darling?' says Bernie as he enters the bedroom.

'Oh, it's just a statue,' replies Becky. 'The Golds next door bought one for their bedroom and when I saw it, I liked it so much, I got one for us too.'

Nothing more was said, not even when they later go to bed for the night.

At 2am, Bernie quietly slips out of bed, goes down to the kitchen and returns with a cold salt beef sandwich on rye and a glass of orange juice. 'Here,' he whispers to the statue, 'eat this. I stood like a *shmuck* at the Golds' for two days and nobody even offered me a glass of water.'

* * *

The birthday treat

Moshe asks his wife Sadie what she'd like for her birthday. 'I'd love to be six again,' she says. So on her birthday, he gets up early, shakes Sadie awake, kisses her and says, 'Happy birthday, darling. Now please get up, I'm taking you on a surprise birthday outing.'

She does as she's told and off they go. After a two-hour drive, Sadie is surprised when they arrive at the Kosher Munchkins Theme Park. And what a day she then has. Moshe makes her go on all the popular rides, including:

• the *Kishkas* Ache Water Slide
• the *Broyges* Ghost House

- the *Menorah* of Fear
- the *Meshugganah* Roundabout
- the Werewolf *Mishpocheh*
- the *Shikker* Swing
- the Cold Water Shpritz
- the Sore *Toches* Dodgems
- the Smelly *Gatkes* Tunnel
- the Klutzy Mountain Railway
- and the *Loch in Kop* Death Ride

In fact, by the end of the afternoon, Moshe has forced Sadie to go on just about everything there is to go on. She staggers out of the theme park with her head going round and round and feeling very dizzy. But Moshe doesn't seem to notice. He takes her to McDavid's, where he orders her a Big Minkyburger with fries and a Pepsi. Then, when they finish eating, he takes her to a movie and buys her a giant tub of popcorn and another Pepsi as they go into the cinema.

Finally they get back home. Sadie wobbles through the front door and with Moshe following behind her goes straight upstairs to collapse into bed. Her stomach feels like it has been forced inside out and she has a bad headache. Moshe leans over her and lovingly asks, 'Well, darling, what was it like being six again?'

Sadie glares at him through her bloodshot eyes and says, 'You *shmuck*, I meant my dress size.'

The moral of this story: even when a man is listening, he's still going to get it wrong.

* * *

Definition
Definition of a *shmuck*: a guy who leaves the shower to take a *pish*.

* * *

Honesty
The phone rings and 80-year-old Victor answers it. 'Hello,' says Victor.

'Can I speak to Moshe, please?' says the woman caller.

'I'm sorry,' says Victor, 'but you've got the wrong number.'

'Are you sure?' asks the caller.

'Listen lady,' says Victor, 'have I ever lied to you before?'

Teaching and Studying

Too clever by half
Little five-year-old Benjy was practising spelling on his fridge using a set of magnetic letters. Freda, his mother, had watched him put together words such as 'mum', 'dad', 'dog', 'cat' and 'car' and was very proud of her clever son. But then Benjy shouted out, 'Look what I spelled, Mummy.'

Freda looked at the fridge and saw that he had put up the three magnetic letters: 'G', 'O', 'D'.

'Why, that's wonderful, Benjy,' she said, 'why don't you leave them on the fridge until Daddy comes home?'

'OK, Mummy,' he said.

But just as Freda was thinking that the Jewish school he went to was starting to have an impact, Benjy's little voice called out, 'Mummy, how do you spell "zilla"?'

* * *

Fairy story

Rebecca is nine years old and is doing her homework. Suddenly, she gets up, goes to her father and says, 'Daddy, could you please tell me what "frugal" means.'

'Yes, of course, replies her father, 'it means something like – to save.'

Rebecca thanks him and goes back to her homework. Later, her father goes over to see how she's getting on. He's reading her story when he comes across the following: *'The beautiful princess Sarah slipped on the wet grass and fell into the lake. As she couldn't swim she starting shouting out, "Frugal me. Oh please, someone frugal me."*

'Luckily for princess Sarah, the handsome prince David was riding by and he quickly frugalled her. They then lived happily ever after.

'The End.'

* * *

Misunderstanding

David went up to his nursery school teacher and said, 'Teacher, I found a cat yesterday.'

The teacher said, 'That's nice, David. Was it dead or alive?'

'Dead,' replied David.

'How do you know that?' she asked him.

'Because', said David innocently, 'I pissed in its ear and it didn't move a bit.'

'You did WHAT?' said the teacher, very surprised.

'You know, teacher,' explained David, 'I leaned over it and went "pssst" and it didn't move.'

* * *

The £1 million essay

The teacher says to her class, 'OK, children, I want you all to write an essay on what you would do if you won £1 million on the lottery.'

At the end of the lesson, Isaac hands in a blank piece of paper.

'Isaac,' says the teacher, 'why haven't you written anything?'

'Because if I had a million pounds, miss, that's exactly what I would do – nothing.'

* * *

School test

During a maths lesson at school, the teacher points to little Benny and asks, 'Benny, what's three per cent?'

Benny sits for a while shaking his head and then replies, 'You're right, miss, what's three per cent?'

* * *

The school inspector

Back in the 1970s, a Russian school inspector is questioning the children. He points to one of the boys and says, 'Who is your father?'

The boy replies, 'The Soviet Union.'

He then asks, 'Who is your mother?'

'The Communist Party,' comes the reply.

'And what do you want to be when you grow up?'

'I want to be a Stankhanovite worker for the glory of the state and the party.'

The inspector then points to one of the girls and asks, 'Who is your father?'

The girl answers, 'The Soviet Union.'

'Who is your mother?'

'The Communist Party.'

'And what do you want to be when you grow up?'

'A heroine of the Soviet Union raising lots of children for the state and party.'

The inspector looks round and sees a Jewish boy tucked away at the back trying to look inconspicuous. He points and says, 'What's your name?'

The boy replies, 'Haim Abramovitch.'

'Who is your father?'

'The Soviet Union.'

'Who is your mother?'

'The Communist Party.'

'And what do you want to be when you grow up?'

Haim replies, 'An orphan.'

* * *

The children's weekly Talmud lesson

Rabbi Levy arrives at his *shul's* weekly children's service. This is when he gathers all the little children around him and gives them a brief Talmud lesson before dismissing them. He never misses an opportunity to give them a suitable message. On this particular *shabbes*, he decides to use squirrels for an object lesson on teaching them the need for industry and preparation. So he starts out by saying to the children, 'I'm now going to describe something to you and I want you to raise your hand when you know what it is.'

The children nod eagerly.

'This thing runs around in trees (pause)…and eats nuts (pause)…'

No hands go up.

'And it's grey or brown (pause)…and it has a bushy tail (pause)…'

The children look at each other, but still no hands are raised.

'And it takes big jumps from one branch to another

(pause)…and it chatters and flips its tail when it's excited (pause)…'

Finally, little Sam tentatively raises his hand. Rabbi Levy breathes a sigh of relief and says, 'Good, Sam, so what do you think it is?'

'Well, rabbi,' says little Sam, 'I know the answer must be Moses…but it sounds just like a squirrel to me!'

* * *

Brotherly love

Miriam, a Hebrew class teacher, has just finished having a discussion with her class about the commandment to honour one's mother and father. She then turns to the class and asks, 'Can anyone here tell me what commandment tells us how to deal with our brothers and sisters?'

Sam immediately stands up and proudly replies, 'Thou shalt not kill.'

* * *

What *saychel*! And in someone so young!

Young Benjy goes to school. Today, there's a new teacher arriving. When class begins, the new teacher decides to make use of her degree in psychology. So she starts her class by saying, 'Will everyone who thinks they're stupid, please stand up!'

After 30 seconds, Benjy gets to his feet. The teacher looks at him and says, 'So you think you're stupid, do you?'

'No teacher,' replies Benjy, 'I didn't want to see you standing there all by yourself!'

* * *

What *saychel!* And in someone so young!

One afternoon, young Benjy's class is taken on a school trip to visit their local police station. When they arrive, Benjy sees a photo of a man pinned on a notice board. 'Why have you put this man's photo on the board?' Benjy asks one of the policemen.

'Because he's a criminal and we're trying to find him,' replies the policeman.

'So why didn't you grab hold of him when you took his picture?' asks Benjy.

* * *

Miriam's shoes

It's late December and little Miriam is getting ready to leave school. But she needs help in putting on her winter boots. So Sharon, her teacher, comes over to help. The boots prove to be quite a challenge and even with Miriam pulling and Sharon pushing, the little boots didn't want to go on easily. It takes Sharon some time to get both the boots on Miriam's feet.

But then Miriam shouts out, 'Teacher, they're on the wrong feet.'

Sharon looks down and sure enough, they are. It isn't any easier pulling the boots off than it was putting them on, but Sharon manages to keep her cool as, together, they work to get the boots back on, this time on the right feet.

But then Miriam shouts out, 'These aren't my boots, teacher.'

Sharon bites her tongue rather than shout at Miriam. 'Why didn't you say so?' Once again Sharon struggles to help Miriam pull the ill-fitting boots off her little feet. No sooner have they got the boots off than Miriam says, 'They're my brother's boots, teacher. My mum made me wear them.'

Now Sharon doesn't know if she should laugh or cry. But she musters up what patience she has left to wrestle the boots on Miriam's feet again. Then, helping Miriam into her coat, Sharon asks, 'Now Miriam, where are your gloves?'

Miriam replies, 'I stuffed them in the toes of my boots, teacher.'

PS: Sharon will soon be coming out of psychiatric care.

* * *

First day of school

A new year is starting at the Jewish Grammar School and on the first day of the new term, many of the children bring presents for their teachers.

Morris, whose mother owns the local florist, brings in a lovely bouquet of flowers for Miss Shapiro, his teacher. When Miss Shapiro receives them, she says to Morris, 'Oh these flowers are lovely, Morris. I'm going to put them in my lounge as soon as I get home and I'm going to look at them and smell them all night.'

Emma, whose father owns the local newsagent, brings in a giant box of Belgian chocolates for Miss Gold, her teacher. When Miss Gold receives it, she says to Emma, 'Oh Emma, that's so nice of you. I'm going to open the box as soon as I get home and make a pig of myself – I just love chocolates.'

Bernie, whose father owns the local kosher wine shop, brings in a big, heavy box for Mr Levy, his teacher. When Mr Levy receives it, he says to Bernie, 'Thank you, Bernie, for my present. I've no idea what's inside it and I can't wait to get home to find out.'

But then Mr Levy notices that the box is leaking a bit. So he touches a drop of the leaking liquid with his index finger, tastes it, then says, 'I bet you've brought me some bottles of wine, Bernie?'

'No, it's not wine,' says Bernie.

So Mr Levy tastes another drop and says, 'Is it champagne then, Bernie?'

'No, it's not champagne either,' says Bernie. 'It's a puppy.'

* * *

Early desires
One day, Rebecca asks her class, 'Children, can anyone tell me what they would like to have when they grow up?

Little Leah puts up her hand and replies, 'Teacher, when I grow older all I want is four animals.'

Rebecca asks, 'Is that so, Leah, and what four animals would they be?'

Leah replies, 'A mink on my back, a jaguar in the garage, a tiger in my bed and an ass to pay for it all.'

Gossips (*Yentas*)

A yenta riddle
Q. What's the plural of *yenta*?
A. *Hadassah*.

* * *

There's no need to worry
As Freda, Hannah, Kitty and Naomi are playing bridge one evening, Freda suddenly says, 'I have a confession to make. We've known each other now for many years so I feel I can now tell you my secret. I'm a kleptomaniac.'

'*Oy*!' moan the other three.

'But there's no need to worry – I've never stolen from any of you and I never will. You're my friends.'

At that, Hannah says, 'OK, since we're having a confession session, I'd like to admit that I'm a nymphomaniac.'

'*Oy oy*!' moan the other three.

'But there's no need to worry – I've never tried to ensnare any of your husbands and I never will. You're my friends.'

'Well then,' says Kitty, 'I'd like to admit that the reason I never married is that I'm a lesbian.'

'*Oy veh*!' moan the other three.

'But there's no need to worry – I will never make any overtures to any of you. You're my friends.'

Naomi then stands up and says, 'I too have a confession to make. I'm a *yenta*. And now could you please excuse me – I have a lot of calls to make.'

'*Gevalt*!' moan the other three.

* * *

Too clever by half

Isaac arrives in London from Canada and takes a job working on the shop floor of Hymie's Supermarket. One day, a customer asks him where he can find half a head of lettuce and Isaac tells him that they only sell whole heads of lettuce. But the customer is insistent and gets Isaac to consult with Hymie. So Isaac goes into the back room and says to Hymie, 'Some idiot wants to buy a half a head of lettuce.'

As he finishes his sentence, Isaac turns to find the customer standing right behind him, so he quickly adds, 'And this gentleman offered to buy the other half.'

Hymie approves the deal and the customer leaves satisfied. Later that day, Hymie says to Isaac, 'I was very impressed with the way you got yourself out of that tricky situation earlier. We like people who can think on their feet here. Where are you from?'

'I'm from Canada, sir,' Isaac replies.

'So why did you leave Canada?' Hymie asks.

'Because too many *yentas* and hockey players live there,' replies Isaac, smiling.

'That's quite surprising,' says Hymie, looking angry. 'My wife is from Canada.'

Isaac replies, 'You don't say? Who did she play for?'

* * *

The great listener

Hannah is talking to her husband Howard. As usual, she's telling him all the latest gossip she's heard about their family and about their friends and about their neighbours. And as usual, she goes on and on and on, non-stop.

Suddenly, Howard can't take any more of this and shouts out, 'Enough, already, Hannah. You're killing me with all this gossip. I can clearly see what will be on my headstone when I'm buried.'

'So what do you see?' asks Hannah.

'Howard replies, 'HERE LIES HOWARD LEVY, A GREAT LISTENER WHO WAS *YENTA'D* TO DEATH.'

Matters of Faith

From the Bible

A Boaz riddle

Q: What kind of man was Boaz before he got married?

A: Ruth-less.

* * *

The soldiers

Privates Benny and Harry are leading a donkey down a muddy road near their barracks when the animal suddenly just drops dead. An officer sees this happen and while Benny and Harry are standing there wondering what they should do, the officer goes up to them. He quickly sizes up the situation and instructs them to get some shovels from the camp and bury the poor animal.

Later, while they are digging the hole, Benny says, 'Wow, is this one big mule.'

Harry says, 'It's not a mule, Benny, it's a donkey.'

As they continue to argue, another officer, this time a rabbi, stops to ask them what they are arguing about. They tell him of their disagreement.

The rabbi looks at the animal and says, 'It's neither a donkey nor a mule. According to the Bible, it is obviously an ass. Now get back to work.' As they continue to dig, another officer arrives on the scene and asks them, 'What are you men digging, a fox hole?'

'No sir,' replies Benny, 'not according to the Bible.'

* * *

Coffee maker

Maurice and Becky are arguing over who should brew the coffee each morning.

Becky says, 'As you get up first in the morning, Maurice, you should make it. Then we won't have to wait too long for our coffee.'

'But you're in charge of all the cooking,' replies Maurice, 'that's your job, so you should make it. And if I have to wait for my coffee in the morning, well, I don't mind.'

'But it says in the Bible that the man should make the coffee,' says Becky.

'OK, responds Maurice, 'if you can show me where it says that, I'll never question you again.'

Next day, Becky borrows a Bible from her neighbour and shows Maurice that on the top of several pages it indeed says: 'Hebrews'.

* * *

A fishy story

As Moses and the children of Israel are crossing the Red Sea, the children of Israel begin to complain that they are very thirsty after walking so far. They can't even drink from the walls of water on either side of them because they're made up of salt water.

While Moses is looking around for some fresh water, a fish from the wall of water tells him that he and his friends are willing to help. They will use their gills to remove the salt from the water and force it out of their mouths like a freshwater fountain for the Israelites to drink from as they walk by.

Moses accepts this kindly fish's offer with gratitude, but the fish says there's a condition. The children of Israel and their descendants always have to be present at the Seder meal that will be established to commemorate the Exodus, since they have a part in the story.

When Moses agrees to this, he gives the fish their name, which remains how they are known to this very day, for he says to them, 'Go Filter Fish!'

* * *

A funny riddle
Q: Who was the greatest comedian in the Bible?
A: Samson – he brought the house down.

* * *

A garden riddle
Q: What did Adam say to explain to his kids why he no longer lived in Eden?
A: Your mother ate us out of house and home.

* * *

Early suspicion
Adam stays out very late for a few nights and Eve becomes upset. 'You're running around with other women,' she tells her mate.

'Eve, darling, you're being unreasonable,' says Adam. 'You know you're the only woman on earth for me.'

The quarrel continues until Adam falls asleep, only to be woken up by a strange pain in his chest. It's Eve poking him rather vigorously about the torso.

'What do you think you're doing?' asks Adam.

'I'm counting your ribs,' replies Eve.

* * *

The kisser

Eve walks over to Adam in the Garden of Eden and kisses him passionately. 'Wow,' says Adam, 'how did you learn to kiss like that?'

* * *

An ark riddle

Q: The ark was built in three stories and the top story had a window to let light in, but how did they get light to the bottom two stories?

A: They used flood lights.

* * *

Marketing message

As Moses is leading the tribes out of Egypt, they come to the Red Sea and they need to be able to cross it to get to the Promised Land on the other side. Moses lifts up his staff and prays to God. The Red Sea immediately parts, leaving enough space for all of them to cross.

Moses goes over to the first tribe and says, 'Please cross now.'

But their leader replies, 'No, we don't want to cross.'

'Be reasonable,' says Moses, 'I've just performed the miracle of the parting of the Red Sea. You must cross.'

'Why must we cross?' asks the leader.

'Because over there, on the other side,' replies Moses, 'we'll find a land overflowing with milk and honey. In any case, you must cross because I've just paid for a full page in the Bible.'

* * *

A babysitter riddle

Q: Who was the greatest babysitter mentioned in the Bible?

A: David – he rocked Goliath to sleep.

* * *

A criminal riddle

Q: Who was the most flagrant lawbreaker in the Bible?

A: Moses, because he broke all Ten Commandments at once.

* * *

Seven reasons why God created Eve

1. God was worried that Adam, being alone, would regularly get lost in the Garden of Eden because he refused to ask for directions.

2. God knew right from the start that Adam would eventually need someone to find the remote and then hand it to him.

3. God knew that Adam didn't have any idea how to choose the latest style of fig leaf when his old one wore out. He would therefore need someone to choose one for him.

4. God knew that Adam would never be able to make an appointment with a doctor, dentist or hairdresser all by himself.

5. God knew that Adam was having difficulty in remembering which days he needed to put the recyclable rubbish in the 'green' bin.

6. God knew that if the world was to be populated, Adam would never be able to handle the pain and discomfort of childbearing.

7. When God finished creating Adam, he stepped back, scratched his head, and said, 'I can do better than that.'

* * *

A giant riddle – 1
Q: Why was Goliath so surprised when David hit him with a slingshot?
A: The thought had never entered his head before.

* * *

A giant riddle – 2
Q: If Goliath is resurrected, would you tell him the joke about David and Goliath?
A: No, he already fell for it once.

* * *

Planting for history
Adam said to Eve, 'I'll wear the plants in this family.'

Cantors (*Chazans*)

How to get ahead
Isaac dies and his three brothers attend his funeral, along with his many friends and family. Just before the service commences, the *chazan* quietly asks each of the brothers what they do for a living. Victor says he's a doctor, Benny says he's a lawyer, but when Cyril says he's a theatrical agent, the *chazan* suddenly bursts into voice and starts to sing music from *Cats*.

* * *

The method
Did you know that whenever a *chazan* hears some really bad news, he always takes his tuning fork from his pocket, taps it on a nearby hard surface to get the right key, then shouts out loud and clear, '*Oy gevalt*!'

Conversing with God

The life of man

One day, God created the cow. God said to the cow, 'You must go to the field with the farmer, suffer under the sun all day, have calves and give milk to support the farmer. For that, I will give you a lifespan of 60 years.'

The cow replied, 'That's a tough life and you want me to endure it for 60 years. Just give me 20 years and I'll give you back the other 40.'

And God agreed.

Then God created the dog. God said to the dog, 'You must sit all day by the door of your house and bark at anyone who comes in or walks past. For that, I will give you a lifespan of 20 years.'

The dog replied, 'That's too long to be barking. Just give me 10 years and I'll give back the other 10.'

So God agreed (sigh).

Then God created the monkey. God said to the monkey, 'You must entertain people, do monkey tricks and make them laugh. For that, I'll give you a 20-year-lifespan.'

The monkey replied, 'How boring having to do monkey tricks for 20 years. Dog gave you back 10 years and I would like to do the same, if that's OK with you?'

And once again God agreed.

Then God created man. God said to man, 'I want you to eat, sleep, play, have sex and enjoy. I want you to do nothing, just enjoy, enjoy. For that, I'll give you 20 years.'

Man replied, 'What? Only 20 years? It's not enough. Why don't I take my 20 years and the 40 cow gave back and the 10 dog gave back and the 10 monkey gave back. That makes 80. Is that OK?'

'OK,' said God, 'you've got a deal.'

Moral: that's why for the first 20 years, man eats, sleeps, plays, has sex, enjoys and does nothing; for the next 40 years, man slaves in the sun to support his family; for the next 10 years, man does monkey tricks to entertain his grandchildren; and for the last 10 years, man sits in front of the house and barks at everybody.

* * *

The magnificent symphony

God is so disenchanted with all the noisy music he keeps on hearing on earth that he decides to do something about it. So he sits down to write a *Rosh Hashanah* symphony. When he finishes, God is very pleased with his effort. It is, he says to himself, 'a magnificent musical symphony, exactly how real music should sound'.

Now that his symphony is ready, God wants it performed as quickly as possible, so he assembles the greatest musicians of all time and invites everyone who ever lived to hear his masterpiece. No one could refuse.

The day of the unique concert arrives and God himself decides to conduct his own composition. He stands in front of a music stand made of solid gold, taps his diamond-encrusted baton for order and then the music begins.

The first movement lasts a whole year, but passes so quickly that no one notices. The second movement is even more beautiful than the first and even though this lasts over two years, no one seems to mind.

Now comes the third movement. This is the longest and loveliest of all and midway through is a special solo part – one note struck on a silver triangle. It is the highpoint of the symphony. And guess who has been personally selected by God to strike that note? It's none other than Moshe. Moshe's family are so proud – it is such an honour to be chosen.

Moshe stands patiently waiting his cue – he doesn't want to miss it. Then it comes. All the other instruments are hushed. Moshe swings and…*oy gevalt*, he misses. There is no sound at all. The orchestra goes deathly quiet and a groan goes up from the audience of billions.

God taps his baton on the gold music stand for order and says, 'OK everyone, let's start again from the top.'

* * *

Alternating light and darkness
God is talking to one of his angels. He says, 'Do you know what I have just done? I have just created a 24-hour period of alternating light and darkness on earth. Isn't that good?'

The angel says, 'Yes, but what will you do now?'

God says, 'I think I'll call it a day.'

* * *

God forbid
The habit of asking God to prevent calamities is a hard one to break. One Jewish businessman, driven to despair by his rival's devious actions, shouted at him, 'You should only drop dead – God forbid.'

* * *

The promise
Moshe is driving off to attend an important meeting. But when he gets there, he can't find a place to park. He drives around, he waits, he even tries a bit farther away, but all in vain. So in desperation he looks up at the sky and says, 'Oh Lord, if you will find me a parking place in the next five minutes, I promise you I will stop gambling, I'll eat only kosher food, I'll stop going with *shiksas* and I'll observe *shabbes* properly.'

Almost immediately, he sees a car pulling out of its parking place and quickly takes its place. Again Moshe looks up at heaven and says, 'Oh Lord, there's no need for you to find me a parking place – I've already found one.'

* * *

How man was created – alternative version

After four weeks in the Garden of Eden, Eve receives a visit from God. 'So Eve, how's everything going?' inquires God.

'It's all so beautiful,' she replies, 'the sunrises and sunsets are breathtaking, the smells, the sights, everything is wonderful. But I have one problem. It's these breasts you've given me, the middle one pushes the other two out and I'm constantly knocking them with my arms, catching them on branches and snagging them on bushes. They're a real pain. Surely God, since many other parts of my body come in pairs, such as my arms and legs, my ears and my eyes, I feel that having only two breasts will make me more symmetrically balanced.'

'That's a fair point,' replies God, 'but it was my first shot at this, don't forget. I gave the animals six breasts so I figured that you needed only half of those. But I can see that you're right so I'll fix it up right away.' And God reaches down, removes Eve's middle breast and tosses it into the bushes.

Three weeks pass and God once again visits Eve in the Garden of Eden. 'Well, Eve, how is my favourite creation?'

'Just fantastic,' she replies, 'but for one oversight on your part. You see, all the animals are paired off. The ewe has a ram and the cow has her bull. All the animals have a mate except me. I feel so alone.'

God thinks for a moment and says, 'You know, Eve, you're right once again. How could I have overlooked this? You do need a mate and I will immediately create MAN from a part of you. Now let's see, where did I put that useless boob?'

* * *

Adam and Eve's choice

After God completed the world, he found he still had two things remaining to give out. He quickly decided to give one to Adam and one to Eve and he'd let each choose which one they wanted. When he told them what he aimed to do, they asked what his give-aways were.

So God explained, 'One of the items is a thingy that allows its owner to pee while standing up. It's very useful. The other thing I have is…'

But Adam was no longer listening. As soon as he heard about the 'stand-up-peeing' device, he started jumping up and down like an excited little boy. 'I'd love one of those,' he said. 'To be able to do that would be just brilliant. Please God, let me have it.'

God turned to Eve and said, '*Nu*? So what do you think?'

Eve just smiled and replied, 'As Adam desperately wants it, let him have it.'

Adam was thrilled to receive it and immediately used it on the flowers. He then ran off to write his name in the sand.

God watched Adam for a few minutes, then turned to Eve and said, 'Well, here's the other thing, it's all yours.'

'What's it called?' said Eve.

'A brain,' replied God.

Heaven

Heavenly home

Yitzhak and Sharon have been eating the healthiest and most organic of foods for over 10 years – mainly at the insistence of Sharon. She also ensures that they regularly attend keep-fit classes, so although they are in their eighties, they are both in excellent health. But their good health doesn't help them when their car collides with a lorry on the M25 motorway and they're both killed.

When they reach heaven, a guide takes them to a beautiful house, furnished in gold and fine silks. All their favourite clothes are hanging in the bedroom's wardrobes and the kitchen is fully stocked. There is even a waterfall in the house's extensive grounds. Yitzhak and Sharon are thrilled when the guide says, 'Welcome to your new home.'

In their previous life, they were not very well off and survived by watching their pennies, so Yitzhak asks, 'How much is this going to cost?'

'Nothing,' replies the guide, 'this is your reward in heaven.'

Yitzhak looks out the window. To the left of the waterfall is a golf course, more beautiful than any he's seen on earth. 'What are the green fees?' he asks.

'This is heaven,' replies the guide, 'you can play for free, every day.'

The guide then takes them into to the clubhouse. 'Wow!' says Yitzhak, when he sees the lavish buffet lunch laid out before them. There is every kind of food, from seafood to steaks to exotic desserts, and plenty of alcohol.

'Don't even ask,' says the guide. 'This is heaven, it's all free for you to enjoy.'

Yitzhak looks around, glances nervously at Sharon and asks, 'Where are the low-fat and low-cholesterol foods, and the decaffeinated coffee?'

'That's the best part,' replies the guide, 'you can eat and drink as much as you like of whatever you like, and you'll never get fat or sick. This is heaven!'

Yitzhak says, 'No gym to work out at?'

'Not unless you want to,' replies the guide.

'No testing of my sugar, cholesterol or blood pressure?'

'Never again. All you do here is enjoy yourself,' replies the guide.

On hearing all this, Yitzhak glares at Sharon and says, 'If it wasn't for your stupid bran cereals, your yucky unsweetened green teas, your tasteless unsalted crisps, your silly small portions, your watery alcohol-free *Kiddush* wine and your mind-numbingly low-fat everything, we could have been here 10 years ago!'

* * *

Adult hide and seek

Mary and Naomi arrive at the Pearly Gates at the same time and soon start to discuss how they died. Mary says, 'I froze to death.'

'*Oy veh*! What a horrible way to die,' remarks Naomi.

'It wasn't so bad, really,' says Mary. 'After I stopped shaking from the cold, I began to feel warm and sleepy and not long after, I died quite peacefully. What about you? How did you die?'

Naomi replies, 'I died of a massive heart attack.'

'So how did it happen?' asks Mary.

'I felt sure that mine Bernie was cheating on me with a *shiksa*, so I came home early to try to catch them in the act. But when I crept into the house, I found Bernie alone watching TV.'

'So then what happened?' asks Mary.

Naomi replies, 'Well, I was sure there was another woman somewhere in the house so I started running all over the place looking for her. I ran upstairs and searched every one of my eight bedrooms and their en-suite bathrooms, checking under every king-sized bed. I searched the games room and then ran downstairs into the garage and looked inside our Bentley convertible. I went through every room in the house, checking every cupboard and looking behind every designer curtain. I even went into our loft. I was running around like a *meshugganah*. Finally, exhausted and stressed, I just keeled over with a heart attack and died.'

'Too bad you didn't look in the freezer,' says Mary. 'If you had, we'd both still be alive.'

* * *

The error in the paper

Hymie and Bernie, both in their nineties, live in a retirement home. One Friday, Hymie gets up very early, extracts the *Jewish Chronicle* newspaper from under his door, and goes down to the lounge to read it. He opens the paper, turns to the obituaries page and gets the shock of his life. There, on page 43, is his own obituary! Even though he quickly realises that it's an error, it both excites him and upsets him. He has to tell someone, so he goes to reception and uses the internal phone to call Bernie's room.

After the phone has been ringing for nearly a minute, Bernie finally picks it up and says, sleepily, 'Which *meshugganah* is ringing me so early, already?'

'Bernie, are you up yet?' shouts Hymie, excitedly.

'Well I am now, aren't I?' replies Bernie.

'Bernie,' shouts Hymie, 'go pick up your *Jewish Chronicle* and turn to page 43.'

'Why, what's so important in the paper that I should do this?' asks Bernie.

'Bernie, don't argue with me. Go get the paper and turn to page 43 and do it now,' shouts Hymie.

'OK, I've got the paper already,' says Bernie, 'so what am I looking for?'

'Bernie, turn to page 43 and look at the bottom of column four!' shouts Hymie.

'All right, already,' says Bernie, 'I'll start reading the column if you stop yelling at me.'

'OK,' says Hymie, 'but read it now.'

The paper rustles for a few seconds, then, following a long silence, Bernie gets back on the phone and quietly asks, 'Hymie, so where are you calling me from right now?'

* * *

The mother of God

Sister Maria, a very devout nun, dies and goes to heaven. She's greeted at the gates by St Peter with a fanfare of trumpets. St Peter then says to her, 'While we're getting your place ready, are there any questions you want to ask me, or is there anything I can do for you?'

'If it's possible,' replies Sister Maria, 'I would love to meet the Holy Mother Mary.'

St Peter immediately takes her to a little building nearby and knocks on the door. 'Come in,' says a gentle voice from inside. Sister Maria enters and sees a middle-aged woman dressed in the clothes of biblical times sitting on a wooden chair, knitting. So Sister Maria sits down at Mary's feet and waits to be addressed.

Mary looks up from her knitting and says, 'Yes, my child, you have a question for me?'

'Reverend Mother,' says Sister Maria, 'you were a simple woman, yet you were chosen from all the women on earth to be the Mother of God. Could you give me just a brief idea of what you were thinking of when Jesus was born?'

With a glazed look in her eyes, Mary replies with a sigh, '*Oy veh. Ich hob dafke gevolt a maydel*' (Well, I was really hoping for a girl).

Eretz Yisrael (Land of Israel)

Bragging

New Zealand's Prime Minister is rudely awoken at 4am by the telephone. 'PM, it's the Health Minister here. Sorry to bother you at this hour, but we have an emergency. I've just been told that the Durex factory in Auckland has burned to the ground and it's estimated that the entire New Zealand supply of condoms will be gone by the end of the week.'

'Oh dear,' says the Prime Minister, 'the economy will never be able to cope with all those unwanted babies – we'll be ruined! We're going to have to ship some in from abroad...how about the UK?'

'No chance,' replies the Health Minister, 'the Poms would have a field day on this one.'

'What about Australia?' asks the Prime Minister.

'Maybe – but we don't want them to know that we're in a mess. Why don't you call Ariel Sharon of Israel and tell him we need one million condoms? Tell him they should be 10 inches long and 8 inches thick. That way he'll know how big we Kiwis really are.'

So the Prime Minister calls Sharon, who agrees to help the Kiwis out in their hour of need, in return for improved diplomatic relations. Three days later, an air express van arrives in Auckland – full of boxes. A delighted Prime Minister rushes out, opens one of the boxes and finds what was ordered – condoms 10 inches long and 8 inches thick. But they are all coloured blue and white and then the Prime Minister notices, in small writing on each and every one, 'MADE IN ISRAEL: SIZE = MEDIUM.'

* * *

A history lesson

An American, an Englishman and an Israeli are indulging in a bit of boasting.

The American says, 'One of my ancestors signed the Declaration of Independence.'

The Englishman says, 'That's nothing. One of my ancestors was present at the signing of the Magna Carta.'

The Israeli quietly says, 'You think that's something? One of my ancestors drew up the Ten Commandments.'

* * *

The trip to Israel – 2
A voice was heard on Israeli Radio: 'This is Station OYVEH Tel Aviv, 1830 on your dial, but to you, 1825.'

* * *

Find this man
The Israeli police are looking for a man who calls himself Joseph. He's wanted for looting offences in Haifa. The suspect is described as the son of a Barcelona ex-nun and a German father. He's a former flautist and works occasionally on a farm.

In short, he's 'A Haifa-lootin', flutin' Teuton, son-of-a-nun from Barcelona, part-time ploughboy Joe.'

* * *

A fast riddle
Q: In what country is the speed of sound faster than the speed of light?
A: Israel, because there can you hear cars hooting half a second before the light changes.

* * *

You know you're an Israeli because
- You dial Directory Enquiries and ask, 'Can I have the phone number of Moshe Levy in Tel Aviv, please?' And when the operator replies, 'Which Moshe Levy do you want?' you say, 'You know, Moshe, the one with the bad limp.'
- You always speak half in Hebrew and half in English.
- You book a room in a nice London hotel and then complain to reception, 'I can't see the ocean from my window!'
- You put on a tight T-shirt with the word SEX written across the front of it in big red letters. Then you smear your lips with thick crimson lipstick and put on five-inch-high,

bright-red platform shoes. Then, when you meet your best friend, you say to her, '*Oy*, did I see such a tart yesterday!'

- As you walk down a main road, you recognise everyone you pass from the days you spent in the Army.
- Before you buy any brand-new car, you check it out by kicking its front tyres.
- When you meet someone who tells you they live in New York, you say, 'Wonderful! So, do you know Shlomo who lives there for three years already?'

Jewish Culture

Identification

Rivkah, an elderly lady travelling to London by train, is sitting next to a very distinguished young man reading the *Financial Times*.

'Excuse me,' she says, 'can I ask you something personal? Are you Jewish?'

'No, I'm not,' replies the man.

A few minutes later, Rivkah asks him, 'Please, are you sure you're not Jewish?'

The man replies, 'No, I've told you I'm not,' and continues to read his paper.

A few minutes later, 'Excuse me, are you absolutely sure you're not Jewish?'

At that, the man gets quite frustrated and replies, 'All right, yes, if you must know. I am Jewish. Now will you leave me alone?'

Rivkah looks at him and says, 'Funny, you don't look Jewish.'

* * *

The new member

Rivkah had been trying for some time to become a member of a very up-market 'English' golf club. Then her husband dies. So Rivah takes elocution lessons, goes to an etiquette class, has her nose altered and changes her surname to Fythe-Smith. It works – she becomes a member.

Unfortunately, at her first golf club dinner, a waiter passing by her table spills a plate of soup over her. Shocked, and especially because she is wearing a rather splendid new evening dress, Rifka jumps up and shouts, '*Oy veh.*'

Then, looking around her, she adds, '…whatever that means.'

* * *

Moshe in conversation

- 'What time is it?' Standard response: 'Sorry, I don't know.' Moshe's response: 'What am I, a clock?'
- 'I hope things turn out OK.' Standard response: 'Thank you.' Moshe's response: 'I should be so lucky!'
- 'Hurry up, dinner is ready.' Standard response: 'OK. Be right there.' Moshe's response: 'All right already, I'm coming. What's with the "hurry" business? Is there a fire?'
- 'Rifka and I just got engaged.' Standard response: 'Congratulations!' Moshe's response: 'She could do with putting on a few pounds.'
- 'Would you like to go riding with us?' Standard response: 'Just say when.' Moshe's response: 'Riding, shmiding! Do I look like a cowboy?'
- 'Isn't it a beautiful day?' Standard response: 'It sure is.' Moshe's response: 'So the sun is out, what else is new?'

* * *

A sour riddle

Q: What's the difference between what you squeeze out of a lemon and members of a religious Jewish movement?
A: One is acidic juice and the other is *Chassidic* Jews.

* * *

Jewish sayings

- Before you read the menu, read the prices. If you have to ask the price, you can't afford it.
- But if you can afford it, make sure you tell everybody what you paid.
- Never leave a restaurant empty handed.
- Never take a front-row seat at a *Bris*.
- The High Holidays have absolutely nothing to do with marijuana.

* * *

Tradition

Rabbi Gold is conducting his very first service at one of London's oldest synagogues. All is going well until he gets to the *Shema* prayer – only half his congregation stand up. Those still seated start yelling, 'Sit down' to those standing and those standing start yelling, 'Stand up' to those sitting. Although Rabbi Bloom is knowledgeable about much of the law, he doesn't know what to do. He thinks it must be something to do with the synagogue's tradition.

After the service, Rabbi Bloom consults Abe, the synagogue's oldest member.

'I need to know, Abe, what the synagogue's tradition is with regard to the *Shema* prayer. Is the tradition to stand during this prayer?'

Abe replies, 'No, that is not the tradition.'

'So the tradition is to sit during *Shema*?' says Rabbi Bloom.

Abe replies, 'No, that is not the tradition.'

'But,' says Rabbi Bloom, 'my congregation argue all the time. They yell at each other about whether they should sit or stand and...'

Abe interrupts, exclaiming, 'Aha, THAT is the tradition!'

* * *

Some Jewish curses

- May all your teeth fall out but one – and may that one ache.
- May you win the lottery – and spend it all on hospital charges.
- May you live in a house with a hundred bedrooms – and may you wander every night from room to room and from bed to bed, unable to sleep.
- May you become very rich – and your widow's second husband never has to worry about making a living.
- May you sell candles for a living – and then may the sun never set.
- May you be like a chandelier – hang by day and burn by night.
- May you eat chopped egg with onion; *haimesher* cucumbers; pickled herring; *gefilte fish* (boiled fish cakes) with *chrayn* (horseradish); *lokshen* (noodle) soup with *knaydlach* (*matzo* balls); salt beef with *latkes*; boiled beef with *tsimmes* (carrots and fruit side dish); potato pancakes with apple sauce; and tea with lemon every day – and may you choke on every bite.
- May you become world famous – in medical records.
- May your mouth never close and your *toches* never open.
- May your wife eat pieces of *matzo* in bed – and may you lie in the crumbs.

* * *

Jewish truths
- Anything worth saying is worth repeating a thousand times.
- Where there's smoke, there may be smoked salmon (wild, of course).
- Next year in Jerusalem. The year after that, maybe a nice cruise.
- Twenty per cent off is a bargain but 50 per cent off is a *mitzvah.*
- Always whisper the names of diseases.
- If it tastes good, it's probably not kosher.
- Without Jewish mothers, who would need therapy?

* * *

Jewish definitions
- Leftovers: something no Jewish meal is complete without.
- *Tsuris:* your son is marrying someone who isn't Jewish.
- Unofficial Jewish dietary law number six: pork and shellfish may be eaten only in Chinese restaurants.
- *Shmata:* a dress that your husband's ex-wife is wearing.

* * *

Yiddish proverbs
- If they give you, take; if they take from you, yell.
- Charge nothing and you'll get a lot of customers.
- Cancer, shmancer – just as long as you're healthy.
- Don't worry about tomorrow, you don't even know what may happen to you today.
- You can't chew with somebody else's teeth.
- If you spit upwards, you're bound to get it back in the face.
- You can't dance at two weddings at the same time; nor can you sit on two horses with one behind.
- Had you gotten up early, you wouldn't have needed to stay up late.
- For dying, you always have time.

Jewish Festivals

The fast day

It's *Yom Kippur* and Aaron is in *shul*, but he's not feeling too good. So during a short break after the rabbi's sermon, he goes over to the rabbi.

'I really need your help, Rabbi Levy.'

'Yes, Aaron, how can I help?' says the rabbi.

'I obviously know that I'm meant to fast today, but I'm so, so thirsty. Please, Rabbi, can I have something to drink?'

Rabbi Levy replies in a firm voice, 'I'm sorry, Aaron, but you know the rules – it has to be a life-threatening situation before I can allow you to break the fast.'

'But Rabbi, it is serious,' says Aaron. 'If I don't get something to drink, I'll faint from thirst. Really I will.'

After much to-ing and fro-ing, Rabbi Levy relents and instructs the *gabbai* to give Aaron a small glass of water kept just for such emergencies. As soon as Aaron has drunk the water, he says, 'Thank you Rabbi, I promise you that it will be the last time I'll eat salt herring for breakfast on *Yom Kippur*.'

* * *

The text message

Avrahom's son Howard is at Cambridge University and Avrahom is worried that Howard might quickly forget that he's Jewish. As *Yom Kippur* is coming, Avrahom sends Howard the following text message: HI HOWARD. *YOM KIPPUR* STARTS ON TUESDAY.

Howard sends the following reply: THANKS FOR THE TIP. PUT ME DOWN FOR £70 ON IT TO WIN.

* * *

The converts

Benjamin is offered a high-powered job as Head of Finance at Utah Life Assurance Inc. He and his Sarah sell their house in New York and move to Utah. But Benjamin is unaware that it had been a difficult decision for the ULA President to offer him the job.

Even after Benjamin starts work, the ULA directors continue to put pressure on the president behind Benjamin's back. 'We're all Mormons on the board and we've never had someone Jewish on the board before. We find this very difficult to accept.' But they also know that Benjamin is proving to be the best. He's a financial genius, a financial guru.

After much careful thought, the president decides on a course of action and calls Benjamin to his office. 'I'm afraid I've run into some opposition to your appointment. If you want to keep your $400,000-a-year position, you'll have to convert. Please let me know by tomorrow what you decide.'

Benjamin has no choice. However difficult it might be to convert, it's easier than losing his great new job. So he goes home and tells Sarah, 'It's simple, from this Sunday we'll be going to church with our children.'

Over the months that follow, Sarah doesn't stop nagging. 'It's so difficult for me...I miss *shul*...*shabbes*....lighting the candles...*kiddush*...festivals etc. You know Benjamin, money isn't everything.'

The more she nags him, the worse Benjamin's conscience bothers him, until finally he's had enough. He goes back to the ULA president. 'I can't go on like this, sir, my troubles are eating me up inside. Money isn't everything to me. Neither I nor Sarah can sleep at night. It's too much for us. I made the wrong decision. We were born Jews and we want to die Jews. If you want me to quit, I'll go without making a fuss.'

The president looks at him in amazement and says, 'Listen

Benjamin, I had no idea it was so tough for you. I thought switching religions would be simple. But you are doing an excellent job here and I don't want to lose you. Stay here and you can be as Jewish as you want – I'll take care of the directors.'

Benjamin goes home to Sarah feeling absolutely great. 'Our troubles are over at last, darling,' he says to her. 'I've spoken to the president and he's letting me keep my job and he said we can go back to being Jewish immediately.'

Sarah looks at him with anger in her eyes. 'Tell me, are you stupid or what?'

Benjamin is shocked. 'But I thought that was what you wanted all along, to be Jewish once more. Don't you want to go back to being Jewish?'

Sarah looks very upset and replies, 'Of course I do, but now, just two weeks before *Pesach*?'

* * *

Yom Kippur service

The phone rings at a leading firm of solicitors. 'Levy, Minkoff and Rokenson,' says the receptionist, in a professional voice, 'can I help you?'

'Yes,' says the caller, 'can I speak to Mr Levy please?'

'Mr Levy is out of the office,' says the receptionist, 'this is *Yom Kippur*.'

'OK, Ms Kippur, please could you tell him his car is fixed and he can now pick it up.'

* * *

The Passover test

Sean is waiting for a bus when another man joins him at the bus stop. After 20 minutes of waiting, Sean is hungry so he takes a sandwich from his lunch box and starts to eat. But noticing the other man watching, Sean asks, 'Would you like one? My wife has made me plenty.'

'Thank you very much, but I must decline your kind offer,' says the other man, 'I'm Rabbi Levy.'

'Nice to meet you, Rabbi,' says Sean, 'but my sandwiches are all right for you to eat. They only contain cheese. There's no meat in them.'

'It's very kind of you,' says Rabbi Levy, 'but today we Jews are celebrating Passover. It would be a great sin to eat a sandwich because during the eight days of Passover, we cannot eat bread. In fact it would be a great sin – comparable to the sin of adultery.'

'OK,' says Sean, 'but it's difficult for me to understand the significance of what you've just said.'

Many weeks later, Sean and Rabbi Levy meet again. Sean says, 'Do you remember, Rabbi, that we met recently and that I'd offered you a sandwich which you refused because you said eating bread on *Passover* would be as great a sin as that of adultery?'

Rabbi Levy replies, 'Yes, I remember saying that.'

'Well, Rabbi,' says Sean, 'that day, I went over to my mistress's apartment and told her what you said. We then tried out both the sins, but I must admit, we just couldn't see the comparison.'

* * *

Eating or fasting – which is it to be?

I'm sure most of you realise that many of our Jewish holidays fall into two categories. Category 1 holidays comprise those on which we must starve ourselves and category 2 holidays comprise those on which we must *fress* and even become *khozzers*. Here are 17 of our Jewish holidays:

- *Rosh Hashanah:* Feast
- *Tzom Gedalia:* Fast
- *Yom Kippur:* More fasting
- *Sukkot:* Feast
- *Hashanah Rabbah:* More feasting
- *Simchat Torah:* Keep feasting
- Month of *Heshvan:* No feasts/fasts for one month. Get a grip on yourself
- *Hanukkah:* Eat potato pancakes
- Tenth of *Tevet:* Do not eat potato pancakes
- *Tu B'Shevat:* Feast
- Fast of Esther: Fast
- *Purim:* Eat pastry
- Passover: Do not eat pastry
- *Shavuot:* Dairy feast (cheesecake, *blintzes*, etc)
- 17th of *Tammuz:* Fast (definitely no cheesecake or *blintzes*)
- *Tish B'Av:* Strict fast, don't even think of cheesecake or *blintzes*
- Month of *Elul:* End of cycle. Enrol in Centre for Eating Disorders before High Holidays arrive again.

* * *

Five positive reasons to celebrate Passover

- You will get to drink a lot of alcohol: you'll have everyone's total permission to drink four glasses of wine and there could even be fifth glass for you if Elijah doesn't turn up.
- You can save money: I'm almost certain that you haven't given thought to eating last year's unused *matzo*. But if you do, you can save money by using it. And it won't even taste any different!
- You can get to sing with a loud and clear voice: did you know that *marror* is a far better treatment for blocked sinuses than any medicine you can buy in the chemist? So enjoy the *marror* and later on you can sing *Chad Gadya* with a voice like an angel!
- You can earn extra money: the extra cash you can get from selling your *chometz* will comes in handy after the spring bank holiday.
- You will save on toilet paper: just think of all the toilet paper you will be able to save by eating *matzo* for a whole week!

* * *

Passover riddle

Q: Why do we read from a *haggadah*?
A: Because we want to be able to *Seder* right words.

* * *

Another Passover riddle

Q: What do we call a person who enjoys eating the bread of affliction?
A: A *matzo*chist.

* * *

Chanukah cards

Sadie is in Israel on holiday and goes to the post office to buy some stamps for her *Chanukah* cards. 'Can I have 50 *Chanukah* stamps please?'

'Of course,' says the clerk, 'what denomination?'

'*Oy veh*,' says Sadie, 'has it come to this already? OK, give me 14 Liberal, 28 Reform and eight Orthodox stamps please.'

Kosher

Sign in butcher's window

Strictly Kosher: the *shochet* kills himself every morning

* * *

A surprise restaurant visit

Rabbi Levy is walking home from *shul* one *shabbes* when he sees Issy in front of him. Issy is a learned and respected man who can hold his own with the rabbi on *Talmudic* discussions. As Rabbi Levy tries to catch up with Issy, he is shocked to see him go into the Chinese Crab restaurant. As he looks through the window, Rabbi Levy sees Issy giving his order to a waiter and a short time later sees the food arrive – a plate of shrimps, lobsters and crabs. As Issy picks up the chopsticks and starts to eat, Rabbi Levy bursts into the restaurant and confronts Issy.

'Issy, just what do you think you are doing coming into this restaurant and ordering this *treif*? You are not only violating everything we are taught about the dietary laws, but you also seem to be enjoying this food.'

'Rabbi,' says Issy, 'did you see me enter this establishment?'

'Yes.'

'And did you see me order this food?'

'Yes.'
'And did you see the waiter bring the food to me?'
'Yes.'
'And did you then see me eat the food?'
'Yes.'
'Then I don't see a problem, Rabbi. Everything was done under full rabbinical supervision.'

* * *

Wrong one
Monty is out on one of his favourite walks, when all of a sudden he gets a strong pain in his stomach and has a desperate need to go to the toilet. As he can't wait, he goes deep into some thick bushes so no one can see him, lowers his trousers and pants, and squats down. Naturally, Monty has not brought any toilet paper with him, so (you should excuse him) he wipes himself with some leaves from a nearby bush, gets dressed and continues on his walk.

But after five minutes, his *toches* starts to itch and after 10 minutes, the itch is almost unbearable. Monty cuts short his walk and goes straight to his doctor. After a brief examination, Dr Myers says, 'Monty, I believe you've wiped yourself with some poison ivy.'

'*Oy veh*,' cries Monty, 'what can I do? The itching is driving me crazy.'

'Don't worry,' replies Dr Myers, 'here's some powder developed just for this purpose. Go home right away, put one teaspoon of powder in a gallon of warm water and soak your *toches* in it for 20–30 minutes. If you repeat this every three hours, it will take away the itching.'

So Monty goes home, puts a teaspoon of the powder into a large pot he finds in the bottom kitchen cupboard, fills it with warm water, puts the pot down in the middle of the kitchen floor, takes off all his clothes and sits in the pot. What bliss!

But then his Sarah comes home. She enters the kitchen, sees him sitting naked in her new pot in the middle of her kitchen floor and shouts out, 'Monty, *bist meshugga*?'

Monty replies, '*Vos tist du*?' and tries to tell her about his walk in the woods, his need to go to the toilet, the poison ivy, the doctor and the powder.

But Sarah screams, '*Nem aroyse dien flayshedika toches fun der milchedika tepple.*'

* * *

The chicken inspector
Freda walks into Harry Minkoff the kosher butcher and asks Harry for the freshest chicken he has. So Harry pulls out a chicken for her to inspect. Freda immediately gets to work. She starts by looking it over inside and out. She then sniffs it at both ends and continues to sniff all around it. Finally, she puts her nose inside the body cavity. Then Freda hands the chicken back to Harry and says, 'You call this a fresh chicken?'

'Mrs Cohen,' replies Harry, 'you could pass such an inspection?'

* * *

The kosher hotel booking
One day, Cyril notices for the first time that his father Nathan is getting on in years and decides to treat him. When next he visits his father, Cyril says, 'Dad, I've done well in business and I'd like to treat you. You haven't been on holiday since Mum died and I think it's time you went again. So I'm going to purchase a return flight to Miami Beach and book you into a nice hotel. I'm sure you'll meet lots of new friends and the weather there will do you good. What do you say?'

'*Oy*, son, what a nice present,' replies Nathan. 'I'd love to go, but only on condition that you book me into a strictly kosher hotel.'

'It's a deal,' says Cyril.

Cyril quickly makes arrangements for his father to stay six weeks at the Kosher Minky Hotel. Two weeks later, he takes his father to the airport and sees him off.

Every Sunday for the next four weeks, Cyril phones his father to check all is well. And the reply is always, 'You didn't need to call me, son, I'm well and I'm thoroughly enjoying myself.'

But Cyril wants to see his father's happiness for himself and decides to visit the Kosher Minky without telling anyone. When he arrives, he looks for his father in the lounges, the dining room and the swimming pool, but there is no sign of him. So he goes to reception and asks where he might find his father. The receptionist tells him that he should try the Goodservice Hotel, room 13.

Cyril immediately takes a taxi to the Goodservice, walks up to room 13 and knocks on the door. The door is opened by a tarty-looking girl in her underwear, and there behind her is his father, in a bathrobe.

'Father,' shouts Cyril, 'how could you? You're a religious man and you made me book you into a kosher hotel. I'm totally shocked by what I see.'

Nathan looks at his son and says, 'I don't know what you're getting so worked up for, son. I don't eat here.'

It's a Miracle

Miracle petrol

Renee is a very caring lady who spends a lot of her spare time visiting and helping sick members of her *shul*. Her car is also well known in the community because it's decorated all over with lots of Hebrew decals and bumper stickers showing the Jewish charities she helps.

One day, as she is driving to one of the care homes she regularly visits, her car runs out of petrol and splutters to a stop. 'Oy veh,' she says to herself, 'and just when I'm late.'

Fortunately, she notices a petrol station only a few hundred yards away, so she walks to the station to get help. 'Hi,' Renee says to the man behind the till, 'I've run out of petrol and I'm hoping you can lend me your petrol can. I'll pay you for the petrol I use and I'll return your can as quickly as possible.'

The attendant replies, 'I'm sorry, lady, but I've lent out my one and only can not more than five minutes ago. I'm expecting it back in about half an hour, so if you want, you can wait here for it.'

But as she's behind schedule, Renee goes back to her car to find something that she could use to fill with petrol. Then, what *mazel*, she notices the bedpan she always keeps handy in case of patient need. So she takes the bedpan to the petrol station, fills it and carries it back to her car.

Two men are passing by and watch her pour in the petrol. One turns to the other and says, 'If the car starts, I'm turning Jewish.'

* * *

A miracle?
Rabbi Levy, one of the wisest of rabbis, is dying. And because he is so loved by his colleagues, many rabbis have gathered around his hospital bedside, trying to make his last moments as rewarding as possible. While the visiting rabbis are praying, one of the nurses comes into the room and offers Rabbi Levy a glass of warm milk to drink. But with what little strength he has left, Rabbi Levy refuses it.

Seeing this, Rabbi Jacobs has an idea. He remembers that he has a bottle of whisky in his car, which he was planning to use for his next *kiddush*. So while his colleagues are watching

Rabbi Levy's laboured breaths, he quickly picks up the glass of milk and creeps out to his car. Rabbi Jacobs then opens the bottle of whisky and pours a generous portion of it into the warm milk. He then goes back to Rabbi Levy's bedside and holds the glass to Rabbi Levy's lips.

'Go on, Rabbi Levy,' says Rabbi Jacobs, 'please drink some of this milk. It will make you feel a bit better. Really it will.'

So Rabbi Levy takes a small sip, stares at the glass, drinks a bit more, then smiles and finishes every drop of the milk-and-whisky mixture.

The other rabbis are humbled when they see Rabbi Levy apparently making some kind of recovery. 'Rabbi Levy,' they say, 'please share some of your wisdom with us before you die!'

At this, Rabbi Levy raises himself up in his bed and with a pious look on his face points out the window and says, 'Don't sell that cow!'

* * *

What's with this?
Eighty-year-old Rebecca, who has never married, is much admired by her community for her kindness and her *tsodoka*. One spring afternoon, Rabbi Levy calls on her. She welcomes him into her house and invites him to sit down while she makes for him 'a nice glass of tea'.

As he is waiting, Rabbi Levy notices a Hammond organ against the wall. On the organ is a cut-glass vase filled with water and he's shocked to see a condom floating in the water. '*Oy veh*,' he says quietly, 'she's gone *meshugga*.'

Rebecca returns with tea and buttered *matzo* and they begin to chat. Although Rabbi Levy tries hard not to mention the vase and its content, he just can't avoid raising the subject. 'Rebecca,' he says, pointing to the vase, '*Vos is dos?*'

'That's my miracle,' she replies. 'I was walking down the street last November when I found a little packet on the ground. When I opened it, the instructions said it would prevent disease if put on the organ and kept wet. And guess what, Rabbi? I haven't had a cold all winter.'

Other Religions

Progress
Hetty is just about to make herself a cup of coffee when her front doorbell rings. She opens the door and there stands a smartly dressed man.

'Good morning, madam,' he says, 'I'm a Jehovah Witness and...' but before he can continue, Hetty says, 'I'm just about to make myself some coffee. Why don't you come in and join me?'

Very surprised, he agrees. After coffee, Hetty says, 'I'm now going to have to make some lunch for myself, so I don't really have much time at this moment to talk to you. But if you'd like to join me in a bite to eat, we can talk later.'

He is shocked at this kind offer. But again he agrees.

When they finish eating, Hetty says, 'OK, I'm all ears. Why don't you start at the beginning and tell me all about the Jehovah Witness movement?'

He's totally surprised by this and replies, 'I can't tell you anything – I've never got this far before.'

* * *

Change of address
It's Christmas 2006 and as Santa Claus is unloading a very heavy bag of gifts, he suddenly mutters, '*Oy Oy Oy!*' instead of his usual, 'Ho Ho Ho!' He's naturally shocked by this uncharacteristic uttering and takes it as divine inspiration.

Soon after Christmas is over, he does some serious thinking on the matter. 'Maybe Judaism is my new path? What would it actually mean if I converted to Judaism?'

'Well, firstly,' he says to himself, 'as there are only three million Jewish children to visit instead of 500 million Christian children, it would lessen my workload and decrease my stress. I was totally overworked and exhausted after last Christmas.'

'And that's not all,' Santa says to himself. 'I would have eight days of *Chanukah* to deliver my gifts, instead of completing the entire lot in one night. And most importantly, Jewish homes have delicious food to offer, such as *gefilte fish*, chicken soup, *blintzes, knishes* and the like. Gosh, my mouth is watering just thinking of them. I've been so bored with the traditional milk and cookies that always await me.'

In the end, it's an easy decision for Santa to make. Even circumcision isn't necessary, because that was taken care of in a freak accident involving frostbite after getting stuck in a tight chimney many years ago. So Santa shouts aloud, 'So let's convert, already!'

He leaves his North Pole home and opens up a new place of work in a Jewish district in north London. He fires all of those annoying elves and replaces them with nice Jewish retirees. Then, finally, he decides to legally change his name to something more in line with his new ethnic surroundings. So beginning *Chanukah* 2008, Santa Claus is to be known as The Clausenburger Rebbe.

Praying

At the races

Jacob goes to the races for the first time. As soon as he arrives at Ascot, not knowing anything about horse racing, he goes straight to the paddock to take a closer look. To his surprise,

Jacob sees a rabbi blessing one of the horses. Jacob thinks he must be on to a good thing so he writes down the number of the horse and places a £3 bet on it. The horse wins and Jacob wins £21.

Jacob immediately returns to the paddock and there, as before, he sees the rabbi blessing another horse. He writes down the number of this horse and bets his £21 winnings on it. It comes in first and Jacob now has over £100.

This process goes on race after race until Jacob has won £4,650.

It's now time for the last race of the day and Jacob watches the rabbi bless the final horse. So confident is Jacob that, although the horse is a 20-1 outsider, he bets his entire £4,650 on it. But, *oy veh*, this time the horse struggles in last, a good 20 lengths behind the field.

Jacob is so upset with this outcome that he runs over to the rabbi and says angrily, 'Why did every horse you bless win except the last one, Rabbi? He came in last.'

The rabbi replies, 'That's the problem with you Reform Jews. You don't know the difference between a *brocheh* and a *kaddish*.'

* * *

Women's prayer
Dear Lord, I pray for:
Wisdom – to understand a man
Love – to forgive him, and
Patience – for his moods
Because, Lord, if I pray for Strength, I'll just beat him to death.

* * *

Change over

Abe goes to see Dr Myers and says, 'I want to become a woman.'

'You must be joking,' says Dr Myers.

'No I'm not,' says Abe, 'I'm serious about it. Are you willing to perform the necessary operations on me?'

'No, definitely not,' replies Dr Myers.

'So who will do it?' asks Abe.

'Well I shouldn't tell you this,' replies Dr Myers, 'but I know the name of a doctor in France who can do it.'

Six months later, Abe returns to Dr Myers and says, 'I'm so glad you gave me the name of Doctor Jean-Pierre. I've had it done and I feel terrific. My new name is Sadie and I now function in every way like a woman, emotionally as well as physically.'

'But…Sadie,' asks Dr Myers, 'don't you have any emotions or desires left over from your previous life as a man?'

'Well now you ask,' replies Sadie, 'some mornings I do have this great urge to lay *tefillin*.'

* * *

Woman's night-time prayer

Now I lay me down to sleep
I pray to God my shape to keep.
Please no wrinkles, please no bags
And lift my *toches* before it sags.
Please no age spots, please no grey
And as for my belly, please take it away.
Please keep me healthy, please keep me young
And thank you Dear Lord for all that you've done.

* * *

The convert

Even though Mordechai has been a *frummer* for over 50 years, one morning, immediately he awakes, he realises he's fed up with all the strict observances to Jewish law. So he turns to his wife and says, 'Bracha, darling, I've had enough of getting up early every morning to put on my *tefillin* and say the same prayers. I've made a decision – I've decided to convert to Catholicism.'

'Don't be so stupid, Mordechai.' says Bracha.

But Mordechai won't be swayed by his wife's arguments. He gets dressed, leaves the house and asks a passer-by for directions to the nearest church. When he gets there, he discusses his intentions with the priest. The following day, he begins taking instruction and on the day after that he's baptised into the Catholic faith.

It's now Thursday morning. Mordechai awakes early as usual and without thinking, puts on his *tefillin* and starts reciting his morning prayers.

'What are you doing, Mordechai?' asks Esther. 'I thought you became a Catholic to avoid ever having to do this again.'

'*Oy veh*,' cries Mordechai, smacking himself on the middle of his forehead with the palm of his hand, '*goyisher kop!*'

* * *

News story: porn sites

Really, it's true. Shlomo Eliahu, chief rabbi in the Israeli town of Safed, composed this prayer to help devout Jews overcome guilt after visiting porn websites on the internet. Eliahu composed the prayer in response to numerous queries from Orthodox Jews worried that the lure of internet sex sites was putting family relationships at risk: 'Please God, help me cleanse my computer of viruses and evil photographs which disturb and ruin my work...so that I shall be able to cleanse myself of sin.'

The rabbi recommended that Jews recite the prayer when they log on to the internet (or programme the prayer to flash up on their computer screens) so that they are spiritually covered whether they enter a porn site, intentionally or by mistake.

* * *

Prayers for two

It's Monday morning and Nathan is in *shul* praying. 'Oh God, please help me. I'm in terrible trouble. My *shmatta* business is making heavy losses; I owe £100,000 to my main supplier; the Inland Revenue is demanding immediate payment of my last two years of tax; mine Sadie is about to leave me; my…'

Just then, Nathan hears the man next to him praying, 'Oh God, please help me. I'm really in trouble. My older son is about to marry a *shiksa*; my younger son is gay; my unmarried daughter is pregnant; my wife wants a sex change; my…'

Nathan takes out his wallet and removes £100. He then turns to the other congregant and says, 'Enough already of your *tsouris*. Here, take this money and go away. I need God to concentrate solely on me.'

Rabbis

The helpers

One *shabbes*, at the end of the service, Rabbi Cohen announces to his congregation that he will not be renewing his contract and that he will be moving on to a larger synagogue in a better part of town for more money. There is immediate silence. He is a popular rabbi and most of the congregation (but not all – after all, he's a rabbi) are unhappy to hear this news.

Suddenly Moshe, who owns several very successful kosher restaurants, gets up and shouts out, 'If Rabbi Cohen agrees to stay with us, I'll provide him and his family with a free three-course meal every day for the next two years.'

Then Abe, a successful property tycoon, stands up and shouts, 'If Rabbi Cohen stays, I'll not only increase his salary by 50 per cent but I'll also guarantee the education of his two children.'

Then Sadie, aged 75, stands up and shouts, 'And if Rabbi Cohen stays, I'll promise him sex.'

Rabbi Cohen, blushing, asks her, 'Sadie, why on earth did you say that?'

Sadie replies, 'Because I've just asked my husband how we could help and he said, "Screw him."'

* * *

The solution

Melvyn and Max were left quite a large plot of land by their rich father. However, this caused the two sons much grief. For months they argued long and hard over how the land should be divided between them. The solution just wasn't that simple, so they took their problem to Rabbi Landau.

'Rabbi,' said Melvyn, 'can you please help us solve our problem?'

As soon as he had heard their case, Rabbi Landau said, 'Come back tomorrow and we'll talk again.'

The next day, Melvyn and Max returned and the rabbi gave them his solution. He gave Max a 50p coin and said, 'You can toss the coin. And you,' said Rabbi Landau to Melvyn, 'can call it, heads or tails. Whoever wins the toss will divide the land.'

'But that won't work,' said Max, 'we'll be right back from where we started.'

'But not,' said Rabbi Landau, 'if the one who wins the toss divides the land and the other one gets first choice!'

* * *

Compared to what?

Issy has six daughters, all married but one – and she is not very beautiful. So one day Issy visits Rabbi Levine. 'Rabbi, I don't know what to do about Becky. She seems to be too ugly for the men around here to want to marry. What do you suggest I do?'

'First of all, can I ask you how ugly Becky is?' says Rabbi Levine.

'Well, Rabbi, if she was lying on a plate with some herrings, I don't think she would stand out from the herrings.'

'OK,' says Rabbi Levine, 'what kind of herrings are we talking about?'

Surprised by the question, Issy replies, 'Err…Bismarck herrings, Rabbi.'

'That's really bad luck, then,' says Rabbi Levine. 'If they were Maatjes herrings, she'd have a much better chance.'

* * *

Sign of the cross

Seventy-five-year-old Hymie is not looking as he's crossing the high street and is hit by a car. It looks quite a bad accident, but luckily for him, he receives only a glancing blow. As he's lying in the road, a priest who saw the accident runs over to help. Just in case it's serious, the priest begins to administer last rites.

'No thanks, Father,' Hymie says as he sits up, 'I'm not a Catholic.'

'What, you're not Catholic?' says the priest. 'So why did you make the sign of the cross immediately after the car hit you?'

Hymie replies, 'I was just checking.'

'Checking? Checking for what?' asks the priest.

'Everything important to me – spectacles, testicles, wallet and watch.'

* * *

What a mitzvah

It's Sunday evening and Rabbi Levy is in deep conversation with his friend. 'I must tell you something, Moshe,' he says, 'I made nine people very, very happy today.'

'A *mitzvah*, Rabbi, a true *mitzvah*,' says Moshe, 'but tell me – how did you manage to achieve this?'

'I performed four marriage ceremonies in my *shul* this afternoon,' replies Rabbi Levy.

Moshe is puzzled. 'I can see how you made eight people happy, Rabbi, but what about the ninth?'

'Do you really believe I did all this for free?' replies Rabbi Levy.

* * *

Plus ça change

Rabbi Morris has just resigned and Issy, the synagogue president, goes to visit him. 'Rabbi,' Issy says, 'I've just heard the news. I'm really sorry that you've decided to leave us.'

'Don't worry,' says Rabbi Morris, 'you'll have nothing to worry about. I'm going to recommend a successor whom I believe will be better than me.'

'But that's exactly what's worrying me,' says Issy. 'Your predecessor told me exactly the same thing.'

* * *

Career mapping

Abe and his young son Sam are in synagogue one *shabbes* morning when Sam says, 'When I grow up, Dad, I want to be a rabbi.'

'That's OK with me, Sam, but what made you decide that?'

'Well,' says Sam, 'as I have to go to *shul* on *shabbes* anyway, I figure it will be more fun to stand up and shout than to sit down and listen.'

* * *

A shaky start

Aaron is soon to be married and is feeling very rough. He's so worried about the commitment he will have to make that he goes to see his rabbi. As Aaron walks in, Rabbi Bloom can't help noticing that he's shaking like a leaf.

'So what's with the shaking, Aaron?' asks Rabbi Bloom.

'I can't go through with my marriage,' he answers. 'I feel so sick that my stomach is cramping up all the time. My legs are like rubber bands and I can hardly walk in a straight line. I don't know whether I'm coming or going, Rabbi.'

Rabbi Bloom smiles, 'Don't worry, Aaron, yours are common symptoms. I get to see them quite regularly. You've got PMS.'

'I've got PMS?' says Aaron, puzzled.

'Yes,' says Rabbi Bloom, 'You've got a dose of Pre-Marriage Syndrome.'

* * *

Meeting with the tax inspector

Abe is due a visit from the Inland Revenue inspector to go through some discrepancies in his accounts. Should he dress up or down for the meeting? He just doesn't know what is best, so he asks both his accountant and his lawyer for their views.

His accountant tells him, 'Wear your worst clothes, *shmattas* even, and an old pair of shoes. Make him believe you're very poor.'

But his lawyer tells him, 'Wear your smartest suit with a good shirt, expensive tie and nice cufflinks. That way you won't be intimidated.'

Abe is confused and goes to see his rabbi about the conflicting advice he has been given.

'Let me answer your dilemma with a story,' says the Rabbi. 'A woman, about to marry, asks her mother what she should wear on her wedding night. Her mother replies, 'Put on a long nightgown that goes right up to your neck and wear woollen socks.' But when the woman asks her best friend, she gets conflicting advice: 'Put on your sexiest, most see-through negligee.'

'I don't understand, Rabbi. What does this have to do with my interview with the Inland Revenue?' asks Abe.

'It means that it doesn't matter what you wear,' replies the rabbi, 'you're going to get screwed anyway.'

* * *

The two questions

Rabbi Bloom gets on a tube train. As soon as the doors close, a priest gets up, goes over to the rabbi and says, 'Good morning, Rabbi. I have a question to ask you. Why is it that everybody thinks Jews are smarter than Gentiles?'

Rabbi Bloom, who is not up for an argument, says, 'I'm sorry, but I am just a simple rabbi and I'm not really able to participate in such a discussion.'

But the priest insists. 'Look, no harm meant, Rabbi, but I have a theory and I need to test it out in the form of a bet. I'll pay you £100 if you can ask me a question that I can't answer. But if I can ask you a question that you can't answer, you must pay me £100.'

Rabbi Bloom replies, 'But I'm a poor rabbi – I only have £10 on me.'

The priest hesitates then says, 'OK, Rabbi, it's my £100 against your £10.'

Rabbi Bloom realises he can't get out of this so he agrees, but on condition that he asks the first question. The priest agrees.

'OK,' says Rabbi Bloom, 'what animal has scaly skin, the body of a cat, the face of a squirrel, the ears of a mouse, webbed toes and swims under water?'

Surprised, the priest admits that he doesn't know and asks the rabbi for a few more minutes to think about it. The rabbi agrees.

Two minutes later, the priest takes £100 from his wallet and gives it to the rabbi. The priest then asks the rabbi, 'So what animal was it?'

Rabbi Bloom replies, 'How should I know?' and gives the priest £10.

* * *

Heavenly needs

Rabbi Bloom is testing the children in his Sunday Hebrew class to see if they understand the concept of going to heaven. So he asks them, 'Boys and girls, if I sell my house and my car and give all the money to the *shul*, would that let me go to heaven?'

'No,' the children shout out.

'OK,' says the rabbi, 'if I clean the *shul* every day, wash all our stained-glass windows, inside and out, and keep every prayer book neat and tidy on the shelves, would that let me go to heaven?'

Again, the answer shouted out is, 'No.'

Rabbi Bloom is beginning to really enjoy this 'test'.

'Well then children,' he asks, 'if I'm the kindest person in the whole world to animals and if I give pieces of halva and kosher sweets to every boy and girl in north London and if I promise never to shout at any of you, would that let me go to heaven?'

Again, all the children shout out, 'No.'

'Well,' Rabbi Bloom continues, 'how then can I get to heaven?'

With that, six-year-old Aaron shouts out, 'You've got to be dead, Rabbi.'

* * *

Start with the easy solution

Faye and Monty have been married for over 30 years when all of a sudden they decide to separate. It shocks friends and family alike.

Monty decides to become more Orthodox and starts to spend much time in *shul* with Rabbi Bloom. Then, two years after they split, Monty and Faye decide to get back together.

Monty now wants Faye to join him in becoming more Orthodox and asks that she does out the kitchen and makes it '*Glatt Kosher*'. But Faye is not at all interested. Monty is very upset with her attitude and goes to see Rabbi Bloom.

'Rabbi,' he asks, 'what can I do? How can I get Faye to become more Orthodox? For example, how can I get her to run a kosher kitchen?'

Rabbi Bloom strokes his beard and nods sympathetically. 'Tell me, Monty, how many Jewish commandments are there in existence?'

Monty has recently learned this and quickly gives the correct answer, 'Six hundred and thirteen.'

Rabbi Bloom replies, 'So why don't you start with ones that don't annoy her?'

* * *

Almost converted

Christine and Daniel fall in love and decide to get married – but only on condition that Christine becomes Jewish. So she goes to see Rabbi Levy for some advice.

Rabbi Levy tells her, 'You will have to learn how to keep a kosher home, light *shabbes* candles, keep two sets of crockery and a few other simple things.'

'That sounds easy to me, Rabbi,' says Christine, 'I can easily do that.'

Then Rabbi Levy says, 'The last thing is, you must go to a *mikva*.'

'A *mikva*?' says Christine, 'What's that?'

'It's a pool of water,' answers Rabbi Levy, 'and you must immerse yourself completely for a few seconds.'

'I'm sorry, Rabbi, but I have a phobia about putting my head underwater. I'll go into the water up to my chin but I won't put my head under the water. Will that be OK?'

'I suppose it will do,' replies Rabbi Levy, 'you'll be mostly Jewish but you will still have a "*goyisha kop*".'

* * *

The wise rabbi

Sadie has a problem, so she goes to see the very wise Rabbi Levy. She asks him, 'Two members of our *shul*, Bernard Himmelfarb and Jacob Gold, are both in love with me, Rabbi. Who will be the lucky one?'

Rabbi Levy replies, 'Jacob will marry you, Sadie, but Bernard will be the lucky one.'

* * *

The visitor

One evening, Rabbi Levy is visited by a stranger. 'Yes,' says the rabbi, 'can I help you?'

'Life is very hard for some,' says the man. 'I thought you should know about the problems facing one of your congregation.'

'So tell me already,' says the rabbi.

'Well,' says the man, 'your Mrs Goldman owes a moneylender over £1,000 and she hasn't got the money to pay him back. She's being thrown out of her house this week, she's too ill to work and she can't feed her children.'

'It's a terrible life, indeed,' says Rabbi Levy. 'Thank you for letting me know. I'll raise some money from the *shul* straight away – I'll even donate £100 of my own money. But tell me, my friend, are you a relative of Mrs Goldman?'

'Don't be silly, Rabbi,' says the man, 'I'm the moneylender.'

* * *

Oh, Rabbi!
Ninety-year-old Abe dies and goes to heaven. The first person he sees there is his own rabbi, Rabbi Bloom, who had died a few months earlier. Abe was shocked to see the rabbi sitting in a heavenly chair with a very busty and tarty-looking blonde on his lap.

'Oh, Rabbi,' cries Abe, 'how could you? In all the time I knew you, you were always the most righteous of men. What has happened to you? Why are you acting in such a disgusting way? Is she your…reward?'

'My dear Abe,' replies Rabbi Bloom, 'you are unfortunately misreading the situation. She is not my reward, I am her punishment.'

* * *

The helpful tornado
Tornados in the UK are not that rare these days. One such tornado lifts off the roof of a house in Manchester very early one morning, picks up the bed on which Rabbi Gold and his wife Beckie are sleeping and sets them down gently in north London.

When Beckie starts to cry, the rabbi tries to comfort her. 'Don't be scared, darling,' he says, 'we're not hurt.'

But Beckie continues to cry. 'I'm not crying because I'm scared,' she says, 'I'm crying because I'm so happy – this is the first time in years we've been out together somewhere other than our *shul*!'

* * *

A question for the rabbi
Rabbi, am I permitted to ride in an airplane on *shabbes* as long as my seat belt remains fastened? Surely it can then be considered as if I'm wearing the plane?

* * *

The special dinner guest
Paul and Natalie have invited their elderly rabbi for dinner. While they're in the kitchen preparing the meal, the rabbi is in the dining room with their five-year-old daughter.

'So tell me, Emma,' asks the rabbi, 'do you know what we're having tonight?'

'Goat,' replies Emma.

'Goat?' says the startled rabbi. 'Are you sure about that, Emma?'

'Oh yes, Rabbi,' replies Emma, 'I heard Daddy say to Mummy, "Today is just as good as any to have the old goat for dinner."'

* * *

Luggage logic

Rabbi Rabinovitz is going on holiday to Israel. He arrives at Heathrow airport and goes to have his luggage checked in.

'Has anyone put anything in your baggage without your knowledge?' asks the girl at the check-in desk.

Rabbi Rabinovitz replies, 'Listen, if it was without my knowledge, how should I know?'

* * *

The book competition

Rabbi Josephs has an appointment to see his old friend Rabbi Bloom and Lionel, the *shammes*, kindly agrees to drive him there. When they arrive, Rabbi Bloom is on the phone and asks them to wait in his study.

As soon as they enter the study, Rabbi Josephs walks over to the well-stocked bookcase and begins to look carefully at the many books on display. Suddenly, Rabbi Josephs pulls a book from the shelf, opens it, scans the pages and goes very pale. Still holding the book, he has to sit down for a moment. When the colour comes back to his face, he gets up, kisses the book and puts it back on the shelf. Lionel doesn't say anything because he doesn't understand what's going on.

But then it happens again. Rabbi Josephs takes hold of another book, opens the pages, stares at what he finds and as before, has to sit down in case he faints. A few moments later, he gets up, kisses the book and replaces it. This time, Lionel decides to ask Rabbi Joseph if everything is OK.

'Rabbi,' Lionel asks, 'what was wrong with that book you just put back?'

'Nothing Lionel, nothing at all,' replies Rabbi Joseph, smiling. 'Just for a moment there, I thought Rabbi Bloom had another book I didn't have.'

* * *

The good wishes

Rabbi Gold is taken ill and is admitted to hospital for treatment. A few days after his admittance, Max, the *shul's* secretary, goes to visit him. 'Rabbi,' says Max, 'I'm here on behalf of our Board of Trustees. They have asked me to bring you their good wishes for a speedy recovery and their hope that you should live to be 110.'

'Thank you,' says Rabbi Gold, 'I'm pleased to hear of their good wishes for me.'

And so you should be, Rabbi,' says Max. 'It was touch and go for a while but the final vote on whether we should send you any good wishes ended up 11 to nine in your favour.'

* * *

Rabbis are just as fallible as we are

Here are three 'Freudian slips' supposedly made by rabbis:

1. A rabbi wished someone in his congregation who was going in for a biopsy, 'I hope you have a successful autopsy.'
2. Another rabbi told his congregation, 'I'm still a bit numb because yesterday I was seduced by my dentist.' He meant 'sedated'.
3. Yet another rabbi was very upset to hear that someone in his congregation had been seen drinking 'pork wine'.

* * *

Advice for the ladies

Rabbi Levy is addressing the 'Enlighten Your Daughter' meeting of the synagogue women's guild. 'Ladies,' he says, 'I'm sure some of you know by now that the unfortunate Jonathan Bloom has been sent to prison for making love to his wife Sadie's dead body.'

A number of '*Oy vehs*' are heard from the ladies present.

'You might also be interested to know', the Rabbi goes on to say, 'that I spoke to Jonathan yesterday and I now firmly believe that his actions were entirely innocent and accidental. So although we are all feeling sorry for Jonathan, there is a lesson to be learned. Ladies, go back home to your daughters and tell them that when making love with a good Jewish husband, they should please make a little wiggle.'

* * *

The synagogue service

Max has been a confirmed atheist ever since he left university. But now that he is approaching his 60th birthday, spiritual issues start to become part of his life and he decides to 'become' a Jew again. The next *shabbes*, Max goes to *shul* for the first time in nearly 40 years.

He enjoys the occasion and even listens attentively to the rabbi's sermon, especially the bit at the end when the rabbi announces that his sermon next week will be about the great flood.

At the end of the service, Max goes over to the rabbi and says, 'Rabbi, I really enjoyed the service. Unfortunately I won't be able to attend next week. But please don't think I will be shirking my duties – I can be as charitable as the next man. So please put me down for £20 for the flood victims.'

* * *

The rabbi's sermons

The *shabbes* service finishes and the congregation is invited to a *kiddush* in the *shul* hall. During the *kiddush*, Mordechai goes over to Rabbi Bloom, shakes his hand and says, 'Rabbi, you gave a good sermon today – you should have it published.'

'Thank you,' says Rabbi Bloom, 'but just between you and me, I'm planning to have all my sermons published posthumously.'

'That's good news,' says Mordechai, 'and the sooner the better.'

Sabbath (*Shabbes*)

The *shabbes* dress
The local synagogue is running its usual popular children's *shabbes* service when it's time for the rabbi to give them a short sermon. All the children are invited to come forward. Little Emma is wearing a really pretty dress and as she sits down, the rabbi leans forward and says, 'That's a very pretty dress, Emma. Is it your *shabbes* dress?'

Emma replies, 'Yes, and my Mummy says it's a bitch to iron.'

* * *

The Orthodox golfer
He never drives on the Sabbath.

* * *

Working boy
It's *shabbes* and Yitzhak and his young son Aaron are on their way to *shul*. Yitzhak is watching Aaron pick his nose. 'Why are you breaking the commandment "Thou shall not work on *shabbes*", Aaron?' asks Yitzhak.

'I'm not, Dad,' says Aaron, 'what work do you think I'm doing?'

'Digging,' replies Yitzhak.

* * *

Shabbes sermons

A good *shabbes* sermon should have a good beginning and a good ending – and they should be as close together as possible.

Synagogues (*Shuls*)

A synagogue visit

Abe and Sadie make a rare appearance in *shul*. It's probably true to say that they are not the most religious of Jews. In fact, they only go to *shul* two or three times every year – and this is one of those days.

At the end of the service, Abe shakes Rabbi Rose's hand and says, 'Sadie and I both thoroughly enjoyed your service today, Rabbi.'

Rabbi Rose replies, 'It's nice of you to say so, Abe. So why don't you and Sadie come here more often?'

'It's difficult,' replies Abe, 'but at least we keep the Ten Commandments.'

'That's really good to hear,' says Rabbi Rose.

'Yes,' says Abe proudly, 'Sadie keeps six of them and I keep the other four.'

* * *

Appearances can be deceptive

It's Friday and Moshe is in Shanghai on business. He asks the hotel's concierge whether there's a *shul* nearby. There is, so he gets instructions on how to get there and arrives just before the start of evening service. Moshe is amazed. It's the largest *shul* he's ever seen and not only that, it's packed with Chinese worshippers. He is lucky and finds the last available seat.

All through the service, Moshe notices the rabbi looking over to where he's sitting and just before the service ends, the rabbi makes his way over to where Moshe is sitting.

'Where are you from?' the rabbi asks.

'I am from Golders Green in London,' replies Moshe.

'Are you Jewish?' asks the rabbi.

Moshe replies, 'But of course I am.'

Then the rabbi says, 'Funny, you no rook Jewish.'

* * *

Shul goer

As Daniel and his wife Naomi are coming out of *shul* one *shabbes*, she says to him, 'That Robson girl has put on a lot of weight, dear. Maybe she's pregnant. What do you think?'

'The Robson girl? If she was there, I didn't see her,' replies Daniel.

'And did you see that flirty Sharon Kay winking at the boys? Disgraceful, don't you think, dear?'

'I must have been looking the other way when that happened,' he replies.

'And what do you think about the short dress Rivkah Levy was wearing? That can't be the right thing for a mother of three children to wear in *shul*. Don't you agree, dear?' asks Naomi.

'Sorry darling,' replies Daniel, 'but I didn't notice her dress.'

'Well then, you must have seen Kitty Usum drinking all those glasses of wine during *Kiddush*,' she says.

'I wasn't watching Kitty,' says Daniel.

'Oh for goodness sake,' shouts Naomi, 'I don't know why you bother to go to *shul* these days.'

* * *

The sleeper

Issy is sitting in *shul* one *shabbes* morning when he falls asleep and starts to snore. The *shammes* quickly comes over to him, taps him softly on his shoulder and says, 'Please stop your snoring, Issy, you're disturbing the others in the *shul*.'

'Now look here,' says Issy, 'I always pay my *shul* subscription in full so I feel I have a right to do whatever I want.'

'Yes, I agree,' replies the *shammes*, 'but your snoring is keeping everybody else awake.'

* * *

Think about it…

It's a very hot August afternoon and Sarah is taking her daily walk. As she nears her local *shul,* she notices that the shrubbery outside the entrance is on fire. She bangs on the *gabbai's* door and when he opens it, she tells him that he should call the fire brigade before the fire causes any damage. The *gabbai* dials 999, identifies himself, gives his location and explains the situation.

'Do you mean to tell me', says the emergency operator, 'that there's a burning bush on the synagogue lawn and you want us to put it out?'

* * *

Learning curve

The Lake District has flooded and little Sam is walking home after *shul* one *shabbes*. As he gets to the crossroads, he meets a little girl.

'Hello,' says Sam, 'what's your name?'

'I'm Naomi,' replies the little girl.

'Where you going, Naomi?' asks Sam.

'I've just been to *shul* and I'm on my way home,' she replies.

'Me too,' says Sam. 'What *shul* do you go to?'

'The Reform *shul* back down the road,' replies Naomi. 'What about you?'

'Mine's the Orthodox *shul* at the top of the hill,' replies Sam.

They soon discover that they both go home the same way so they decide to walk back together. But they come to a halt at a low point in the road where the rain has partially flooded the road and they can't find a way to get across without getting wet.

'If I get my new *shabbes* dress wet, my mummy's going to really tell me off,' says Naomi.

Sam says, 'My mummy might even stop my pocket money if I get my new *shabbes* suit wet.'

'Tell you what I think I'll do,' says Naomi. 'I'm going to take off all my clothes, hold them over my head and walk across.'

'That's a good idea,' says Sam. 'I'll do the same thing.'

So they both undress and wade across to the other side without getting their clothes wet. As they are waiting to dry before putting their clothes back on, Sam says to Naomi, 'You know, I never knew how much difference there is between a Reform and Orthodox Jew.'

* * *

The board meeting
Rabbi Levy finishes yet another of his long, dry and somewhat boring sermons. This time, however, before he sits down, he announces to his congregation that he wishes to meet with the *shul's* Board of Representatives immediately after the service.

The first man to arrive and greet Rabbi Levy is a total stranger to him. 'Thanks for coming,' says the rabbi, 'but you must have misunderstood my announcement. This is a meeting of the Board.'

'Yes I know,' says the man, 'but if there's anyone here more bored than I am, then I'd like to shake his hand.'

* * *

Overheard in *shul* – 1

'So Henry, is your son Simon a good doctor?'

'Good? He's such a lovely boy that last year, when I needed an operation and couldn't afford it, he touched up my X-rays.'

* * *

Overheard in *shul* – 2

'Diane, the summer holidays will soon be with us and I was wondering where you'll be going this time?'

'Well, as you know Fay, we took a trip around the world last year. This year, we're thinking of going somewhere different!'

* * *

Overheard in *shul* – 3

'You tell me, Arnold, that you have a relative staying with you over the holidays. Is this relative of yours a religious man?'

'Well let me tell you, Benny. My relative is so Orthodox that when he plays chess with me, he doesn't use bishops, he uses rabbis.'

Language (including *Yiddish*)

Roman salesman

Marcus Brutus Goldstein earned his living in the great market of ancient Rome. He was a tailor and made togas, which he would sell from his market stall. His marketing ploy was to shout out his wares for sale: 'Togas! Come buy your togas here – the finest togas in all of Rome!'

Unfortunately, business was not good. His friend Moshe suggested that the problem was due to the cold weather. He should therefore line the garments with a fine-quality wool lining.

Marcus Brutus Goldstein decided to use the finest quality Kashmir linings. From that day on, he could be heard plying his trade in the market, shouting to passers-by, 'Kashmir in togas!'

* * *

The court proceedings

Judge Allen enters Court Number 1 and sits down. He feels ready for the day's business. However, the first case involves Moshe Cohen and as soon as Judge Allen sees this elderly man with his long white beard, *peyess and kippot*, without even asking a question, he says to the court clerk, 'Get me a translator.'

When the translator arrives, Judge Allen points to Moshe and says to the translator, 'Ask him his name, his age and where he's from.'

The translator says to Moshe, '*Die judge vilt vissen, vos is dein namen, vie alt bist du, and fun vie kumst du?*'

Moshe smiles, looks at Judge Allen and replies in perfect English, 'Your honour, my name is Moshe Cohen, I shall be 82 tomorrow and I live in Oxford University where I'm professor of Hebrew Philosophy.'

The translator then turns to Judge Allen and says, '*Ehr zukt, ehr is Moshe Cohen, ehr is tzwei und achtzig yur alt, und ehr is, mit sach Yiddish philisoph, areingekummen fun Oxford.*'

* * *

At the country club

Aaron and Rivka move to the suburbs and join the new, very elite, country club. But just before their first meal at the club, Aaron is feeling somewhat anxious about Rivka's lack of finesse and so decides to give her some advice.

'Rivka,' he says, 'ven ve go to dee club and dee vaiter asks you vaht you vahnt for ah drink, please don't say, "Ah glass Manishevitz vine." At a club like dis, you don't esk for Manishevitz vine.'

'Well, Aaron,' she replies, 'if I can't esk for Manishevitz, vot should I esk for?'

'You should esk for ah martini,' replies Aaron. 'Every lady drinks martini. You'll like it.'

That evening at the club, as the smartly dressed drinks waiter arrives at their table to take their order, Rivka is ready. 'Madam, may I bring you a cocktail?'

Rivka replies, 'Yes, I'll have ah martini.'

'Dry?' asks the waiter.

'No,' replies Rivka, '*Tzvei iz genug*' (Two is enough).

* * *

The hot spot

Unusually for a mid-August day in London, it's very, very hot. Sadie has been busy. She's washed the floor, made the evening's roast meal and taken the washing out of the washing machine and hung them up. Then she leaves the house to go pick up some dry cleaning. As Sadie walks to the shops, she's perspiring profusely, so when she comes to a pub, she says to herself, 'Gootness, it's hotter dan hell today, so vy nodt? I must go ged a drink or I'll pass out.'

She enters. When the bartender asks what she would like to drink, all she can think of is a cold beer, her Nathan's favourite drink when he's hot. So she replies, 'Ya know, it is zo hot, I tink I'll have myself a cold beer.'

'Anheuser Busch?' asks the bartender.

Sadie blushes and replies, 'Vell fine, tanks, und how's yu pecker?'

* * *

The Hebrew lesson

'Hello Cyril,' says Fred, 'I hear you know Hebrew?'

'Yes, I do,' replies Cyril.

'I was wondering what the Hebrew for "he" is?' says Fred.

'*Hu*,' says Cyril.

'No one in particular,' says Fred, 'I just wanted to know what is "he"?'

'*Hee* is "she",' says Cyril.

'Who?' says Fred.

'No, *hu* is "he",' says Cyril.

'I thought you said he is she?' says Fred.

'Yes, that's correct,' says Cyril.

'What is correct?' says Fred.

'*Hee* is "she",' says Cyril.

'I have no idea what you said. Who is she?' says Fred.

'No, *hu* is "he",' says Cyril.

'I don't want to know who he is, now I want to know what she is in Hebrew?' says Fred.

'*Hee*,' says Cyril.

'He who?' says Fred.

'Yes that's correct, but *Hee* is "she",' says Cyril.

'Who is she?' says Fred.

'No, *hu* is "he",' says Cyril.

'Why do you keep asking me who is he?' says Fred.

'I thought you were asking me what "he" is in Hebrew?' says Cyril.

'Me?' says Fred.

'That's *hu*,' says Cyril.

'Who is me?' says Fred.

'No, *hu* is "he", *mee* is "who",' says Cyril.

'I don't want to know who you are, I want to know who is he,' says Fred.

'That's correct,' says Cyril.

'But I've no idea what I'm saying,' says Fred.

'But you say it so well,' says Cyril.

'Who, me?' says Fred.

'Why are you asking me who he is?' says Cyril.

'No, I'm asking you what is "he"?' says Fred.

'*Hee* is "she",' says Cyril.

'Who is she?' says Fred.

'No, *hu* is "he",' says Cyril.

'I'm very lost. Me is who? Who is he? He is she?' says Fred.

'Very good, you said that very well,' says Cyril.

'What did I say?' says Fred.

'*Mee* is "who", *hu* is "he" and *hee* is "she",' says Cyril.

'Well if you must know, you're crazy. I don't know who he is and if she is a he, I'm sure I don't want to know her,' says Fred.

* * *

Knowledge is a dangerous thing

Peter is a street trader who has set up his pitch right outside the local synagogue. One day, Jed, a friend of Peter and also a trader, happens to walk past the *shul* and sees Peter. 'Hey Peter, I hear you're doing very well here. What's your secret, then?'

'It's easy,' replies Peter, 'when one of my clients comes out of the *shul*, I always say something like, "Good *shabbes*, Mr Levy, how was the *kiddush*?' or, "Good *yontif*, Mr Cohen, how was the service today?" '

'But how do you remember all these words?' asks Jed.

'It's easy,' says Peter, pointing to his head, 'I keep them right up here in my *toches*.'

* * *

Identity problems
'Hello, have I dialled the right number for Benjy?'
    'Ah-ah, mit whom you vish to talk?'
    'Benjamin. Is Benjamin Levy at home?'
    'Vat! At dis time of the day? Mr Levy is voiking.'
    'Well OK. Is his daughter Ruth at home then?'
    'Ruth is mit boyfriend.'
    'OK. OK. How about his son Simon? Can I speak to him?
Is he at home?'
    'Simon? In de hospitel is Simon. He is gute docketor.'
    'It seems that no one is in. Am I talking to Mrs Levy?'
    'Mrs Levy, she shoppink in de supermakkit.'
    'Well, who am I talking to, then?'
    'Dis is Mildred, de au pair.'

* * *

A Yiddish saying
'If I live, I'll see you Monday, if not, Tuesday.'

* * *

What are friends for?
Ruth has just been to see her doctor for the first time in years
and returns home with a little plastic beaker. When her
husband Henry sees the beaker, he asks Ruth, 'So *nu*, darling,
what's the beaker for?'
    'Dr Myers wants me to bring him a specimen in it.'
    'So provide him with one, already,' says Henry.
    'Well I would if I could,' says Ruth, 'but what's a specimen,
darling?'
    'How the hell should I know,' replies Henry, 'we haven't
seen a medical person for years. Why don't you ask your
friend Rifka – she's always going to see her doctor.'
    So Ruth goes out to talk to Rifka. She returns 30 minutes
later. Her dress is torn and she has two black eyes and a cut lip.

'What on earth has happened to you?' Henry asks.

'You wouldn't believe it,' she replies. 'When I asked Rifka what a specimen was, she said, 'Go pee in a bottle.' So I told her to *'Gay kakken af en yam'* and that's when the fight started.

* * *

Translation problems

Hyman and Isaac are discussing the problems in translating from one language to another. Hyman says, 'Did you know, Isaac, that there are some English words and expressions that are very difficult to translate into Yiddish?'

'You surprise me,' says Isaac. 'Can you give me an example?'

'Well,' replies Hyman, 'I've always had difficulty in finding a Yiddish word that adequately covers the meaning of the English word "disappointed".'

Isaac thinks for a while and says, 'Mmm, I see what you mean, Hyman. Look, I'll tell you what I'll do. My mother speaks only Yiddish, so I'll ask her tonight how one says, "disappointed" in Yiddish.'

That night, Isaac says to his mother, 'Mum, I always come here for dinner on Friday nights. So how would you feel if I were to tell you that I won't be coming here next Friday?'

Isaac mother replies, *'Oy! Ich'll zein zayer* disappointed.'

* * *

Only for those who understand a bit of Yiddish

Hyman and Isaac are *davening* in *shul*. But Hyman can't take his eyes off the very attractive lady he's noticed in the women's section.

So Isaac says to Hyman, *'Kuk nisht tzu di froien. Dafst davenen.'*

Hyman returns to the prayers, but soon he is looking at the woman again.

So Isaac says, this time a bit more angrily, '*Kuk nisht tzu di froien. HAINT IZ YOM KIPPUR.*'

Hyman replies, '*Bai mir in di oizn iz haint SIMJES TOIRE.*'

* * *

A primer on practical Yiddish for lawyers
In the heat of litigation, tempers often flare and lawyers sometimes have difficulty expressing their frustrations. When English fails, Yiddish may come to the rescue. So, it happened that a defence counsel, arguing in a recent summary judgment motion in federal court in Boston wrote, in a responsive pleading: 'It is unfortunate that this Court must wade through the *dreck* of the plaintiff's original and supplemental statement of undisputed facts.'

The plaintiff's attorneys, not to be outdone, responded with the following motion that could double as a primer on practical Yiddish for lawyers:

'Plaintiff, by her attorneys, hereby moves this court pursuant to Rule 12(f) of the Federal Rules of Civil Procedure to strike as impertinent and scandalous the characterization of her factual submission as "*dreck*" on page 11 of Defendant's Rule 56.1 Supplemental Statement of Disputed Facts, a copy of which is attached hereto as Exhibit A.

'As grounds therefore, plaintiff states: for almost four years now, plaintiff and her attorneys have been subjected to the constant *kvetching* by defendant's counsel, who have made a big *tsimmes* about the quantity and quality of plaintiff's responses to discovery requests. This has been the source of much *tsouris* among plaintiff's counsel and a *gantzeh megillah* for the Court. Now that plaintiff's counsel has, after much time and effort, provided defendants with a specific and comprehensive statement of plaintiff's claims and the factual basis thereof, defendant's counsel have the *chutzpah* to call it "*dreck*" and to urge the Court to ignore it.

'Plaintiff moves that this language be stricken for several reasons. First, we think it is impertinent to refer to the work of a fellow member of the bar of this Court with the Yiddish term "*dreck*" as it would be to use 'the sibilant four-letter English word for excrement". (*Rosten, The Joys of Yiddish*, Simon & Schuster, New York, 1968, p.103.)

'Second, defendants are in no position to deprecate plaintiff's counsel in view of the *chozzerai* which they have filed over the course of this litigation. Finally, since not all of plaintiff's lawyers are *yeshiva buchers*, defendants should not have assumed that they would all be conversant in Yiddish. WHEREFORE, plaintiff prays that the Court puts an end to this *mishegass*.'

* * *

**Please preserve the English language
(author unknown)**

'To all the *shlemiels, shlemazels, nebbishes, nudniks, klutzes, putzes, shlubs, shmoes, shmucks, nogoodniks* and *mumzers* that are lurking out there in the crowd, I just wanted to say that I, for one, get sentimental when I think about English and its place in our society.

'To tell the truth, it makes me so *farklempt*, I'm fit to *plutz*. This whole *schmeer* gets me *broyges* when I hear these *mavens* and *luftmenschen kvetching* about our national language. What *chutzpah!*'

'These *shmegeges* can tout their *shlock* about the cultural and linguistic diversity of our country and of English itself, but I, for one, am not buying their *shtick*. It's all so much *dreck*, as far as I'm concerned. I exhort you all to be *menshen* about this and stand up to their *fardrayte* arguments and *meshugganah*, *farshtunkene* assertions. It wouldn't be *shayich* to do anything else.'

'Remember, when all is said and done, we have English and they've got *bubkes*! The whole *myseh* is a pain in the *toches*!'

A Mirthful Miscellany...

Cars and Drivers

Drive-in cash

Hyman received the following letter from his bank:

The President of the Bank is pleased to announce that two 'drive-through' cash dispensers have now been installed to enable customers to withdraw cash without leaving their cars.

To help our customers make the most effective use of this new service, we have come up with the following guidelines. These were drawn up following intensive behavioural studies of drive-in services.

PROCEDURES FOR MALE CUSTOMERS
1. Drive up to the cash machine
2. Wind down your car window
3. Insert card into machine
4. Enter PIN number
5. Enter amount of cash required
6. Retrieve card, cash and receipt
7. Wind up window
8. Drive off

PROCEDURES FOR FEMALE CUSTOMERS
1. Drive up to the cash machine
2. Reverse a bit to align the car window with the cash machine
3. Re-start the stalled engine
4. Wind down your car window

5. Find handbag, empty contents on to passenger seat to locate card
6. Turn down the radio
7. Attempt to insert card into machine
8. Open car door to access cash machine due to its distance from car
9. Insert card into machine
10. Re-insert card the right way up
11. Empty handbag again to find diary with the PIN number listed
12. Enter PIN number
13. Press 'cancel' and re-enter correct PIN number
14. Enter amount of cash required
15. Check make-up in rear-view mirror
16. Retrieve card, cash and receipt
17. Empty handbag again to locate purse and place cash inside
18. Place receipt in back of chequebook
19. Re-check makeup in rear-view mirror
20. Drive away and then stop after 8 feet
21. Reverse car back to cash machine
22. Retrieve card
23. Restart stalled engine and drive away
24. Drive for 2–3 miles
25. Release handbrake

* * *

Life's little problems
One day, as Rachel is cleaning her daughter's bedroom, she notices a letter on the pillow addressed to her. With a worried feeling, Rachel reads the letter. This is what it says:

Dear Mum
   I'm sorry to have to tell you this but I've eloped with my

new boyfriend. He's so different, Mum. What with his pierced tongue, his tattoos and his big motorcycle, I've found real passion with him. But that's not all. I'm pregnant. But don't worry, Mick says that we will be very happy living in his caravan. He even shares my dream of having a big family and he wants to have more children with me.

He's very clever as well. He's taught me how to grow marijuana and I agree with him that it doesn't hurt anyone. So we'll be growing it not only for us but also all his friends.

Don't worry about our finances. Mick has arranged for me to appear in some homemade video films. I can earn £150 per scene, more if there are three men involved. But don't worry, I'm 15 years old and know how to take care of myself.

In the meantime, Mum, please pray that science will soon find a cure for AIDS. Mick deserves to get better.

Love Rebecca

PS: This letter is not true – it's all make believe. Actually, I'm at our neighbour's house. I just wanted to prove to you that there are worse things in life than denting your Lexus car.

* * *

A driving riddle
Q: What kind of motor vehicle is mentioned in the Bible?
A: David's Triumph was heard throughout the land.

* * *

Old cars
One day, little Rachel asks her mother, 'Mummy, what happens to old cars when they stop working?'

'Someone sells them to your father,' replies her mother.

* * *

The car sale

Rivkah drives a big Lexus to her local Lexus dealer and tells him she wants to sell it. 'How much do you want for it?' he asks her.

'I'll be happy to accept £100,' she replies.

The dealer is very suspicious. Well he would be – the car is almost new and is worth at least £40,000. 'I'm not sure I want to take it,' he says to Rivkah.

'Don't get worried,' says Rivkah, 'let me explain. There's nothing wrong with the car, as well you know, as you sold it to us only recently. But mine Bernie died two weeks ago and he was having an affair with his *shiksa* secretary. I've just attended the reading of his will and in it he says his secretary should have the proceeds from selling his car. So here I am.'

* * *

Serious negotiation

In 1946, after many years of endeavour, Norman, Hymie and Maxwell Goldberg finally invent the first air-conditioning unit that can be fitted inside a car. So thrilled and confident are these three brothers that they decide to sell it to the largest car manufacturer in the world – Ford.

They install their only working unit in one of their cars and choosing a hot day, drive to Ford's Head Office in Detroit. On arrival, they ask to see Henry Ford himself, but as they don't have an appointment, they have to use all their charm to persuade his secretary to help them. Within minutes, she's telling Mr Ford that sitting in her office are three well-dressed gentlemen with a most exciting invention that will help sell more Ford cars.

Henry Ford immediately asks them to join him in his office. But they refuse, asking him instead to go with them to the car park to see their invention. He agrees and when they reach the Goldbergs' car, all four get in. As it's now very hot outside, the Goldbergs turn on their air-conditioning unit. Almost immediately the car begins to cool down. Henry Ford is very excited and asks if they have patented their invention – which they are pleased to confirm. So he invites them back to his office for some discussion.

One hour later, the Goldbergs are offered $3 million for their invention. But they refuse. They not only want $5 million but they also desire recognition by having a label on every one of their units saying, 'A Goldberg Air-Conditioning unit.'

But Henry Ford says that there is no way he is going to put the name 'Goldberg' on millions of his Ford cars (everyone in America knows that he is more than a little bit anti-Semitic). So they go back to haggling and eventually reach an agreement for the product. The offer now is $4.5 million plus the display in each car of just the first names of the three brothers.

And so today all Ford air-conditioning units show their names on the air-conditioning controls as 'Norm' 'Hi' 'Max'.

Information Technology (IT)

Kosher PC

My rabbi came over yesterday and we had a *Bris* for my computer – he cut a little piece off the tail of the mouse. He also told me that I should buy a kosher computer, called a KPC. If I did, he said I would need to know the differences.

- The KPC comes with two hard drives, one for *flayshedig* business software and one for *milchedig* computer games.
- Internet Explorer comes with a spinning Star of David in the upper right corner.
- Microsoft Office includes, 'a little byte of this and a little byte of that'.
- *Hava Nagila* plays during the KPC boot up.
- The *Chanukah* screen saver shows Flying Dreidels.

- The KPC automatically shuts down at sundown every Friday.
- The KPC start button is labelled, 'Let's go already, I'm not getting any younger.'
- When disconnecting external devices from the back of the KPC, the screen message says, 'Please remove cable from the *toches.*'
- KPC scandisk opens with the prompt, 'You vant I should fix this?'
- When the KPC processor is working hard, it broadcasts a loud, '*Oy gevalt.*'
- After 30 minutes of inactivity, the KPC goes *shloffen.*
- KPC email always opens with, 'You don't write and you never call.'
- The KPC options button is labelled, 'But on the other hand.'
- When delete is chosen, the KPC Dialogue Box says, 'Listen, you never know – you might need this someday. So do you really want to cancel?'
- The KPC comes with a monitor cleaning solution from Manischewitz to get rid of *shmutz* from the monitor.
- Computer viruses on the KPC are quickly cured with chicken soup.

* * *

Man versus machine
On his way to work one morning, Nathan arrives at the railway station a bit early. While he's waiting for his train, he notices a new machine on the platform – the sign on it says it's a state-of-the-art talking, weighing machine. So Nathan stands on it, puts in a £1 coin and the machine says, 'You weigh 160 pounds and you are Jewish.'

Nathan can't believe what he's just heard. So he gets on it again and inserts another £1 coin. 'You weigh 160 pounds, you are Jewish and you're waiting for the 7.35am train to take you to your job at Rothschild's Bank.'

He is totally shocked, but he's determined to beat the machine. He goes into the Gents' toilet, ruffles up his hair, puts on a pair of dark sunglasses, removes his tie, takes off his jacket and drapes it over his arm, and puts a first-aid plaster on his chin. He then goes back outside, steps on the machine and puts in another £1 coin. The machine instantly says, 'You're still Jewish and weigh 160 pounds. You're also a *shmuck*. While you've been testing me out, you've just missed your train.'

* * *

For computer nerds only
There are 10 types of people in the world – those who understand binary and those who don't.

* * *

The stork brought you
One day, five-year-old Arnold asks his father, 'Daddy, how was I born?'

His father replies, 'Arnold, my son, I guess one day you'll need to find out so I'll tell you. Well, you see your mummy and I first got together in a chat room on MSN. Then I set up a date via email to meet her at a cyber-cafe. We then sneaked into a secluded room where your mummy agreed to a download from my hard drive. As soon as I was ready to upload, we discovered that neither of us had used a firewall and since it was too late to hit the delete button, nine months later a little Pop-Up appeared and said, "You've Got Male!"'

* * *

Satire
(True story): Following the death of Morris Gorski, a popular and wealthy businessman, it was discovered that a clause in his will stated that his heirs would only be entitled to get their share of his money by visiting his grave on a weekly basis. Surprisingly, the Jewish Board has agreed to put a special cash machine near his grave to allow his heirs to collect up to £750 a time when they turn up. A special debit card has been issued to 25 of Morris's heirs, which they can use at the graveside as well as being able to use elsewhere.

'When Uncle Morris said he was going to do this, we thought he was joking,' said his niece. 'I would have visited his grave anyway, but I guess Uncle Morris wanted to ensure that other family members got an incentive to visit him.'

According to the Board, 'If the test project involving Mr Gorski proves popular, other people will get the opportunity to have cash machines near their graves. As the forward-thinking Jewish group we are, we like to consider all ideas. Before Mr Gorski died, he asked us if such a special cash machine was something we would consider for him. We listened and thought it was a wonderful idea especially as he felt it was a way to encourage family members to visit him. We consulted with members of the Board who agreed that when the time came to honour Mr Gorski's request, we would.'

* * *

It's curtains for you
Becky walks into the haberdashery department of a large department store and says to the sales girl, 'I'd like a pink curtain for my computer screen, please.'

The sales girl is surprised by this request and replies, 'But madam, computers don't have curtains.'

'Becky says, 'Maybe most, but mine's got Windows!'

* * *

The amazing robot

Moshe builds one of the most advanced talking robots ever invented. This robot can answer just about any question asked of it, whatever the subject. Moshe announces his achievement in the *Jewish Chronicle* and invites scientists to the launch. As the guests arrive, there stands the robot with a sign around its neck: ASK ME ANY QUESTION AND I'LL GIVE YOU THE CORRECT ANSWER.

For the first 30 minutes, dozens of questions are asked and the robot always gives the correct answer. Everyone is amazed. Then Hymie goes up to the robot and asks, 'Where, at this very moment, is my father?'

The robot immediately replies, 'Your father is at present lying on the beach in front of the Dan Hotel in Tel Aviv accompanied by a gorgeous woman.'

'Well you're totally wrong,' says Hymie. 'My father is Aaron Minkoffsky and just before I arrived, I spoke to him on the phone. He's at home with my mother in north London.'

'Yes, it's true that Aaron Minkoffsky is at home with your mother in north London,' says the robot, 'but your father is at present lying on the beach in front of the Dan Hotel in Tel Aviv accompanied by a gorgeous woman.'

* * *

What was it like before computers?
- Memory was something you lost with age.
- An application was for employment.
- A program was a TV show.
- A cursor used profanity.
- A keyboard was a piano.
- A web was a spider's home.
- A virus was the flu.
- A hard drive was a long trip on the road.

- A mouse pad was where a mouse lived.
- And if you had a three-inch floppy…you just hoped nobody ever found out!

* * *

Not on a kibbutz
Aharon, Bracha and their son Mordechai have lived an extremely isolated life in a kibbutz without any form of modern convenience. There is no TV, no radio, no PC – in fact there is no electricity. And not one of them has ever left the kibbutz since they were born. But when Aharon reaches 90 years of age, they decide to take their very first overseas trip to London. Today, they are visiting a shopping mall.

While Aharon is walking around inside an electronics shop, being amazed by the variety of equipment on display, Bracha and Mordechai are outside the shop, being fascinated by two shiny, silver walls that move apart by magic and then slide back together again. 'What are those, Mother?' asks Mordechai

Bracha replies, 'Son, I have never seen anything like them in my life. I just don't know what they are.'

Suddenly, an obese elderly man with white hair and walking stick hobbles over to the silver walls and presses a button. The walls open, he walks between the doors into a small room, and the walls close behind him. Bracha and Mordechai then see some small numbers above the walls light up and change sequentially from one to six. Then they notice the numbers start changing, this time from six down to one. The walls open up again and a very handsome young man steps out. Bracha watches him walk away and, not taking her eyes off him, says quietly to Mordechai, 'Son, go get your father.'

* * *

PC trouble

Sarah is having trouble on her PC with her Outlook emails, so she telephones Joshua the computer expert and asks him to come over and sort it out for her. As soon as he arrives, it takes Joshua only a few minutes to solve the problem. He then gives Sarah an invoice for £25, his minimum service charge, and turns to leave. As he's walking away, she shouts after him, 'So *nu*? What was wrong with it, Joshua?'

'It was an "ID ten T" error,' he replies.

Sarah doesn't want to appear stupid, but nonetheless asks him, 'An "ID ten T" error? What's that...in case I need to fix it again?'

Joshua grins and replies, 'Haven't you heard of an "ID ten T" error before?'

'No,' she replies.

'So write it down,' he says, 'and then I think you'll figure it out.'

So Sarah writes out...I D 1 0 T.

PS: She used to like Joshua, but doesn't any more.

* * *

The watch

Hymie is in his local shopping centre when he sees someone he knows. It's Estelle, a rather attractive widow, and she's sitting all alone on a bench. So, being both a widower and a bit of a playboy, he walks over to the bench and quietly sits down next to her. He gives her a quick glance then casually looks at his watch for a moment. Then he looks up at her again and then glances down at his watch.

Estelle turns round and sees it's Hymie. 'Oh hello Hymie,' she says, 'is anything the matter? Are you waiting for someone, because you keep on looking at your watch, then at me?'

'Oh no,' replies Hymie, 'I've just bought one of the world's most advanced watches and I'm testing it out.'

Estelle is intrigued. 'An advanced watch?' she says. 'So what's so special about it, Hymie? Why is it any different to mine?'

'OK, I'll tell you why,' replies Hymie. 'It's special because it uses Bluetooth waves to talk to me telepathically.'

'OK then,' says Estelle, 'so what's it telling you right now?'

'It's telling me loud and clear,' replies Hymie, looking very serious, 'that you're not wearing any panties.'

'Well it must be broken then,' Estelle says, giggling, 'because I'm definitely wearing panties!'

At that, Hymie starts to tap on the face of his watch and says, '*Oy veh*, the watch must be an hour fast.'

* * *

Gender confusion

A Tel Aviv college professor of IT knew that ships are referred to as 'she' and 'her'. But what gender, he thought, should computers be considered? So he decided to ask his class.

He set up two groups of computer experts, one comprising women and the other men. Each group was asked to recommend whether computers should be referred to in the feminine or masculine gender and give four reasons for the choice.

The women said that computers should be referred to in the masculine gender:

• in order to get their attention, you have to turn them on
• although they have a lot of data, they are still clueless.
• they are supposed to help solve problems but most of the time they are the problem
• as soon as you commit to one, you realise that had you had waited a little longer, you could have had a better model.

The men, on the other hand, said that computers should be referred to in the feminine gender:

- no one but God understands their internal logic
- the native language they use to communicate with other computers is incomprehensible to everyone else
- even smallest mistakes are stored in long-term memory for later retrieval
- as soon as you commit to one, you start spending money on accessories for it.

Entertaining

The old ones are the best ones – some well-known quickies

- I've been in love with the same woman for 49 years. If my wife ever finds out, she'll kill me!
- A car hits an elderly Jewish man. The paramedic says, 'Are you comfortable?' The man says, 'I make a good living.'
- Someone stole all my credit cards, but I won't be reporting it. The thief spends less than my wife did.
- We always hold hands. If I let go, he buys some more useless electronic gadgets.
- My wife and I went back to the hotel where we spent our wedding night, only this time I stayed in the bathroom and cried.
- The doctor gave me six months to live. I couldn't pay his bill, so the doctor gave me another six months.
- The doctor called Mrs Cohen, 'Mrs Cohen, your cheque came back.' Mrs Cohen answered, 'So did my arthritis!'
- I just got back from a pleasure trip. I took my mother-in-law to the airport.
- Q: Why do Jewish divorces cost so much? A: They're worth it.
- Q: Why do Jewish men die before their wives? A: They want to.

* * *

Bedtime games

Benjy and Hannah are in bed watching *Who Wants To Be A Millionaire?* when Benjy turns to Hannah and says, 'Do you want to have sex?'

'No,' she answers.

'Is that your final answer?' asks Benjy.

'Yes,' replies Hannah.

'Then I'd like to phone a friend,' says Benjy.

* * *

£35 is £35

Manny and his wife Ethel go to the Farnborough Air Display every year. Every year, Manny says, 'Ethel, I'd like to take a ride in a plane,' and every year she replies, 'I know, but a ride in a plane is expensive.'

At this year's Air Display, as Manny and Ethel are walking past the plane ride, Manny says, 'Ethel, I'm getting old. If I don't go up in that plane today, I'll never get another chance.'

Ethel replies, 'But Manny, that ride costs £35, and £35 is £35, you know.'

The pilot hears their conversation, 'Hey you two, I'll make a deal with you. I'll take you both up for a ride and if you can both stay absolutely silent for the entire trip, I won't charge you a thing. But if I hear just one sound, I'll charge you £35.'

Manny and Ethel talk it over and agree to the offer. So up they go.

The pilot tries very hard to get them to shout out in fear – he puts the plane in a series of dives; he twists and turns the plane at speed; he even rolls the plane on its back, but he doesn't hear a sound from his elderly passengers.

When they land, the pilot turns to Manny and says, 'You're very brave, I tried everything to make you shout out aloud, but you didn't utter a word.'

Manny replies, 'Thanks. To be honest, I was going to say something when Ethel fell out, but £35 is £35 you know....'

* * *

The famous writer
Benny is on holiday in Israel and goes to a concert at the Minkovsky Auditorium. When he gets to his seat, he looks around and is very impressed with the architecture and the acoustics.

After the concert is over, Benny asks one of the officials, 'I was wondering whether this magnificent auditorium is named after Dovid Minkovsky, the famous biblical scholar?'

'No,' replies the official, 'It's named after Harry Minkovsky, the writer.'

'I've never heard of him,' says Benny, 'what did he write?'

'A cheque,' replies the official.

* * *

Moshe's 18 questions
Here is a well-known riddle. Q: What is a genius? A: An average pupil with a Jewish mother.

OK, so you're a genius. But how smart do you think you are without your mother's help?

Write down the answers to the following 18 questions, then check your answers with those given at the end of these questions. Will you still be a genius?

1. 'Do they have a 4th of July in England?'
2. 'How many birthdays does the average Jewish man have?'
3. 'If some months have 31 days, how many months have 28?'

4. 'Why can't Jewish men living in London be buried in Jerusalem?'

5. 'Is it legal for a Jewish man living in Tel Aviv to marry his widow's sister?'

6. 'Moshe and Abe play five games of tennis. Each wins the same number of games. There are no ties. How can this be so?'

7. 'Divide 30 by 1/2 and add 10. What's the answer?'

8. 'Moshe builds a house rectangular in shape and all sides have a southern exposure. Moshe asks, "If a big bear walks by the house, what colour is it?"'

9. 'If Moshe has three apples and you take away two, how many do you have?'

10. 'Moshe has two US coins totalling 55 cents. One is not a nickel. What are the coins?'

11. 'Moshe has only one match and he walks into a room where there is an unlit gas fire, an oil lamp and a fireplace with dry wood in it. Which one does Moshe light first?'

12. 'How far can my dog run into the woods?'

13. 'Moshe's doctor gives him three pills and tells him to take one every half hour. How long do Moshe's pills last?'

14. 'Moshe has 17 sheep and all but 11 die. How many sheep does Moshe have left?'

15. 'How many animals of each sex did Moses take on the ark?'

16. 'Moshe works as an assistant in Minkoff Butchers and is 5 foot 10 inches tall. What does he weigh?'

17. 'How many 12p stamps are there in a dozen?'

18. 'What was the prime minister's name in 1950?'

* * *

Answers to Moshe's 18 questions

1. Yes, but it's not celebrated
2. One, all the rest are anniversaries of his birthday.
3. All 12 of them have at least 28 days
4. They can't be buried if they aren't dead.
5. No, because if his wife is a widow, then he's dead.
6. They aren't playing each other.
7. 70.
8. White. The house is at the North Pole so it is a polar bear.
9. Two.
10. 50 cent piece and a nickel. (The other one is a nickel.)
11. The match.
12. Halfway. Then he is running out of the woods.
13. One hour.
14. 11.
15. None – Noah took them on the ark.
16. Meat.
17. 12.
18. Same as it is now.

* * *

Well organised

Ruth is visiting the local shopping centre when she meets Esther. It's the first time they've met since leaving school and they quickly get talking. Ruth says, 'You were always so well organised in school, Esther, so I'm wondering, are you now living the well-planned life you always said you would?'

'Oh yes, Ruth, I certainly am,' replies Esther. 'My first marriage was to a multi-millionaire property developer; my second marriage was to a West End musical star; my third marriage was to Rabbi Levy, and at present I'm married to the chairman of The United Synagogue Burial Society.'

'But I don't understand, Esther,' says Ruth. 'What on earth do your marriages have to do with a well-planned life?'

'Well it's easy really,' replies Esther. 'It's…one for the money, two for the show, three to get ready, and four to go.'

* * *

Memories

Joseph is thrilled to be taking Bracha, his 95-year-old mother, to see the hit show *Fiddler on the Roof*. He's excited not only because Bracha hasn't seen it before, but also because she came to America in the late 1930s from one of the many Anatevka-like Russian *shtetls*.

Not only does Joseph book the most expensive seats in the theatre, but he also buys Bracha some smart new clothes to wear. And on the night of the show, he even orders a stretch limo to take them there and back. He wants it to be a memorable evening and doesn't want to leave anything to chance.

On the night of the show, they arrive in style, take their seats and watch the performance. And as soon as the final curtain comes down, Joseph asks Bracha, 'Well Mom, what did you think of the show? Be honest. Did it bring back any memories for you?'

Bracha sits there for a while, then turns to Joseph and gives both a nod and a classic JMS (Jewish mother Shrug). 'Yes *bubbeleh*, it did,' she replies, 'but I really don't remember that much singing.'

* * *

Who's got talent?

Moshe is lucky enough to meet Arthur Rubinstein, the famous concert pianist, and within minutes of meeting him, Moshe persuades him to drop by his house to listen to his wonderful daughter Emma play the piano.

As soon as Emma finishes her favourite piano piece, she looks at Rubinstein and asks, 'So what do you think I should do now, Mr Rubinstein?'

Rubinstein immediately replies, 'I think you should get married.'

* * *

News story: competition winners

Really, it's true. Moshe and Sadie enter a competition where the first prize is a holiday for two in Israel. They've always wanted to go there, but they get the second prize of 'A year of passion'.

When they receive their prize, it turns out to be 365 condoms. Later, Moshe tells a reporter, 'I can't believe it. I'm 64 and I have a bad back. My wife Sadie has just had her hip replaced. If I was a young chap, still able to do the business, I suppose I'd be happy. But these days, I'm lucky if I get a stiff neck.'

He is now trying to sell his prize.

* * *

Thomashefsky Joke – 1

Boris Thomashefsky, a star of the Yiddish theatre, was as famous for his romantic pursuits as for his acting, and there was always an attractive woman waiting for him at the stage door. One night, the story goes, Thomashefsky went home with an alluring young lady. In the morning, he handed her a gift – two front-row tickets to that evening's performance. The young lady was evidently disappointed and she began to cry.

'What's wrong?' asked the actor in astonishment.

'Oh, Mr Thomashefsky,' she said. 'I'm very poor. I don't need tickets. I need bread!'

'Bread?' cried Thomashefsky. 'Thomashefsky gives tickets. You want bread? Sleep with a baker!'

* * *

Thomashefsky Joke – 2
In a small Yiddish theatre the great Boris Thomashefsky had a heart attack and died while acting in the middle of a scene. The stage manager came over and felt Thomashefsky's pulse and told the packed theatre that unfortunately the great man was indeed dead.

An old lady in the front row yelled up to the manager, 'Give him some chicken soup.' When she was ignored, she yelled even louder, 'Give him some chicken soup.'

To this the manager replied, 'Madam, I don't think you understand – the Great Thomashefsky is dead. What good will chicken soup do?'

The old lady replied, 'What good? What harm?'

* * *

The following is just for you, dear reader
Dear reader

If you had great sex last night, please don't say anything to anyone, just smile.

Thank you.

PS: Did I catch you smiling just then?

* * *

A new TV programme – *Who Wants to be a Kosher Millionaire?*
You have three lifelines to help you as follows. You may call your rabbi for his opinion. You may ask the congregation for their opinion. You may consider your wife's opinion...or not! OK, so let's play, already.

Q: Who is Israel's favourite internet provider?

A: Netanyahoo.

Q: What's the name of the face lotion made especially for Becky?

A: Oil of *Oy veh*.

Q: What's the title of a horror film for Jewish women?

A: *Debby Does The Dusting*.

Q: What is the technical term for a divorced Jewish woman?

A: Plaintiff.

Q: In Jewish doctrine, when does a foetus become human?

A: When it wins a place in medical school.

Q: What does Sadie do to keep her hands soft and her nails long?

A: Nothing at all.

Q: Define 'genius'.

A: An average student with a Jewish mother.

Q: Why did the *mohel* retire?

A: He just couldn't cut it any more.

Q: If Tarzan and Jane were Jewish, what would Cheetah be?

A: A fur coat.

* * *

Here are some new reality TV shows to look out for

The Minyanaire: three nice, homely-looking young men go to an Orthodox singles event and tell the girls they match up with what they *daven* for every day. Watch one girl's reaction when she discovers that her man hasn't been inside a *shul* since his *Bar mitzvah* and spends every morning and afternoon at McDonald's.

The London Sheitel Fashion Show: Jewish women appear on the show wearing their *shabbes* head-coverings and viewers phone in to vote for the woman wearing the best-looking one.

The Schmeer Factor: in each episode, contestants compete to see who is the bravest by trying out some new bagel-and-cream-cheese combinations, such as shiitake mushroom bagels with lemon-and-Marmite-flavoured cream cheese or tortellini bagels with sheep's-brain-and-quince-flavoured cream cheese.

Meet My Parents (Don't): in each episode, three Jewish sons take their girlfriends home to meet their parents. But the catch is that one of the girlfriends is a *shiksa*. Parents try to guess which son is in an interfaith dating situation so they can throw him out of the house and threaten to sit *shivah* for him.

Jewish Survivor: the 10 participants attend rounds of Jewish fund-raising dinners. Each week, one participant is voted off the show for falling asleep during the guest speaker, or complaining about the chicken being dry, or eating three extra desserts, or changing seats so he doesn't have to sit with Mrs Levy, or snapping his fingers at the rabbi, who looks just like one of the waiters, etc. The final 'survivor' wins £100,000 – to be donated, of course, to his or her favourite Jewish charity.

Gamblers

The butcher

Shlomo walks into Harry Kosher Butchers, goes over to Harry and says, 'So, Harry, I hear that you're something of a betting man.'

'Yes,' replies Harry.

'Well,' says Shlomo, 'you're a tall man, so I bet you £50 that you can't reach those pieces of meat hanging on those hooks up on that wall.'

'I'm not taking your bet,' says Harry.

'Why not?' says Shlomo. 'I thought you were a betting man.'

'I am,' says Harry, 'but the steaks are too high!'

* * *

A betting man

Abe is reading the *Jewish Chronicle* when his wife Ruth walks up behind him and smacks him on the back of the head with her hand.

'What on earth was that for?' shouts Abe.

'That', she replies, 'was because I found a piece of paper in your pocket with the name "Judith Pasha" written on it.'

'You've got it all wrong, darling,' Abe says. 'Don't you remember last week when I went to Ascot races? Well, "Judith Pasha" was the name of one of the horses I bet on while I was there.'

Ruth gives a shrug and walks away muttering to herself.

A few days later, Abe is reading his *Times* newspaper when Ruth again walks up behind him and smacks him on the back of the head, but this time much harder.

'What was that for?' Abe shouts, rubbing the back of his head.

Ruth replies, 'Your horse just called.'

Inventors

Moshe's three inventions

Moshe is an inventor, or at least he thinks he is. After spending many months in his study working on his latest ideas, he rings the Patent Office and books an appointment. When he arrives, the receptionist greets him, 'Good morning Mr Levy. I see you're booked to meet with one of our consultants to discuss your three new inventions. Before you do so, however, I have to fill in this form. I only need to ask you some basic questions. Is that OK with you?'

'Yes, it's fine, thank you,' replies Moshe.

After asking Moshe the usual questions, such as name, address, nationality and age, the receptionist goes on to ask, 'And what is your first invention, Mr Levy?'

'I've invented a folding bottle,' replies Moshe, proudly.

'And do you have a name for it?' she asks.

'Yes, I call it a Fottle,' replies Moshe.

'And what's your second invention?' she asks, smiling ever so slightly.

'I've invented a folding carton,' replies Moshe.

'And what do you call that?' she asks.

'I call it a Farton,' replies Moshe.

At that, she can't help laughing as she says, 'If I may say so, Mr Levy, those are rather silly names for new products. And the name of your carton is a bit rude too.'

Moshe is not prepared to take any further ridicule from her and walks out of the office. He doesn't even tell her about his third invention, his folding bucket.

Magic Arts

The mermaid

It's Sunday morning, and as usual, Abe, Issy and Benny are out fishing. Suddenly, Benny catches a mermaid. The mermaid begs him to set her free. In return, she will grant each of them a wish.

Abe doesn't believe her and says, 'If you can really grant wishes, double my IQ.'

The mermaid says, 'Done.'

Shazzam. Abe starts reciting Shakespeare flawlessly and analyses what he's recited with great insight.

Issy is amazed and says to the mermaid, 'Triple my IQ.'

The mermaid says, 'Done.'

Shazzam. Issy starts to spout solutions to problems that have been puzzling the greatest scientists of the world – the mathematicians, atomic physicists and chemists.

Benny sees the changes in his friends, so he says to her, 'Quintuple my IQ.'

The mermaid looks at him with a worried look and says, 'You know, I normally don't try to change people's minds when they make a wish, but in this case, I really think you should reconsider. You just don't know what you're asking for. It will change your entire view of life as you now know it. Please, ask for something else. Ask for £1 million and I'll give it to you. Ask for anything, please.'

Benny replies, 'I hear what you're saying but I'll take the chance. I want you to increase my IQ to five times its usual power. If you don't, I won't set you free.'

So the mermaid sighs and says, 'Done.'

Shazzam. Benny turns into a woman.

* * *

No help

Mary is woken from her sleep. There's a bat in her room, which must have got in through the open window. The bat swoops around the room and Mary watches in horror as it transforms itself into...a vampire.

'Oh my God,' she says, as she grips her pillow tightly.

As the vampire slowly approaches her, Mary remembers the cross around her neck. She grabs it, points it towards the vampire and with a trembling cry says, 'You can't come any closer. Look, I have a cross.'

The vampire looks Mary in the eye and says, 'Lady, *Es vet dir gornisht helfen*!' (It won't help you.)

* * *

The English lesson

Harry has reached 60 and for some reason seems to have lost the ability to make love to his wife Kitty. She is not amused and tells him, 'So get it sorted out already, Harry.'

Harry goes to see Dr Myers. Two weeks later, after many tests and some lotions, potions and powders, nothing has improved for poor Harry, so Dr Myers says, 'May I suggest that you go see Vivian Agra, someone I met recently at a doctors' convention. She's very nice and specialises in erectile problems using ancient Indian treatments.'

Harry goes to see Vivian and after a thorough examination, she says, 'I can help you.' She then takes some blue powder from a glass jar and throws it into a candle flame. There's a bright flash and Harry is suddenly covered with billowing blue smoke. When the smoke clears, Harry says, 'Is that it? I'm cured?'

Vivian replies, 'Sort of. Even though it's a powerful medicine, it's only given you the chance to make love once a year. To do that, all you have to do is say, "One, two, three" and you'll be able to "stay up" for as long as you want.'

'But,' asks Harry, 'what happens when it's over and I don't want to continue?'

'All you or your wife has to do,' replies Vivian, 'is say "One, two, three, four" and it will "go down". But I must warn you – you won't be able to enjoy another erection for 12 months.'

When Harry gets home, he has a wide smile on his face as he tells Kitty, 'It's done. You just wait until tonight, my little sex kitten.'

That night he gets ready for the main event. He showers, shaves and smears on his expensive aftershave. As he gets into bed with Kitty, he says, "One, two, three." Immediately, he becomes more aroused than ever before, exactly as Vivian predicted. But as he climbs on top of Kitty, she says to him, 'What did you say "One, two, three" for?'

(And now you know why you shouldn't end a sentence with a preposition.)

* * *

A few kind words

Moshe walks into the bar at his golf club, sits down and orders a whisky. As he sips his drink, he hears a soothing voice say, 'Nice tie, Moshe.'

He looks around but notices that there is no one else in the room except for himself and the barman. A few sips later, another voice says, 'Beautiful shirt, Moshe.'

Moshe calls over the bartender. 'I must be losing my mind,' he says. 'I keep hearing voices saying nice things to me yet there's no one in here except the two of us.'

'It's the peanuts, Moshe,' says the barman, smiling.

'What on earth are you talking about? Are you *meshugga*?' says Moshe.

'It's the peanuts,' repeats the barman, 'they're complimentary.'

Some Naughtier Jokes

Far reaching

Three senior citizens – Sarah, Becky and Estelle – are sitting on a park bench having a quiet chat when a flasher approaches. He walks up to the bench, stands right in front of them and all of a sudden, with a loud shout, 'Aha!' he opens his raincoat.

Sarah immediately has a stroke. Becky also has a stroke. But Estelle, who is much older and feebler than the other two, can't reach that far.

* * *

Another clever answer

Rivkah, an experienced teacher, reminds her class of the following day's final exam. 'Now class, I won't tolerate any excuses for you not being here tomorrow. I'll only consider a nuclear attack or a serious personal injury or a death in your immediate family, but nothing else, no other excuses whatsoever.'

Lawrence, sitting at the back of the class, raises his hand and asks, 'What would you say, teacher, if tomorrow I said I couldn't come in because I was suffering from complete and utter sexual exhaustion?'

The entire class does its best to stifle its laughter. When silence is restored, Rivkah smiles sympathetically at the student, shakes her head, and replies, 'Well, Lawrence, I guess I'd say you'd have to write the exam with your other hand.'

* * *

A good sex life

Sadie and Becky are having coffee one morning while discussing life in general. 'So how long have you and Harold been married, Becky?' asks Sadie.

'Next week, please God, it will be twenty-five years,' replies Becky.

'That's a long time, Becky,' says Sadie. 'How's your sex life been all this time?'

'It's been OK,' replies Becky, 'especially the S&M.'

'You're really into S&M?' asks Sadie with surprise.

'Oh yes,' replies Becky, 'Harold and I have been into S&M for some time now – he snores and I masturbate.'

* * *

The staff of life

Moshe and Solly are in a shopping centre having a man-to-man chat. Moshe says, 'I'm so embarrassed to have to tell you Solly, but am I having trouble keeping up an erection.'

'You're in luck, Moshe,' says Solly, 'you're talking to the right man on this one. I have just the solution for you – eat a lot of rye bread. It worked for me.'

After they leave, Moshe thinks about what Solly has said and although he doesn't really believe it, he decides it wouldn't hurt to try it out. So he goes to the Grodzinski's bakery and says to the lady behind the counter, 'I'll take a large loaf of your rye bread, please.'

'Do you want it sliced?' she asks.

'What's the difference?' replies Moshe.

'Well,' she says, 'when it's sliced, it gets hard quicker.'

Moshe cries out aloud, '*Oy veh*, how come everybody knows about this but me?'

* * *

Familiar faces

Lionel and his wife Sharon have just done their weekly shopping at Marks & Spencer food hall and are now queuing to pay. Suddenly, remembering that she needs some money, Sharon leaves Lionel to pay while she goes outside to look for a cash dispenser.

Lionel pays for the food, but as he's wheeling the trolley outside the store, he sees a gorgeous woman smiling at him. Then, to his surprise, she says to him, 'Hello.'

He starts to think, 'She looks a bit familiar but I just can't place where I might know her from.' So Lionel replies, 'Hello. Do I know you?'

'I'm not sure,' she replies, 'I could be mistaken, but I think you might be the father of one of my children.'

Lionel is shocked and immediately starts thinking back to

the time of his one and only indiscretion. So, blushing heavily, he says to her, 'Oy veh, are you the lady I met some years back at my shul's Chanukah party when my wife was at home in bed with the flu? When you and I had too much Palwin wine to drink? Where we found a nice quiet room in the secretary's office and made great love, with you scratching my back with your nails in your excitement?'

There is a short pause.

'No, you've got the wrong woman,' she replies with a smile. 'I'm your son's science teacher!'

* * *

End of an affair?
Yitzhak comes home one day to find his wife Rivkah crying. 'What's the matter, darling?' asks Yitzhak.

'I've just found out that you've been having an affair with your secretary. How could you do this to me? Haven't I always been a good wife to you? Haven't I cooked for you, raised your children and always been by your side when you needed me? What have I done to make you unhappy?'

Yitzhak confesses, 'It's true, you really are the best wife a man could hope for. You make me happy in all ways – except one.'

'What's that?' asks Rivkah.

'You don't moan when we make love,' replies Yitzhak.

'Do you mean that if I did moan,' says Rivkah, 'you'd stop running around? In that case, let's go to bed now so I can show you that I can moan during lovemaking.'

So they go upstairs, get undressed and get beneath the sheets.

As they kiss, Rivkah asks, 'Now, Yitzhak, should I moan now?'

'No, not yet.'

Yitzhak begins fondling Rivkah. 'What about now? Should I moan now?'

'No, I'll tell you when.'

He climbs on top of Rivkah and they begin to make love.

'Is it time for me to moan, Yitzhak?'

'Wait, I'll tell you when.'

Then, seconds before reaching climax, Yitzhak yells, 'Now, Rivkah, moan.'

'*Oy veh, Yitzhak*! You wouldn't believe what a day I've just had!'

* * *

Sleeping problems

Leah has a problem with her Issy and goes to see her therapist. 'Doctor, I need your help with a serious problem. Whenever my Issy and I are in bed together, he always lets out a loud scream when he climaxes.'

'But that's quite common, Leah, in fact it's completely normal. There really isn't anything I can do.'

'But Doctor, my problem is that it wakes me up.'

* * *

Decisions, decisions

Sadie bumps into her friend Rachel while out shopping. 'You're looking very tired today, Rachel. Did you have a late night?'

'Yes,' replies Rachel, 'but it was all very strange. While doing some gardening yesterday, I found a lamp, so I rubbed it and out popped a genie. He gave me a choice of two wishes.'

'Wow, fantastic,' says Sadie, 'so what were the options he gave you, Rachel?'

'He said he could either give me an excellent, sharp, hundred-per-cent memory or else he could give my Issy a bigger penis.'

'So tell me already, Rachel, what did you choose?'

'I can't remember,' replies Rachel.

* * *

Inflation

Hannah has had a tiring day at the office and is now on her way home to Hendon. She gets on a tube train at Bank station and, as usual, is dismayed to find it packed. Everyone is squashed together like sardines. But this time, things get worse.

During the next 10 minutes, she becomes more and more aware of the man standing behind her – so much so that when the train reaches Euston, she turns to him and without attracting other passengers' attention, says, 'I can feel something hard rubbing against my backside. Please remove it.'

The man quietly replies, 'There's no need to get panicky. I got paid today and what you feel is a roll of £50 notes in my pocket.'

'So are you telling me that between Bank and Euston your salary doubled?' says Hannah.

* * *

Surprise in a lift

Moshe, just 5 feet tall, is in a lift on his own when, on the third floor, a giant of a man gets into the lift with him. He's so big that Moshe just can't help staring up at him. The giant sees Moshe staring at him and says, 'Yes, I'm big, aren't I? I'm 7 feet 3 inches, 330 pounds, 15-inch penis, two pounds each testicle, Turner Brown.'

Moshe says, '*Oy veh,*' and immediately faints to the floor. The giant kneels down and starts to gently slap Moshe's face and shake him. When Moshe gains consciousness, the giant asks him, 'Is there anything wrong with you?'

In a croaky voice, Moshe replies, 'What exactly did you say to me just before?'

The giant replies, 'I saw the look on your face when you first saw me and thought I'd give you answers to the questions going through your mind. So I told you I'm 7 feet 3 inches tall, weigh 330 pounds, have a 15-inch penis, each of my testicles weighs two pounds and my name is Turner Brown.'

Moshe says, 'Thank goodness, I thought you said, "Turn around."'

* * *

The warning

Issy, Benny and Howard went everywhere together. They were not only friends but also three very different people. Issy was an alcoholic, Benny was a heavy smoker and Howard was gay. However, over the years, all three became desperately ill, so one day they decided to see a doctor to discuss their options.

The doctor examined each one in turn and when he had written up his notes, he looked up and with a very serious look on his face, addressed all three of them. He said, 'It's very clear to me that if you continue to indulge in your abhorrent vices, even just once, you will die. Please believe me, I know what I'm talking about.'

Each one left the surgery determined never again to indulge in his vice. However, on their way home, they passed a wine bar. Issy heard the loud music, he smelled the drink and without thinking, led his friends inside and ordered a glass of wine. As soon as he had finished the drink, he fell dead on the floor.

Benny and Howard were totally shaken when they left the bar. They now realised more than ever the seriousness of their doctor's warning.

As they continued home, Benny saw a cigarette end lying in the gutter. It was still alight but before Benny could do anything, Howard put his hand on Benny's shoulder and said, 'You know, if you bend down to pick up that cigarette end, we're both dead.'

* * *

Slippery customer
Ruth was having a conversation with her best friend Sadie.
'Do you know what happened last night, Sadie? Mine Abe
walks into our bedroom and gives me a tube of KY Jelly.'

'Why did he do that?' asks Sadie.

'Well, he told me he bought it for me to make me happy.
But immediately he gave it to me, he goes downstairs to
watch football on TV. What a *chutzpah*, and me with my new
sheets.'

'But did it work?' asks Sadie.

'Yes, Abe was right – it did make me happy. When he left
the room, I squeezed it over the bedroom door handle and
mine Abe couldn't get back in.'

* * *

Definition of a Jewish ménage-à-trois
Two headaches and a hard-on.

* * *

A useful hobby
Rose is talking to her friend Sharon. 'Did you know, Sharon,
that I've been married three times?'

'No I didn't,' replies Sharon. 'Did you love all three of your
husbands equally?'

'No I didn't,' replies Rose. 'My first husband Alan was a
gynaecologist, but he would only look at it. My second
husband Henry was a psychiatrist, but he would only talk to
it. But I loved my third husband David the best. He was a
stamp collector.'

* * *

Yiddish story

Fay and Ethel are two *alte maidel shvesters* (old sisters), both of whom are virgins. One evening, Fay says to Ethel, '*Ich vilt nish shtarben a virgin*' (I don't want to die a virgin). *Ich gayen arum and ich nist kimpt ahaim until I've been shtupped*' (I'm going out and I'm not coming home until I've been laid).

Ethel replies, 'Vell OK, but make sure you're home by 10 o'clock so I shouldn't vurry about you.'

Ten o'clock comes and goes and there's no sign of Fay, then 11 o'clock and midnight. Finally, just after 1 o'clock in the morning, the front door opens and in walks Fay. She heads straight for the bathroom.

Ethel is worried so she knocks on the bathroom door and shouts, '*Do bist goot, Fay?*' (Are you OK Fay?)

No answer, so she opens the bathroom door and sees Fay sitting there with her panties around her ankles, legs *ousgashprait* (wide apart) and her head stuck between her legs looking in her '*knish*' (you figure it out!).

'*Vous is de mair?*' (What's the matter?) asks Ethel.

Fay replies, 'It vuz ten inches long ven it vent in and only five inches ven it *kimpt oise* (came out). Ven I find the other half, Ethel, you too can have the time of your life.'

* * *

Money first

Sadie and Becky have been best of friends for some time. Then, one day in the local shopping centre, Sadie notices that Becky is not only wearing new gold and diamond jewellery but also the latest in designer clothes. She's also had her hair done immaculately and her nails are well manicured. So she says, 'Becky, how come all this new gear? Where did you find the money?'

'I get my extra money by charging mine Issy £5 every time we have sex,' Becky replies.

'Wow,' says Sadie.

'And you can do the same with your Benny,' says Becky. 'It really adds up quickly, but you must remain firm, you mustn't let him talk you into accepting less and you must never let him coax you into doing it for nothing.'

'OK,' says Sadie, 'that sounds easy enough. I'll start tonight. Benny will certainly be surprised.'

That night, when Benny is ready to make love, Sadie says to him, 'From now on, darling, you'll always have to give me £5 before we have sex.' She then tells him why.

'Oh, I see,' he says and gets out of bed to get the money. But he quickly realises that he has only £4 in his wallet.

Sadie refuses to accept it. 'Rules are rules,' she says. 'If you want sex, you'll have to give me the full amount – £5.'

'All right,' says Benny, 'so we can't have sex. But can I touch you for £4? We'll just make out, OK?'

'OK,' says Sadie.

Benny starts to kiss her and fondle her body. He rubs against her, and engages in the usual foreplay. Quickly, Sadie starts to get hot and bothered and finally she's so turned on that she says, 'If it's all right with you, Benny, I'll lend you the £1 until tomorrow.'

* * *

Forgotten ticket

Arnold leaves for a two-day business trip to Paris. As he's walking to the station, he realises that he's left his British Airways ticket on the bed. So he returns and quietly enters the house.

There in the kitchen is his Ruth. She's wearing her skimpiest negligee and she's standing at the sink washing the breakfast dishes. She looks so inviting that Arnold tiptoes up behind her, reaches out, and squeezes her right breast.

'Leave only one pint of milk,' she says without turning, 'Arnold won't be here for breakfast tomorrow.'

* * *

The photographer

Shlomo and Sadie have been unable to have children and in desperation decide to use a proxy father to start their family. On the day the proxy father is to arrive, Shlomo kisses Sadie and says, 'He should be here soon so I'd better be off.'

But just after Shlomo leaves, a door-to-door baby photographer calls at their house hoping to make a sale. 'Good morning madam. You don't know me but I've come to....'

'There's no need to explain,' says Sadie, 'I've been expecting you. Do come in.'

'Oh, really?' says the photographer. 'Well then, let me say that I've made a specialty of babies.'

'That's what my husband and I had hoped,' says Sadie, blushing. 'So where do we start?'

'Leave everything to me,' says the photographer, 'I usually try two in the bath, one on the armchair and perhaps a couple on the bed. On the floor is fun too – you can really spread out.'

'In the bath, on the floor? No wonder it didn't work for me,' says Sadie.

'Well, madam,' says the photographer, 'none of us can guarantee a good one every time. But if we try several different positions and I shoot from six or seven angles, I'm sure you'll be pleased with the results.'

'I hope we can get this over with quickly,' gasps Sadie.

'Madam,' says the photographer, 'in my line of work, a man must take his time. I'd love to be in and out in five minutes, but you'd be disappointed with that, I'm sure.'

'Don't I know it!' Sadie exclaims.

The photographer opens his briefcase and takes out a portfolio of his baby pictures. 'This was done on the top of a bus in Hampstead, London.'

'Oh my God,' says Sadie.

'And these twins turned out exceptionally well when you consider their mother was difficult to work with,' says the photographer, as he hands Sadie the picture.

'What do you mean she was difficult?' asks Sadie.

'Well, I had to take her to Hyde Park to get the job done right,' he replies, 'and people were crowding around us five deep to get a good look.'

'Five deep?' says Sadie, with her eyes wide open in shock.

'Yes,' the photographer says, 'and it lasted for four hours with the mother constantly squealing and yelling. I could hardly concentrate. Then darkness approached and I began to rush my shots. Finally, when the squirrels began nibbling on my equipment, I just packed up and left.'

'Your...equipment?' says Sadie.

'That's right. Well if you're ready, I'll set up my tripod and we can get to work.'

'Tripod?' says Sadie, looking extremely worried.

'Oh yes, I have to use a tripod to rest my Canon on. It's much too big for me to hold while I'm getting ready for action. Madam? Madam? Oh dear, she's fainted!'

* * *

The professionals
Maurice, Isaac and Hannah are sitting at a bar in the heart of London's financial district – the City – talking about their professions.

Maurice says, 'I'm a yuppie. You know – young, urban, professional.'

Isaac says, 'I'm a dink. You know – double income, no kids.'

They then turn to Hannah and say, 'And you?'

She replies, 'I'm a wife. You know – wash, iron, fuck, etc.'

* * *

The Rabbi's cough drops

It's bitterly cold outside the *shul*. Inside, Rabbi Bloom is getting fed up with the constant coughing that's disturbing his sermon, so after the service ends, he goes over to old Hyman the *shammes* and tells him that he needs his help to solve the problem. Rabbi Bloom tells Hyman to have a large bowl of cough drops ready in *shul* for his next sermon and instructs him to give one cough drop to any *shul* member who begins coughing.

So next *shabbes*, during the rabbi's sermon and following orders, every time a member coughs, Hyman walks over and hands out a cough drop. Rabbi Bloom watches this out of the corner of his eye and notices that each time Hyman does this, the member immediately gets up and walks out of the *shul*. At the end of the service, half the members are gone, so Rabbi Bloom goes over to Hyman and asks, '*Nu*, Hyman? So what did you say to the members that made them leave the *shul*?'

Hyman replies, 'So vat did I say? All that I said wuz, "The rabbi said for cough."'

* * *

Bubbeh's first cruise

Ethel, an 80-year-old *bubbeh*, is going on her first cruise, courtesy of her children and grandchildren. As she boards the ship, Ethel shows her ticket to the purser. He looks at it and says, 'Oh, I see you have UD.'

'UD? Voos is UD?' asks Ethel.

'UD is Upper Deck,' replies the purser.

Ethel goes to the upper deck and when she shows her ticket to the purser there, he says, 'I see that in addition to UD, you also have OC.'

'OC? Voos is OC?' asks Ethel.

'OC is Outside Cabin,' replies the purser.

Ethel is delighted. She goes down the corridor and when she shows her ticket to the cabin boy, he says, 'Oh, I see that you also have BIB.'

'BIB? Voos is BIB?' asks Ethel.

'BIB is Breakfast In Bed,' replies the cabin boy.

'*Oy-yoy-yoy*,' says Ethel, 'mine children and grandchildren are vonderful.'

Next morning, bright and early, two waiters enter Ethel's room with trays of food for her breakfast in bed. She wakes up with a start, looks at them and says, 'FUCK.'

Shocked, one of them asks, 'FUCK? What do you mean FUCK?'

'FUCK is Foist U Could Knock,' replies Ethel.

* * *

The powerful desire

Yossel Abramovitz works in a pickle factory. Unfortunately, he suddenly develops a very powerful desire to put his *shlong* in the pickle slicer. After three months of restraint, Yossel can't stand it any more and decides to seek professional help for this infatuation of his. He then spends many sessions with a psychiatrist who finally gives up on him.

'Yossel,' says the psychiatrist, 'because your desire to put your penis in the pickle slicer is so powerful, the only way to get over it is to actually do it.'

'OK,' says Yossel, 'I'll do it first thing tomorrow morning at work. I promise.'

And next day, Yossel does what he promised. But at 11am, he arrives back at his house. This worries his wife Sarah and she asks him why he's home so early. Yossel tells her for the first time about his desire; that he couldn't take it any more, and that today he did it and got fired as a result.

Sarah gasps, runs over to him, pulls down his trousers and pants – and sees his *shlong* perfectly normal and intact. She looks up at him and says, 'I don't understand, Yossel, what happened to the pickle slicer?'

'She got fired too,' replies Yossel.

* * *

What an ass

Sidney goes to Dr Myers for a check-up and returns home with a thermometer. His wife Miriam asks him, 'So what's with the thermometer, darling?'

'Dr Myers says I must put it in my rectum, but I don't know what he means,' he replies.

'Well I don't know either,' says Miriam, 'so call him and ask.'

'Isn't it a bit late to call the doctor?' asks Sidney.

'But you've no choice,' says Miriam.

So Sidney calls the doctor. When he puts the phone down, Miriam asks, 'So what did he say?'

'The doctor told me to put it in my anus,' replies Sidney.

They are now both *farfufket* as to what an anus is.

'So call him again,' says Miriam.

'But it's very late already,' says Sidney, 'I'm sure he's going to be mad.'

'Maybe, but please call him and ask him,' insists Miriam.

So very reluctantly Sidney calls Dr Myers yet again and after a very brief conversation puts down the phone.

'So what did he say this time?' asks Miriam.

'See, I told you he'd be *broyges*,' replies Sidney, 'he shouted at me and told me to shove it up my arse.'

* * *

The dumb father

As part of his growing-up process, Isaac and Renee take their six-year-old son Aaron to a nudist beach. As Isaac and Aaron take a walk along the sands, Aaron notices that many of the women have boobs bigger than his mum's, so he runs back to ask her why.

'The bigger they are, Aaron, the sillier the lady is,' explains Renee.

Aaron is pleased with her answer and goes away to play. But five minutes later he returns to tell Renee that many of the men have larger things than his dad has.

'The bigger they are, Aaron, the dumber the man is,' explains Renee.

He is again very pleased with her answer and goes back to play.

Five minutes later, Aaron is back again and promptly tells Renee, 'Mum, Dad is talking to the silliest lady on the beach and the longer he talks to her, the dumber he gets.'

* * *

The real thing

Jonathan and Talia are celebrating their 20th wedding anniversary. In all those 20 years, every time they've make love, Jonathan has insisted they do it with the light off. Talia thinks it's all to do with his not wanting to be seen naked. But today, on their anniversary, she decides to try to rid him of his embarrassment – she really believes that she can cure him of his habit. That night, while they're having a great *shtup*, Talia suddenly turns on the bedside lamp and sees Jonathan with a vibrator in his hand – a soft, penis-shaped one, but much larger than the real thing. She is shocked and very, very angry.

'You impotent *momzer*,' she screams at him, 'how could you have lied to me all these years? You'd better explain or you won't see me again.'

Jonathan looks at her and calmly says, 'OK. I'll explain the vibrator…you explain our children.'

* * *

At the tattoo parlour

Miriam goes into a tattoo parlour in Tel Aviv and says to the artist on duty, 'I'd like the words "Happy Purim" tattooed on my right thigh please, just below my bikini line.'

'Of course, madam,' he says, 'anything else?'

'Yes,' replies Miriam, 'put a picture of a *hamentash* underneath the words.'

'No problem,' he says, 'will that be all?'

'No,' replies Miriam. 'On my other thigh, also just below my bikini line, I'd like the words, "Happy Pesach" with a picture of a *matzo* underneath the words.'

So the artist gets going and some time later completes his work of art. The tattoos look great. As Miriam is getting dressed, he says to her, 'I don't mean to pry, but why did you want such unusual tattoos on your thighs?'

'Because I'm fed up with my husband always complaining that there's nothing good to eat between *Purim* and *Pesach*,' she replies.

* * *

His new shoes

Abe, a *shlemiel*, walks to work every day and each day stops to look in the window of a shoe shop to admire a particular pair of Giovani hand-made black leather shoes. Every time he sees them, he falls more in love with them. To him they look fantastic – they're shiny, stylish and very, very expensive. He says to himself, 'They might be expensive, but the girls will just love me in these shoes. I must have them.'

Two months later, he's saved the £400 for the shoes and

buys them. He then wears them for the first time at his *shul*'s Sunday Singles Dance. During the evening, he asks Judith to dance with him. As they dance he says, 'Judith, I bet you're wearing red knickers.'

Startled, Judith replies, 'Yes, I'm wearing red knickers. How did you know?'

Abe replies, 'I saw their reflection in my new £400 Giovani leather shoes.'

Later, he asks Leah to dance with him. As they dance he asks, 'Leah, I bet you're wearing blue knickers.'

Startled, Leah replies, 'Yes, I'm wearing blue knickers. How did you know?'

Abe replies, 'I saw their reflection in my new £400 Giovani leather shoes.'

Later on, as the end of the evening grows near and the last song is being played, Abe asks Ruth to dance with him. As they are dancing, Abe's face turns bright red. He says, 'Ruth, I'm very worried. I don't think you're wearing any knickers tonight. Please tell me if I'm right.'

'Yes Abe,' replies Ruth with a naughty smile, 'it's true – I'm not wearing any knickers tonight.'

Abe utters a sigh of relief and says, 'Thank God. I thought I had a crack in my new £400 Giovani leather shoes.'

* * *

The *chassid*'s dilemma

A *chassid* is standing near his hotel's reception desk about an hour before *shabbes*, all dressed up in his special *shabbes* clothes, when an utterly gorgeous blonde El Al air hostess checks in. As she starts to walk towards the lifts, she sees the *chassid* and stops dead in her tracks. She walks quickly over to him and with a big friendly smile says, 'Hello.'

'Hello to you too,' he replies.

'I have a confession to make to you,' she says.

'Really?' he asks.

'Yes really,' she says. 'I have a sexual fantasy.'

'What kind?' he asks.

'I've always wanted to be with a *chassidic* man,' she says. 'I want to run my hands over his *tzitzit*, twirl his *peyess*, take off his *gatkes*, squeeze his *hinten*, and cradle his *baitsim*. In fact I want to *yentz* right now. I have a room upstairs, so will you join me right now for half an hour of excitement?'

He looks at her thoughtfully and replies, '*Vemen bares du*?' (What's in it for me?)

* * *

The prize toast

Hymie's golf club is giving a prize for the best toast of the evening. When it's Hymie's turn, he raises his glass and says, 'Here's to spending the rest of my life between the legs of my wife!'

And that wins him the top prize and everyone at the club congratulates him. When he returns home, he tells his wife Sadie, 'Guess what, darling? I won the prize for the best toast of the night.'

'That's nice,' says Sadie, 'So tell me already. What was your toast?'

Hymie replies, 'Here's to spending the rest of my life sitting next to my wife in *shul*.'

'Oh Hymie,' says Sadie, 'that's a really beautiful toast.'

The next day, as she's going to the local supermarket, Sadie meets one of Hymie's golf club friends. When he sees her, he smiles in a leery fashion and says, 'Hi Sadie. Did Hymie tell you he won first prize last night with a toast about you?'

'Yes he did tell me,' replies Sadie. 'But I was a bit surprised because he's only been there twice in the last six months. The first time he fell asleep, and the second time, on *Yom Kippur*, I had to pull him by the ears to make him come.'

* * *

Can you see this?

Leah goes to see Doctor Levy, a Harley Street optician, for an eye test. After asking Leah some basic questions, Dr Levy holds up a chart and says, 'Can you read the letters on this chart, Leah?'

'No,' replies Leah.

Dr Levy holds up another chart, this time with bigger letters. 'Can you see the letters on this chart, Leah?'

Again, Leah replies, 'No.'

So Dr Levy holds up yet another chart, this one has very large letters, and asks Leah, 'So, Leah, you must be able to see these letters?'

But once again Leah replies, 'Sorry, but I can't.'

Feeling very exasperated, Dr Levy takes out his *shlong* in front of Leah and asks, 'Can you see this, Leah?'

'*Oy veh*,' says Leah, 'that I can see very clearly.'

'Well that's your problem, then,' says Dr Levy, 'you're cock-eyed.'

* * *

Dog tricks

Aaron and Lionel are good friends and meet in the local shopping mall for a chat. Soon they are talking about their wives. 'Would you mind, Aaron,' asks Lionel, 'if I ask you a very intimate question?'

'Of course not,' replies Aaron, 'you're my friend.'

'OK,' says Lionel, 'tell me – do you and your lovely Rebecca ever make love "doggy style"?'

'Well not exactly,' replies Aaron, 'Mine Rebecca is much more into the dog tricks aspect of lovemaking.'

'Oh, I see,' says Lionel, 'she's a bit kinky, is she?'

'Well, not exactly,' replies Aaron, 'I sit up and beg and she rolls over and pretends to be dead.'

* * *

When Miriam met Arnold

Miriam meets Arnold at her Israeli dance class and they agree to see each other again at the weekend. When they meet, they get on so well that she invites him back to her flat. After a few drinks, things begin to get very steamy – and that's when Miriam starts to notice some odd behaviour in Arnold. First of all, as soon as he takes off his shirt, he goes straight into the kitchen and washes his hands. Then five minutes later, as soon as he takes off his trousers, he again goes into the kitchen and washes his hands.

'I bet you're a dentist,' says Miriam, who always likes to speak her mind.

This surprises Arnold. 'Yes, I am,' he replies. 'How did you come to that conclusion?'

'Oh, it was easy,' replies Miriam, smiling, 'you keep on washing your hands. Now let's get into bed.'

After they finish making love, Miriam turns to Arnold and says, 'You must be an extremely good dentist.'

'Well…yes I am,' says Arnold, modestly, 'how did you know?'

'Because I didn't feel a thing,' replies Miriam.

* * *

Moshe the *Jokenik*

Moshe the *Jokenik* is an official in King Arthur's court, but unfortunately for Moshe, he's got an obsession with the beautiful Queen Guinevere's breasts. He wants to touch them, even to kiss them, but Moshe is not *meshugga*. He knows that the penalty for doing this is – *oy veh* – death by a thousand cuts.

One day, Moshe reveals his secret desire to his friend, Aaron the Doctor, who is King Arthur's senior physician. When Aaron learns of Moshe's problem, he comes up with a great idea to make himself some money. 'I think I can help you satisfy your desire, Moshe,' he says, 'but it will cost you a hundred gold nuggets. What do you think?'

'If the idea is good,' replies Moshe, 'then I'll pay you. What's your scheme?'

When Aaron finishes explaining, Moshe instantly agrees.

Next morning, Aaron makes some itching powder and while Queen Guinevere is taking a bath, pours a little powder into her 36D bra cups. When she later gets dressed, she starts to itch and the itching grows more intense by the minute. When Aaron is summoned to her room, he examines her and then informs the King, 'Your Majesty, to cure the Queen's problem, she needs a special kind of saliva to be applied to her breasts for 30 minutes.'

'And where are we to get this special saliva?' asks King Arthur.

'I know from one of my earlier tests,' replies Aaron, 'that only fresh saliva from Moshe the *Jokenik* is going to work.'

Moshe arrives soon after being summoned. He has the real antidote to the itching powder hidden neatly inside his mouth. Then his dream comes true – for the next 30 minutes, he has his mouth on Queen Guinevere's breasts and when her itching finally goes, Moshe leaves in a state of ecstasy.

When he returns to his room, Aaron is waiting for him. 'I've come for my hundred gold nuggets.'

But with his obsession now satisfied, Moshe is no longer willing to keep his side of the bargain. 'I don't think what you did was anything special, nor did it cost you much money. So here are ten gold nuggets. Please now leave, the matter is closed.'

Moshe knows, of course, that Aaron can never report this treachery to King Arthur. But the next day, Aaron slips a large dose of itching powder into King Arthur's codpiece. Later, the King quickly summons Moshe the *Jokenik*.

The moral of this story is: 'Please pay your bills in full.'

* * *

EXCHANGE OF LETTERS: Part 1 – To my dear wife
During the past year I have tried to make love to you 365 times. I have succeeded 36 times, which is an average of once every 10 days. The following is a list of why I did not succeed more often:

- 54 times the sheets were clean
- 57 times it was too late
- 49 times you were too tired
- 20 times it was too hot
- 24 times you pretended to be asleep
- 22 times you had a headache
- 17 times you were afraid of waking the baby
- 16 times you said you were too sore
- 12 times it was the wrong time of the month
- 19 times you had to get up early
- 9 times you said weren't in the mood
- 7 times you were sunburned
- 6 times you were watching the late show
- 5 times you didn't want to mess up your new hair-do
- 3 times you said the neighbours would hear us
- 9 times you said your mother would hear us

Of the 36 times I did succeed, the activity was not satisfactory because:

- 6 times you just lay there
- 8 times you reminded me that the ceiling needs painting
- 4 times you told me to hurry up and get it over with
- 17 times I had to wake you and tell you I finished
- 1 time I was afraid I had hurt you because I felt you move

* * *

EXCHANGE OF LETTERS: Part 2 – To my dear husband
I think you have things a little confused. Here are the reasons
you didn't get more than you did:

- 41 times you did not come home that night
- 38 times you worked too late
- 10 times you got cramps in your toes
- 29 times you had to get up early to play golf
- 11 times you had a cold and your nose was running
- 20 times you lost the notion after thinking about it all day
- 107 times you were too busy watching football, baseball,
  etc on TV
- 33 times you came too soon
- 40 times you went soft before you got in

* * *

Do you have one of these?
Sixty-year-old Rivkah goes into her local sex shop. As soon
as she enters, everyone there notices how unstable she is on
her feet. Very shakily, she wobbles the few feet across the
shop to the counter, grabs it for support, and asks the
assistant behind the counter, 'D-d-d-o-o y-o-u-u-u s-e-l-l-l d-
d-i-i-l-l-d-o-s-s?'

The assistant, trying not to laugh, replies, 'Yes, we have
many different types of dildo in stock.'

'D-d-o-o y-y-o-u c-c-a-r-r-y a-a-a p-p-p-in-k-k o-n-n-e-e,
t-t-e-n inches-s-s-s l-l-long a-a-and a-a-b-b-o-u-t-t t-t-woo
inches-s-s th-th-ick-k?' asks Rivkah.

The assistant replies, 'Yes we do.'

'M-a-a-z-z-e-l-t-o-v-v-v. D-d-o-o y-y-ou kn-n-ow h-how t-
t-o t-t-u-r-r-r-n i-t-t-t o-f-f-f-f?'

* * *

A beautiful display

Sixty-five-year-old Hymie meets his 70-year-old friend Sidney in town one day. '*Nu*, what's new?' Sidney asks.

'*Oy*! You'll never believe what's happened to me,' replies Hymie.

'So tell me already,' says Sidney.

'I vent for a holiday last veek to Bournemouth,' says Hymie, 'and I found this place where all the girls do sometink. And I meet a beautiful lady there. And vat lovely *tsitskehs* she had. Then she takes me to see her room. As soon as ve're inside, she removes my trousers and pants and she…vell you know…she makes me hard. Then she sprays vipped cream from a can around my *putz*, shprinkles on some nuts and raisins, puts a glazed cherry on top and then…and then…'

'Go on Hymie,' says Sidney excitedly, 'so tell me what she did next.'

'She ate it all up,' replies Hymie.

'*Mazeltov*, you lucky old *momzer*,' says Sidney. 'I'm going to Bournemouth next week. Can you give me her name and phone number?'

'Of course, Sidney,' replies Hymie, 'for you, anything.'

A few weeks later they bump into each other again. '*Nu*,' Hymie asks, 'so vat happened on your holiday?'

'It was just like you told me,' replies Sidney. 'I get to Bournemouth, I ring her, she meets me, she takes me to her room, she takes off my trousers and pants, and she makes me hard. Then she sprays whipped cream around my *putz*, sprinkles on some nuts and raisins, puts a glazed cherry on top and then and then…oh Hymie, what a *groisser potz* I was, it looked so good that I ate it myself.'

* * *

A diaphragm riddle

Q: Why do Princesses wear gold diaphragms?

A: Because their husbands like coming into money.

The Universe

Leadership

Abe is sunbathing in his back garden one Sunday afternoon when a small spaceship appears out of nowhere and lands near him. A strange-looking spaceman gets out, walks over to Abe and says, 'Take me to your leader.'

'I can't,' replies Abe, 'mine Hetty is away with the grandchildren.'

* * *

The test for oxygen

At last, after a long journey, the landing module sets down safely on Mars. Within minutes, Gerry and John, the two astronauts on board, take their first steps on the planet. Their mission is very important to the future of mankind – they must check whether there is oxygen on the planet. Gerry says, 'OK, John, pass me the box of matches and I'll try to light one. It will either burn, in which case there's oxygen, or nothing will happen.'

Gerry takes the box from John, removes a match and is just about to strike it when a Martian suddenly appears in front of him waving his arms frantically. 'No, no, don't do that!' the Martian shouts at Gerry.

Gerry and John are puzzled. Could there be an unknown explosive gas on Mars that their module hasn't detected? Gerry doesn't think so, so he continues with his plan to strike the match. But now there's a whole group of Martians around him, all of them looking very serious and waving their arms.

'No, no,' they shout, 'please don't do that!'

'What are they afraid of?' John asks Gerry.

'I don't know,' replies Gerry, 'but we're here for the benefit of mankind and we've a job to do.'

So Gerry strikes the match. It instantly flares up, burns slowly down and then goes out. Nothing else happens. So Gerry turns round to the Martian leader and asks, 'Why didn't you want me to strike the match?'

The Martian leader replies, 'Because today is *shabbes*!'

Philosophers

The birthday presents

Because Luigi and Moshe live very close to each other in Milan and also share the same birthday, they grow up together. Luigi is the son of a jeweller and Moshe is, unfortunately, the son of a 'hit man'.

On their 14th birthdays, Luigi gets a Rolex watch and Moshe gets a gun. Next day, when they compare their presents, they decide that they like what the other has received – and so decide to swap gifts.

When Moshe goes home and shows his father his watch, his father is angry.

'What are you, nuts?' says his father. 'Let me tell you something, you idiot! One day you're gonna meet a nice girl and you're gonna wanna settle down with her and get married. You'll have some kids, all that stuff. Then one day, you're gonna come home early and find your wife in bed with another man. Then what the hell ya gonna do? Are you going to look at your watch and say, "Hey, how long you gonna be?" '

* * *

The helper

Maurice, a motivational consultant, is just getting into his car when a lovely woman walks up to him and says, 'Can you give me a lift, please?'

Maurice replies, 'Of course I can. You're beautiful, intelligent and there's nothing in the world you can't do. Go for it.'

* * *

The important discussion

Leah and Rose always meet every week at the local shopping centre and always end up having a light lunch there. One day over lunch, Leah says to Rose, 'All we ever seem to do is talk about the unimportant things in life. Today, for example, we've talked about the rudeness of our local kosher butcher, what the weather's like in Bournemouth, and our rabbi's recent poor sermon. Next time we meet, why don't we have a serious discussion on world affairs?'

'A good idea,' says Rose.

So the following week, while they are waiting for their lunch to arrive, Rose says, 'So let's talk already.'

Leah says, 'OK. What do you think about the situation with Red China?'

Rose replies, 'Not much – it won't go with your green tablecloth.'

* * *

Philosophical questions

Moshe believes himself to be a clever thinker, a philosopher, even. How do I know this? Well, he keeps on asking me questions such as:

- If man evolved from monkeys and apes, why do we still have monkeys and apes?
- Is there another word for synonym?
- What was the best thing before sliced bread?
- Do infants enjoy infancy as much as adults enjoy adultery?
- Why are haemorrhoids called 'haemorrhoids' instead of 'asteroids'?
- Why is there an expiry date on sour cream?

* * *

A question of noodles

Aharon asks his friend Monty, 'Tell me, Monty, you're a clever guy. This has been puzzling me for years. Why do we call noodles "noodles"?'

'Well,' says Monty, 'it's simple, really. They're soft like noodles, aren't they? They're also long like noodles, aren't they? And they certainly taste like noodles, don't they? So why shouldn't we call them noodles?'

* * *

Seeing double

As Morris and Sidney are walking down the street together, Sidney says, 'Morris, if you had two top-of-the-range Lexus cars, would you give me one?'

'Sidney,' replies Morris, 'we've been best friends for over 30 years now, ever since we left school, and if I had two top-of-the-range Lexus cars, yes, I would give one to you.'

They continue walking. After a couple of minutes, Morris

turns to Sidney and says, 'Sidney, if you had two luxury, playboy-type jet planes, would you give one of them to me?'

'Morris,' replies Sidney, 'you and I are like twins. You were my best man at my wedding and we've both attended the same *shul* for 30 years. So if I had two luxury, playboy-type jet planes, then yes, I would give one to you.'

They continue walking. A couple of minutes later, Sidney turns to Morris and says, 'Morris, if you had two 32" flat-screen HD-ready LCD televisions....'

'Hey, hold on a minute,' interrupts Morris, 'you know I've got two 32" TVs.'

* * *

The complainer

Morris and Isaac are constant companions. Morris is calm and laidback and never complains, whereas Isaac is a nervous person and is always complaining about something or another.

One day, Isaac says, 'How do you manage to get along so well with everyone you meet, Morris? I'd love to know.'

'Oh, that's easy,' replies Morris, 'I just never disagree with anyone.'

'Morris,' says Isaac angrily, 'I think you're a liar!'

'Don't I know it,' says Morris with a smile.

* * *

A philosophical thought

It's funny how 'big' £100 looks when you make a *shul* donation, but so 'small' when you spend it at the shopping centre.

* * *

Inner peace

Abe is talking to his friend. 'If there's one piece of simple advice I can give you, Mervyn, it's this. I read it in *The Times* yesterday and it worked immediately for me. I've finally found inner peace. I'm sure it will work for you too.'

'So give me this advice, already,' says Mervyn.

'OK, here it is,' replies Abe. 'The way to achieve inner peace is to finish all the things you've started.'

'Really?' says Mervyn.

'Yes,' replies Abe. 'I looked around to see all the things I had started but hadn't finished. So, I finished one bottle of Kiddush wine, a bottle of whisky, my Prozac, three bottles of Maccabi beer and a large box of organic chocolates. You have no idea how good I felt.'

Keeping Fit

The exercise class

Freda says to her daughter, 'Ever since I reached 65, Lisa, I'd been feeling that my body had gotten totally out of shape. So I made a big decision – I went to my doctor and got his OK to start doing some exercise. And yesterday I went to LA Fitness and booked into their aerobics class for seniors.'

'That was brave of you, Mum, So how did you get on?' asks Lisa.

'Well, for 30 minutes I sweated by bending, twisting, pulling, pushing and hopping up and down. But then, by the time I got my leotard on, the class was over.'

* * *

The new golf course

Maurice wakes up one morning feeling lousy. 'Becky, he shouts, 'I'm feeling terrible, I'm sore all over, what should I do?

'So go see Dr Myers,' she replies.

After a thorough examination, Dr Myers says, 'I am sorry to have to tell you this, Maurice, but I have bad news for you. You're very ill and in my opinion you don't have very long to live – anything from a few days to three months. I suggest you go home and make the necessary arrangements.'

Maurice is devastated.

Later that evening, after the crying is over, Maurice tells Becky that as he is a devoted golfer, he would like to be buried with his golf clubs. If there's a golf course in heaven, he would then have his clubs to play with.

But Becky says, 'Maurice, as neither of us knows if there is a golf club up in heaven, I think you should go see Rabbi Levy and ask for his opinion.'

Maurice goes to see Rabbi Levy. 'Rabbi, is there a golf course in heaven?'

Rabbi Levy says, 'I'll speak to God for you. Come back in a few days time.'

Two days later, Maurice returns. 'Rabbi, have you any news?'

Rabbi Levy says, 'Yes, Maurice, I have spoken to God and I have some good news and some bad news for you. The good news is that God says there is the most wonderful golf course you could imagine in heaven. The sun shines every day, 365 days a year, and you can play golf to your heart's content.'

Maurice says, 'That's wonderful news, Rabbi, but what's the bad news?'

Rabbi Levy replies, 'Tomorrow morning, 8 o'clock – you tee off.'

* * *

A round excuse

Benjy the dentist was also a golf fanatic and would often take time off work for a round of golf. One day, he told his secretary to cancel all his appointments. She was also to leave the following voice-mail message on his phone: 'Dr Benjamin is fully occupied today as he needs to fill 18 cavities. Please ring tomorrow for an appointment. Thank you.'

* * *

The fishing trip

Lionel, Benny, Max and Hyman are out fishing early one Sunday morning. After an hour of fishing, Lionel suddenly breaks the silence and says, 'You three have no idea what I had to do before I could come out fishing today. I had to promise my Rivkah that I would decorate our bedroom next Sunday.'

'That's nothing,' says Benny. 'I had to promise my Leah that I would build her a new terrace by the swimming pool.'

'Well,' says Max, 'you both had it easy. I had to promise my Sharon that I would completely refit our kitchen with new mahogany cupboards and the latest state-of-the-art equipment.'

But Hyman has not said a word so they ask him what he did to come out fishing. Hyman replies, 'I just set my alarm for 5.30am. When it went off, I gave my Faye a firm nudge and said, 'Fishing or Sex?'

She replied, 'Don't forget your sweater.'

* * *

Fore!

Moshe and his friend Issy are halfway through a round of golf when a golf ball arrives out of nowhere and strikes Moshe on the back of his head. '*Gevalt*!' Moshe cries out, rubbing the back of his head.

Almost immediately, Hymie arrives to apologise. But Moshe is having none of it.

'You call yourself a golfer?' yells Moshe. 'If I had my way, I'd ban you from every golf club in town. Do you see what you've done to me? My head is bleeding. I'm going to call my solicitor as soon as I get to the clubhouse. I'll sue you for £5,000.'

'But…but,' says Hymie, 'didn't you hear me? I shouted FORE.'

'OK,' says Moshe, 'I'll take it.'

* * *

The Jewish jogger

At 50 years of age, Moshe decides to take up jogging. So remembering an advert he saw in the *Jewish Chronicle*, he goes to Kosher Runners' Needs to buy a pair of running shoes. When he enters the shop, he's astounded by the wide selection of jogging shoes available. The assistant shows him one particular pair of shoes and says, 'These might be the ideal shoes for someone of your age, sir. They're called Nike Energy Savers.'

As Moshe is trying them on, he notices the left shoe contains an unusual pocket next to the heel, so he asks the assistant, 'What's this little pocket thing for?'

'You can carry spare change in there, sir,' replies the assistant, 'so you can call your wife to pick you up when you've jogged enough.'

* * *

Faster than lightning
It's the Maccabi Games in Tel Aviv and just before their race, an American sprinter asks an Israeli opponent, 'So what's your best time for the 100 metres?'

'Just over eight seconds,' replies the Israeli.

'But the world record is around nine seconds,' says the astonished American.

'Yes,' says the Israeli, 'but I know a short cut.'

* * *

Half-time advice
It is half-time during a Maccabi youth team football match and Henry, the manager of one of the sides, calls over Lawrence, one of his nine-year-old players, and says to him, 'Do you understand what co-operation is, Lawrence? Do you know what a team is?'

'Yes,' replies Lawrence.

'Do you therefore understand', continues Henry, 'that it's the team that counts and what matters most is whether we win or lose together as a team?'

Lawrence again replies, 'Yes.'

'OK,' Henry says, 'so when the referee sees a foul and blows his whistle, one shouldn't swear, argue, attack him or call him a *shmuck* head and a *putz*. Nor is it good sportsmanship to call a manager "a dumb asshole". Do you agree?'

Again Lawrence says, 'Yes.'

'Good,' says Henry, 'Now go over there and explain all that to your dad.'

* * *

The avid golfer

Gary, an 80-year-old avid golfer, moves to a new house just to be near a golf club. So keen is Gary that not long after the last removal lorry has left, he gets into his car, takes a short trip to the local country club and quickly becomes a member. Two days after that, he goes to play his first round there.

When he arrives, he's told by Harold the on-duty pro that as everyone is out on the course he won't be able to play today. But our Gary doesn't give in easily and nags that he really, desperately, with all his heart, wants to play. Harold gives in and says he himself will play with Gary, but only if they play for a £50 bet. Gary agrees.

On their way to the first hole, Harold asks Gary, 'How many strokes do you want?'

'I don't need any strokes,' replies Gary, 'I've been playing quite well this year and the only problem I have is getting out of sand traps.'

Gary then begins his first round of golf at the club and for the next three hours he plays 'out of his skin'. Coming to the par four 18th, Gary and Harold are level. Harold produces a great drive that allows him to get onto the green in two and is then able to two-putt for a par. Gary also drives well, but his approach shot lands in the sand trap next to the green. Gary gets into the bunker and hits a high ball, which lands on the green and gently rolls into the hole. Match and £50 to Gary!

Harold immediately walks over to Gary and says, 'That was a fantastic shot for an 80-year-old, but I thought you told me you have a problem getting out of sand traps?'

'I do,' replies Gary, 'could you please give me a hand?'

Child-friendly Jokes

If you have young children or grandchildren, here are some clean, hopefully easy-to-understand jokes you can share with them.

* * *

Little Leah is on holiday. One day, she goes to the beach with her mummy and daddy. 'Mummy,' says Leah, 'I think the sea is very friendly.'

'Why do you say that, Leah?' says her mummy.

'Because,' replies Leah, 'it waved.'

* * *

'Dad,' asks Bernie, 'where did Morris the cow go last night?'

'I don't know son, where did he go?' says his dad.

'He went to the moo-vies,' replies Bernie.

* * *

Q: What did the big *shabbes* candle say to the little *shabbes* candle?

A: I'm going out tonight.

* * *

Q: Why was the man sneezing on the Post Office Tower so sad?

A: Because it was Atisha above.

* * *

The Hebrew teacher asks Moshe, 'Do you think Noah did a lot of fishing when he was on the ark?'

'No,' replies Moshe, 'how could he? He only had two worms.'

* * *

Q: Do you know a dirty joke?
A: Sam fell in the mud.

* * *

'Dad,' asks Daniel, 'where would you be able to weigh Jonah's whale?'

'I don't know, Daniel,' says his dad. 'Do you know where?'

'Yes,' replies Daniel, 'at a whale-weigh station.'

* * *

The Hebrew teacher says to her class, 'We have recently been learning how powerful kings and queens were in Bible times. But there is a higher power. Can anybody tell me what it is?'

'Aces,' says Sarah.

* * *

Q: What did the cockney Jew say about the hard luck of Haiman?
A: Poor 'im.

* * *

As the Hebrew teacher is describing to his class how Lot's wife looked back and turned into a pillar of salt, little Sam interrupts, 'My Mummy looked back once, while she was driving, and she turned into a telephone pole.'

* * *

'Mummy,' says Sarah, 'do you know that road they've built above our neighbourhood?'

'Yes,' replies her mum.

'Well,' says Sarah, 'do you know what name my friends have given it?'

'No, what are they calling it?' asks her mum.

'The Passover,' replies Sarah.

* * *

Nine-year-old Isaac is asked by his mother what he has learned in Hebrew school.

'Well, Mum,' says Isaac, 'our teacher told us how God sent Moses behind enemy lines on a rescue mission to lead the Israelites out of Egypt. When he got to the Red Sea, he had his engineers build a pontoon bridge and everyone walked across safely. Then, he used his walkie-talkie to radio headquarters for reinforcements. They sent men to blow up the bridge and all the Israelites were saved.'

'Really Isaac,' says his mother, 'is that really what your teacher taught you?'

'Not really, Mum,' replies Isaac, 'but if I told it the way the teacher did, you'd never believe me.'

* * *

Q: What did Hannah's mum say to her when she came home with a new Audi?
A: Han – new car?

* * *

Emma, Hannah and Melissa walked into a house. You'd think one of them would have been looking.

* * *

Q: How do you stop a cockerel crowing on Monday morning?
A: Have him for dinner on Sunday night.

* * *

Q: Why is the Bible red?
A: Because it's interesting.

* * *

Emma, Hannah and Melissa are robbing a greengrocer's shop when suddenly they hear a security guard coming, so they all jump into three nearby sacks.

The security guard kicks the first sack and says, 'What's in here?'

Emma says, 'Meow.'

The security guard goes to the second sack, kicks it and says, 'What's in here?'

Hannah says, 'Woof woof.'

The security guard goes to the last sack, kicks it and says, 'What's in here?'

Melissa says, 'Potatoes.'

* * *

Q: Where would you weigh a pie?
A: Somewhere over the rainbow, weigh-a-pie.

* * *

One day, two lovely babies are sitting in their carrycots while their mothers are having coffee. All is quiet. Suddenly, one baby says to the other, 'Are you a little boy or are you a little girl?'

The other baby says, 'I have no idea.'

'Why don't you know?' asks the first baby.

'Because I don't know how to tell the difference,' says the second baby.

'Well I can tell,' says the first baby. 'I'll come over and find out for you.'

So the first baby crawls into the second baby's carrycot and goes under the blankets. A few seconds later, the first baby comes back out.

'You're a little girl, and I'm a little boy,' he says.

'You must be very clever,' says the baby girl, 'how can you tell?'

'It's easy peasy,' replies the baby boy, 'you're wearing pink boots and I'm wearing blue boots.'

* * *

Q: Why didn't the Vienna appear on stage?
A: Because the role wasn't good enough

* * *

Mixed-up riddles: In the following, the answer to each riddle has been put against the one above it by mistake. (The answer to the first riddle has been put against the last riddle.)

Q: Why did the bull wear bells?
A: To get to the other side.
Q: Why did the chicken cross the road?
A: Because he wasn't peeling well.
Q: Why did the banana go to the doctor's?
A: Because it was a man-eater.
Q: Why didn't the woman run away from the lion?
A: Because she wanted to be a Smartie.
Q: Why did the female jelly bean go to school?
A: Because she over swept.
Q: Why was Mrs Broom late?
A: Because he was crackers.
Q: Why did a stupid person eat lots of biscuits?
A: Because he didn't have mushroom.
Q: Why was the farmer feeling a bit squashed?
A: He stuck up an umbrella.
Q: What did the man stick upwards when rain came downwards?
A: Computer chips.
Q: If babies drink milk and monkeys eat bananas, what do computers eat?
A: Water.
Q: What runs but never walks?
A: A jelly copter.
Q: What's red and flies and wobbles at the same time?
A: Apricots.
Q: Where do baby apes sleep?
A: Curtains.
Q: What did the artist want to draw before he went to bed?
A: You're too young to smoke.
Q: What did the big chimney say to the little chimney?

A: I'm looking for Pooh.

Q: What did Tigger say as he put his head down the toilet?

A: Leaving out the swear words, he didn't say anything at all.

Q: What did Daddy say when he fell into some dog poo?

A: Phew York.

Q: What's the smelliest city in America?

A: Peking.

Q: What Chinese city cheats at exams?

A: Wavy.

Q: What kind of hair do oceans have?

A: Flood lighting.

Q: What did Noah use to see the animals in the Ark at night?

A: A coconut with a cold.

Q: What is hairy and coughs?

A: A snowball.

Q: Where did the snowman dance?

A: It had a fright.

Q: Why did the milk shake?

A: Because it couldn't blow its horn.

* * *

I was once in a play called *Breakfast in Bed*.
Did you have a big role?
No, just toast and marmalade.

* * *

I want a hair cut please.
Certainly, which one?

* * *

Q: What's brown and sticky?
A: A stick.

* * *

Abraham is walking home alone late one foggy night when he hears a strange sound coming from behind him. BUMP BUMP BUMP. He starts to walk faster, then he looks behind and through the fog he sees an upright coffin bouncing its way down the middle of the road toward him. BUMP BUMP BUMP.

Frightened, he starts to run toward his house, but the coffin continues to bounce after him.

Abraham runs faster, but so does the coffin. BUMP BUMP BUMP. He runs even faster, but so does the coffin. BUMP BUMP BUMP.

When Abraham reaches his house, he runs up to his front door, fumbles with his keys, opens the door, rushes in and slams and locks the door behind him. But suddenly, the coffin CRASHES through his front door and begins to bounce towards him, with the coffin lid banging up and down all by itself. Clappity – BUMP. Clappity – BUMP. Clappity – BUMP.

Even more terrified now, Abraham thinks, 'Who's in the coffin?' He rushes upstairs to the bathroom as fast as he can and locks himself in. His heart is pounding and his breath is coming in sobbing gasps. But with a loud CRASH, the coffin breaks down the bathroom door. Now it's bouncing and banging toward him again. Clappity – BUMP Clappity – BUMP Clappity – BUMP.

Abraham screams and reaches for something! Anything! But all he can find is a bottle of cough medicine. Desperate, he throws the cough medicine at the coffin.

AND GUESS WHAT? The coffin stops.

* * *

Shlomo the tomato was out walking one day with his wife and young son, Benjy the tomato. Unfortunately, Benjy the tomato was not walking fast enough and he kept falling behind his parents. So Shlomo the tomato turned round and shouted at Benjy, 'You *meshugganah*, ketch-up.'

Humour Test for Couples

Dating (Kosher Humour)

Here, for the second time in print, is the dating test for couples wishing to gauge their 'kosher humour compatibility'.

Married couples take this test at their peril!

How often do you hear or read of someone saying, 'I'm looking for a partner with a 'GSOH' (good sense of humour)?

So humour must be an important characteristic – and I can think of an example as to why. What if a couple are watching a show or a film or a comedian, or see some slapstick, or are listening to someone telling a joke? What if one is laughing out loud while the other just has a bemused expression on their face? You've probably seen this happen. So how compatible can they be? Well, probably not at all in the humour stakes.

Why not take this test to see how compatible you are in 'kosher humour'? You can come to your own conclusion on compatibility when you see the results.

Following are 15 jokes taken from this book. Each joke has a reference name against it. Each of you should read the 15 jokes (separately) and then decide which five you liked the best, or laughed at loudest, or smiled at widest, or most tickled your fancy. Each of you should write down the names of your own favourite five jokes on a piece of paper. Alternatively, you could photocopy the table following and write the scores in the table.

Then, when both of you have done this, you can compare your selections as follows:

KOSHER HUMOUR COMPATIBILITY QUOTIENT (KHCQ)
5 the same – WOW! Great kosher jokes compatibility (or you're cheats)

4 the same – very good kosher jokes compatibility
3 the same – good kosher jokes compatibility
2 the same – some kosher jokes compatibility
1 the same – there is still some hope for you both
0 the same – oh dear!

Health warning: please don't jump to any meaningful conclusion as a result of taking this test. I've no idea what a 'kosher humour' mismatch' means to a couple's overall compatibility rating – very likely nothing at all. This is just a fun test for you to hopefully enjoy and has no scientific basis – at least, I don't think it has. At least after taking this test, you will both know a few more jokes to tell.

THE JOKES

A year in the life
As Sadie and Manny are leaving Brent Cross shopping centre, they see their neighbour's son Paul and his fiancée Sharon just going in.

"Did you see that?" Sadie says.

"See what?" asks Manny, pretending not to know what Sadie is referring to.

"Paul's fiancée, that's who," Sadie says, "She's dressing all wrong. She's probably 37-23-35 and with big breasts like hers, she shouldn't be wearing such a skimpy see-through top. And such a tight leather skirt she's wearing – I don't know how she can breathe properly. And it's so short, it make her legs look too long. I know she's got a beautiful face but I don't think blonde dyed hair suits her. Believe me, Manny, that marriage won't last more than one year."

With a deep sigh, Manny replies, "Please God I should have such a year."

The charges

Sarah and Max get married. On their wedding night, just when Max is highly aroused, Sarah surprises him by demanding £25 for their lovemaking. Max readily agrees.

Over the next 30 years, this scenario is repeated each time they make love – and lovemaking is very frequent because they are both passionate people. Max always regards the payment as a cunning way to let Sarah buy new clothes and go regularly to the hairdressers.

One day, Sarah arrives home just after lunch to find Max at home. He is stressed out and in tears. He tells her, 'My company's been taken over and I've been made redundant. What on earth will I do? I'm not young anymore and finding another job quickly will be difficult.'

Without saying a word, Sarah opens her bureau and hands Max her Nationwide Building Society passbook. When he opens it, he's surprised to see it showing deposits plus interest over 30 years totalling nearly £1 million. Sarah then hands him share certificates worth nearly £2 million and says, 'Darling Max. For the last 30 years, I've been carefully investing my "£25 lovemaking charges" and what you see is the result of my investments. So we don't need to worry about money.'

When he hears this, Max gets even more distraught and agitated than before, so Sarah asks him, 'Why are you so upset at such good news, Max?'

Max replies, '*Oy veh.* If I had known what you were doing, I would have given you all of my business.'

House move

Little Esther is talking to her friend Rebecca. 'Have you moved into your new house, Rebecca?'

'Yes,' replies Rebecca, we moved in last Sunday.'

'Do you like it?'

'Oh yes, it's a much bigger house than the one we had

before. We all now have our own bedrooms. All except my poor mum – she's still in with dad.'

Yes it's true

Nathan meets his friend Harry in the Edgware Bagel Factory. 'I hear that your mother-in-law has sold her house and moved in with you. Is this true Harry?'

'Yes it's true,' replies Harry.

'And I also hear that she's recently become quite ill,' says Nathan.

'Yes it's true,' replies Harry.

'In fact, I hear that she's so ill that she's been taken into hospital,' says Nathan.

'Yes its true,' replies Harry.

'So how long has she been in hospital?' asks Nathan.

'In two days' time, please God, it will be two weeks,' replies Harry.

The *Bar mitzvah* space boy

Abe has done very well in business and has amassed a small fortune. Now he's looking to create the most unique and spectacular *Bar mitzvah* ever for his son David. But what should it be? He dismisses the *Bar mitzvah* safari – too many families have already done it. But then, after much investigation, Abe is sure he has cracked it – he'll rent a spaceship and David can be the first *Bar mitzvah* space boy. He starts on the plans immediately.

In due course, the spaceship takes off with his family and friends (and his rabbi, of course) on board. When they return, the media are there to find out how the journey has gone.

The first person off the shuttle is the *bubbeh*.

'How was the service, grandma?' asks the Jewish Chronicle reporter.

'OK,' she replies.

'And how was David's speech?'

'OK.'

'So how was the food?'

'OK.'

'Everything was just OK? Why aren't you more enthusiastic? What went wrong?'

'There was no atmosphere,' she replies.

The son

Victor and Rivkah have always wanted a son to join their two stunningly gorgeous teenage daughters and so they try one last time for 'their boy'. After months of trying, Rivkah gets pregnant and nine months later delivers a healthy baby boy.

Victor is at first ecstatic but as soon as he sees his son he is horrified – it's the ugliest baby he's ever seen. He turns to Rivkah and says, 'This can't be my son, Rivkah. Anyone can tell this just by looking at the two beautiful daughters I've fathered. Have you been unfaithful to me?'

Rivkah smiles sweetly and replies, 'No, not this time.'

Insomnia cure

Dr Myers has been looking after one of his patients, 80-year-old Freda, for most of her life. But he retires and passes all his patients over to the newly qualified Dr Faith who has just joined the practice. One of the first things Dr Faith does is to ask to see Freda and that she should bring with her a list of all the medicines that have been prescribed for her. Eventually, Freda has her appointment.

As Dr Faith is looking through Freda's list, he is totally shocked to see that she has a prescription for birth control pills.

'Mrs Cohen,' he says, 'do you realise that these are birth control pills?'

'Yes doctor,' replies Freda, 'they help me sleep at night.'

'Mrs Cohen,' says Dr Faith, 'I can assure you that there is absolutely nothing in birth control pills that could possibly help you sleep better at night.'

When she hears this, Freda reaches over to Dr Faith, lovingly pats him on his knee and says, 'Yes, doctor, I know that, but every morning I get up very early, grind up one of the pills and mix it in the glass of orange juice that my 16-year-old granddaughter Suzy drinks when she awakes. Believe me doctor, this helps me sleep at night.'

A doctor's solution

Ruth's baby boy is born with only one eyelid. '*Oy veh*! What am I going to do?' she says to her doctor.

'Don't worry,' he replies, 'after the *bris*, we will take the little bit of skin from down there and make him a nice new eyelid.'

'But if you do that,' says Ruth, 'won't it will make him cockeyed?'

'On the contrary,' says the doctor, 'it will give him good foresight.'

Family fortunes

Renee is talking to her friend Talya. 'So Talya,' she says, 'you're telling me that you want to divorce your Mervyn due to incompatibility problems?'

'Yes, you've got it in one,' Talya replies.

'Why? Aren't your relations any good?' asks Renee.

'Well,' replies Talya, 'mine are wonderful, but Melvyn's …..Oy! what *yachnas* and *krechtzers*!'

Living in the past

Morris and Ruth have just celebrated their 25th wedding anniversary. That night, as they are getting ready for bed, Morris looks carefully at Ruth.

'What are you staring at?' Ruth asks.

'Darling,' he replies, 'I've been thinking. When we got married 25 years ago, we lived in a small apartment, we drove a cheap Ford car, we watched TV on a small 15-inch black and white television and we couldn't afford a proper bed so we had to make do with a sofa-bed. However, despite all of that, I was proud to be sleeping with a sizzling 25-year-old blonde. Now, however, we have a large house in Hampstead, we drive a Lexus, we have a 42-inch Sony LCD television set with Sky digital and we have a king-sized water bed. But here's my problem – I'm now sleeping with a 50-year-old woman. You're obviously not holding up your side of things and I don't know what to do.'

Ruth, being a very reasonable and sensible lady, says to Morris, 'I've got a solution to your problem, Morris. Go out and find a sizzling 25-year-old blonde. When you find one, I'll make sure that you'll once again be living in a small apartment, driving a cheap Ford, sleeping on a sofa bed, and watching a 15-inch black-and-white television set.'

What I want in a wife
Lionel tells his friend Sidney that he's at last looking for a wife.

'So what kind of wife are you looking for?' asks Sidney.

'Well,' replies Lionel, 'she needs to be ultra beautiful, she needs to be very kind to me, and she needs to have lots of money.'

'But you can't marry three women at the same time,' says Sidney.

Courtesy seating
Young Benny arrives home from school and says to his mother, 'Mummy, when Daddy was taking me to school on the bus this morning, he asked me to give up my seat to a lady who was standing next to us. So I did. But do you think I should have given up my seat?'

'Well Benny,' replies his mother, 'I think it was a very nice thing to do. I always appreciate someone giving up their seat for me when all the seats are taken.'

'I know that, Mummy,' says Benny, 'but I was sitting on Daddy's lap at the time.'

I wish you long life

Rivka and Bernie have been married for 50 years and are being interviewed by a reporter from the *Jewish Chronicle*.

'So Rivkah,' asks the reporter, 'I know today is your Golden Wedding Anniversary, but how old, exactly, are you?'

'I am 78 years old,' replies Rivkah, 'and *kin-a-hora* I should live to be a hundred.'

'Well I hope your wish comes true,' says the reporter. He then turns to Bernie and asks, 'And how old are you, Bernie?'

'I'm also 78 years old,' replies Bernie, 'and please God I should live to be a hundred and one.'

'But why,' asks the reporter, 'do you want to live one year longer than your wife?'

'Well, to tell you the truth,' replies Bernie, 'I would like to have at least one year of peace and quiet.'

Our little secret

Harry and Kitty are celebrating their 60th wedding anniversary with a party for their family and friends. During the party, Max and Betty walk over to them and say, '*Mazeltov*. We're so pleased for you both. But you must let us in on your secret – how have you managed to stay married for so long, especially in this day and age?'

Harry turns to Kitty and asks, 'OK for me to reply to this?'

Kitty replies, 'Yes dear.'

'Well,' continues Harry, 'our secret is quite simple. On the very day we got married, Kitty and I came to an agreement which we've stuck to all these years. We decided that I would make all the major decisions and Kitty would make all the minor decisions. And I can truthfully say that over the 60 years of our marriage, I have never needed to make a major decision.'

Time and motion

Miriam gets married and a year later goes into hospital and gives birth to triplets. All her family and friends are shocked when they hear the news – they know of no-one who has had triplets before.

As soon as she hears the news, Miriam's *shviger* Fay goes to visit her daughter-in-law in hospital. As soon as she arrives, Fay hands over the bunch of grapes and says, 'What a surprise, Miriam. No one on our side of the family has ever had twins before, yet alone triplets.'

'Yes, it was a bit of a shock,' replies Miriam, 'but I'm getting over it. In fact my doctor tells me that triplets only happen once every hundred thousand times.'

'*Oy veh*, Miriam,' says Fay, 'how on earth did you find the time to do your housework?'

SCORE SHEET

TICK ONLY IF TOP 5 RANKING	JOKE NAME
	A year in the life
	The charges
	House move
	Yes it's true
	The *Bar mitzvah* space boy
	The son
	Insomnia cure
	A doctor's solution
	Family fortunes
	Living in the past
	What I want in a wife
	Courtesy seating
	I wish you long life
	Our little secret
	Time and motion

The Best Punchlines in this Book

You've probably heard the story of the group of jokers who only tell each other the joke 'numbers' and one of them got no laughs when he said, 'number eight', because he told it wrong.

Well, here is the Jewish version. Why not just tell the punchlines of the jokes:

'How on earth did you find the time to do your housework?'

'I know, darling, but your daddy's insured.'

'I think Uncle Hymie wants to buy Mummy.'

'But I was sitting on Daddy's lap at the time.'

'There's a two-inch deductible.'

'It will give him good foresight.'

'You're right, miss, what's three per cent?'

'I can't find a card that mine Sarah will believe.'

'I would like to have at least one year of peace and quiet.'

'There was no atmosphere.'

'If I had known what you were doing, I would have given you all of my business.'

'Please God I should have such a year.'

'My feelings towards the ring haven't changed.'

'Howard's got full-blown pneumonia.'

'I feel like I already had it.'

'Harry hasn't put in an appearance at home for four years.'

'You call that living?'

'You get rid of the whole *shmuck*.'

'Yes, he was my daddy last year.'

'Then why do I smell her perfume?'

'Believe me, Doctor, this helps me sleep at night.'

'I'm hiding – I'm hiding in the bedroom wardrobe.'

'Mine Sadie doesn't need a subject.'

'But you can't marry three women at the same time.'

'In two days' time, please God, it will be two weeks.'

'*Nu*, so it takes two hours to get run over?'

'Oh dear, it's started.'

'I married his widow.'

'When I asked you for that a little while ago, you told me to go fly a kite.'

'But I was in love and I didn't notice it.'

'I didn't think anybody could celebrate that long.'

'But at least I'm suffering in comfort.'

'My husband's first wife.'

'What problem can there be that's greater than this one?'

'You're never home.'

'She can drive at night.'

'That's because we aren't married yet.'

'Put me down for Mondays.'

'I would have got out today.'

'Smoked Whitefish.'

'Sadie, for goodness' sake, sing a little something.'

'Well Jacob, some say yes...and some say no.'

'But darling, if you don't go out, how do you expect to meet anyone?'

'On him it looks good.'

'OK, *Bubbeleh*, but don't go too close.'

'I've only been a Gentile for two hours and already I hate three Jews.'

'The air bag on your new Lexus works very well.'

'I would like a second opinion.'

'No doctor, but I do get some crackling from time to time.'

'They're all out looking for your dog.'

'Mind you, if it wasn't for Issy, we would all be starving.'

'But then we found out he's going out with a nice Jewish doctor.'

'What, and lose my hard-won independence?'

'I know, but I'm a big tipper.'

'From that one old chicken, we got ourselves four *mitzvahs*!'

'From your house they could walk?'

'The first thing ve are going to do is fix the brakes on our run-down fire engine.'

'How much does one tip for a thing like that?'

'I've had second thoughts. Maybe you shouldn't bother looking for him.'

'No, I always walk like this.'

'*Oy veh, kreplach.*'

'I never had a saucepan that was large enough!'

'Thank you sir, we always aim to please.'

'I'm tired of her telling me what to do. I'll have the chicken soup and *flanken* nosh-up.'

'Oh I do apologise, the waiter brought you the Peking Duck by mistake.'

'Who asked for the clean glass?'

'I don't know about the others, but I use the spoon.'

'For crying out loud, Hetty, don't you ever stop?'

'She also stole a can of peas.'

'I can see the moon, how far is that?'

'So *nu*, your Lordship, vat vould you haf said?'

'I told you my partner's side of the case.'

'You want my blood as well?'

'Because then I'll be sure my wife will visit me twice a week.'

'Well, you could try wearing a veil.'

'And is this woman giving you a hard time?'

'You've always told me I'm luckier than my friends – who knows, maybe this time I'll strike it rich.'

'So how long do you think you can stay dead on that kind of *gelt*?'

'I may be many things, darling, but inquisitive I'm not.'

'Of course not, I told her I was 90.'

'I wish I had given you all my business. We could have owned half of London by now.'

'When it comes to my health, money is no object!'

'Mine Jacob gets either real respiration or he gets notting at all.'

'I might have guessed it would be a Jewish diamond.'

'Lady, do you want a singer or a dancer?'

'I tella you he no looka so good.'

'She's up on the roof fixing a tile.'

'Listen lady, have I ever lied to you before?'

'But for an outside line you need to dial 9 first.'

'For £280, you'd have thought they would have ironed it for me.'

'I bought her a pack of cards.'

'But if I get well, please God, then I'll stay *broyges* with you.'

'Her clothes would never have fitted you.'

'You mean…I can check my email from here?'

'Then I'll take the other one.'

'That's nothing, my Sadie dreams she's married to a millionaire during the day.'

'It doesn't matter, let's just look for your Judith.'

'Why not just leave your car in our heated garage this time?'

'Because down there I've got no worries.'

'You don't say? Who did she play for?'

'Go ahead, maybe it'll attract some business.'

'These are what I started with. Everything else is profit.'

'If you don't have sufficient capital, you mustn't begin to build.'

'So go tell him it will shrink.'

'Listen, *bubbeleh*, ask him how much he'll charge to paint my kitchen.'

'Have you tried doing the experiments with a different female ape?'

'With marks like these, and you still felt like singing?'

'About nine months after I get home.'

'I know, but at least it's steady work.'

'I'm not sure, but I think it's Veranda.'

'I personally can't sell much salt, but, *oy veh*, the sales rep who sold me the salt – can he sell salt!'

'I put in a lot of overtime.'

'OK everyone, let's start again from the top.'

'Hymie, so where are you calling me from right now?'

'You think that's something? One of my ancestors drew up the Ten Commandments.'

'Of course I do, but now, just two weeks before Pesach?'

'Because I wouldn't want you to die suddenly.'

'Mrs Cohen, you could pass such an inspection?'

'I don't know what you're getting so worked up for, son. I don't eat here.'

'If the car starts, I'm turning Jewish.'

'Don't sell that cow!'

'You don't know the difference between a *brocheh* and a *kaddish*.'

'Well now you ask, some mornings I do have this great urge to lay *tefillin*.'

'If they were Maatjes herrings, she'd have a much better chance.'

'Do you really believe I did all this for free?'

'Jacob will marry you, Sadie, but Bernard will be the lucky one.'

'Don't be silly, Rabbi, I'm the moneylender.'

'She is not my reward, I am her punishment.'

'They should please make a little wiggle.'

'So please put me down for £20 for the flood victims.'

'Yes, Sadie keeps six of them and I keep the other four.'

'Funny, you no rook Jewish.'

'Oh for goodness sake, I don't know why you bother to go to *shul* these days.'

'Yes, I agree, but your snoring is keeping everybody else awake.'

'No, *tzvei iz genug.*' (Two is enough.)

'I keep them right up here in my *toches.*'

'I know, I heard it snoring!'

'I think you should put a new battery in your hearing aid.'

'Broccoli – 75p a pound.'

'Arnold, believe me, just then, for the first time in many, many weeks, I didn't feel your dentures!'

'Ach. In the old days, you could be ill for at least two years for that kind of money.'

'Miracle, shmiracle, he just gave me a longer walking stick.'

'It's very serious. They've already called three doctors.'

'Never mind, you'll just have to talk about your old operation for yet another year.'

'And 95 taps means, "I'll do the drying up."'

'As a result, I've changed my will three times already.'

'I told you that 'you've got a heart murmur...be careful.'

'I just turned out the light.'

'Anna, I'm so glad you saw this thing. Now I think I know where my hearing aid is.'

'She's still upstairs in the bathroom changing out of her hospital gown.'

'Ah, a thing of beauty and a *goy* for ever.'

'But those are the only foods we can slide under the door.'

'I won the first prize as Best Dried Arrangement.'

'He was up a ladder looking at me through the bedroom window.'

'Oh no, Mum, I don't take abnormal psychology until next term.'

'OK, who's responsible for labelling my mother "bananas"?'

'Certainly not, it's just that I've never learned to read Hebrew.'

'What's the matter? Are none of my friends good enough for you?'

'Stop your crying, Isaac. Don't worry. I'll get married again!'

'Can you believe my *meshugga* Hymie is out golfing?'

'You lying *momzer*. You've been playing golf again.'

'They're under your pillow in a plastic bag.'

'*Oy veh zmir*, Schwartz is dead.'

'I noticed it twice last night, Doctor, and once again this morning.'

'Nothing much, he came and he went.'

'She doesn't know it yet but she's only got a few more weeks to live.'

'Because I'm making you eggs and the egg timer's broken.'

'What do you mean 30 minutes? Where were you yesterday?'

'*Oy veh*, how come everybody knows about this but me?'

'No, you've got the wrong woman, I'm your son's science teacher!'

'But Doctor, my problem is that it wakes me up.'

'But I loved my third husband David the best. He was a stamp collector.'

'If it's all right with you, Benny, I'll lend you the £1 until tomorrow.'

'Thank God. I thought I had a crack in my new £400 Giovani leather shoes.'

'*Vemen bares du*?' (What's in it for me?)

'Well that's your problem, then, you're cock-eyed.'

'It'll keep the sheets off his legs.'

'Aha, THAT is the tradition!'

'But I really don't remember that much singing.'

'But then, by the time I got my leotard on, the class was over.'

'I am, but the steaks are too high!'

'Never mind, Sharon, it's the first time since we started playing that I've known what the man has in his hand.'

'Not much – it won't go with your green tablecloth.'

'So why shouldn't we call them noodles?'

'So you can call your wife to pick you up when you've jogged enough.'

'Maybe most, but mine's got Windows!'

'But thank God I'm now wealthy enough that my Moshe doesn't have to walk.'

'That's Isadore, the kosher butcher.'

'Ah, so you work for El Al.'

'Well, she was here and you could have.'

'Please send me the pearl and re-bait the trap.'

'Oy, vas I thirsty…Oy, vas I thirsty.'

'*Oy vey*! And he was such a healthy man.'

'*Oy veh*, it's nearly the end for my Maurice – he's getting delirious.'

'I know, darling, now be quiet and let the poison work.'

'Hardly worth going back home, is it?'

'When I said I was, he took out a penknife and started cutting up my suit.'

'*Oy veh*! Am I driving?'

'How soon do you need to know?'

'That's what you can do when you're old and rich.'

'I forgot your mother's name about five years ago.'

'But, my dear Shlomo, thank God I still have my driver's licence.'

'Because I woke up this morning and nothing hurts.'

'I'll take the soup, please.'

Glossary of Yiddish and Hebrew Words and Terms

Alav hasholom: May he or she rest in peace.

Aliyah: To be called up to read a portion of Torah scroll in synagogue; the immigration of Jews to Israel.

Alteh mold: A spinster, an old maid.

Baitsim: Balls, testicles.

Bar mitzvah: Religious ceremony marking coming of age of 13-year-old Jewish boy or 12- or 13-year-old Jewish girl.

Baruch Ha-Shem: Blessed be name of the Lord – used like 'God willing'.

Bashayrt: Destined by fate; intended (fiancée).

Blintzes: Pancakes, usually spread with cream cheese, or jam or strawberries rolled within a thin dough pancake.

Borsht: Beetroot soup.

Boychick: Bit of a lad; young boy.

Bris (pl. Brisses): Circumcision ceremony, performed on a boy on the eighth day after birth.

Broyges: Angry.

Bubbeh: Grandma.

Bubbeleh: Term of endearment (like dear, pet, honey).

Bupkes: Nothing; something trivial, worthless.

Chad gadya: A Passover song.

Challah: Braided white Sabbath bread made with egg, eaten on the *shabbes* (q.v.).

Chanukah: The Festival of Lights, a Jewish festival that falls in December.

Chassid; Chassidic: (Lit. pious) Member of an ultra-orthodox religious sect.

Chazan: Cantor, the singer who leads synagogue services.

Cholent: Potted meat and vegetables simmered overnight.

Chometz: Bread to be removed from the house prior to Passover.

Chozzerai: Junk, trash; awful food; anything disgusting or loathsome.

Chrayn: Horseradish.

Chutzpah: Insolence, impudence, unmitigated cheek, effrontery.

Daven(ing): Pray(ing), or lead(ing) prayers, often with strong swaying from the hips.

Dreck: (vulgar) Excrement.

Farfufket: Befuddled, disoriented.

Farmisht: Mixed-up, befuddled, confused.

Flanken: Brisket.

Fortz: (vulgar) Fart.

Fress: Eat and enjoy lots of food and maybe even pig out!

Frum: Religious.

Frummer: Very religious person.

Gabbai: Synagogue warden.

Gantzeh megillah: Big deal (sarcastic); a long, boring story or speech.

Gatkes: Underpants, long johns.

Gay kakken af en yam: (vulgar) Go shit in the sea.

Gefilte fish: Fish, ground, seasoned with spices and made into balls or patties, then shaped into fishcakes and boiled or fried. Often made from carp.

Gefilter: (play on words) gefilte, filled, stuffed.

Gelt: Money.

Gesheft: Business.

Get: A Jewish religious divorce.

Gevalt: Exclamation of fear, terror.

Glatt: kosher; strickly kosher.

Gonif: Thief; crook.

Goy (pl goyim): Non-Jew.

Goyisher kop!: Gentile brains!

Groisser potz: Big idiot.

Groisser sheeser: A big shot.

Hadassah: Woman's organisation in America. Also the Hebrew version of the name Esther.

Haggadah: Passover prayer book.

Hamentash: A pastry stuffed with poppy seed (or prune), usually eaten at *Purim*.

Ha-Shem: God; literally 'The Name'. Jews consider that saying the name of God is blasphemy.

Hava Nagila: Famous Israeli music.

Havdalah: Ceremony marking the end of *shabbes* (q.v.).

Hinten: *Toches*, backside.

Kabbalah: Jewish mysticism.

Kabbalat shabbat: An early-evening service welcoming *shabbes*.

Ketubah: Jewish marriage certificate.

Khozzer: A pig, a gluttonous person.

Kichel: Small, round, plain biscuit.

Kiddush: A special blessing said before a meal on *shabbes* (q.v.) and festivals, and after the *shabbes* synagogue service, usually including the blessing over the wine or/and bread.

Kin-a-hora: Expression used to ward off evil eye.

Kinder: Children.

Kippa: Skullcap; see also *yarmulka*.

Klop: Whack.

Kol Nidre: Prayer said just before sunset on eve of *Yom Kippur*. The name is that of the first two words of the prayer beginning 'All our vows'.

Kol Nidre Appeal: On *Kol Nidre* evening in the synagogue, an appeal is made for charity, and the members make pledges but they cannot write cheques as it is forbidden to write on festivals, so they have to send the cheque subsequently.

Kosher: Food that complies with the Jewish dietary religious laws that can be found in Leviticus, chapter XVI. By extension, anything that is pure, good, whole, prepared according to Jewish dietary laws; legitimate; genuine.

Krechtzer: A complainer, someone who grunts and groans all day.

Kreplach: filled dumplings.

Kunyehlemel: A naïve, gullible man.

Kurveh: Trollop, a prostitute, a woman who trades on her sexuality for money, gifts or position.

Kvell: To gush with pride.

Kvetch(ing): Complain(ing).

Latke: Potato pancake, a sort of hash brown made from raw, grated potatoes.

Levoyah: Funeral.

Lox: Smoked salmon.

Ma nishtana halaila hazeh mikol halelot shebechol halelot anu ochlin hamatz umatza: Jewish Passover prayer.

Maariv: Daily evening religious service.

Makes aliyah: Emigrates.

Marror: Bitter herb, usually grated horseradish.

Matzo: Unleavened bread eaten during week of Passover; a *matzo* ball is a dumpling made from ground *matzos*.

Mazel: Luck.

Mazeltov: Congratulations; good luck.

Mekheiyeh: A pleasure.

Mensh: Man of fine qualities; a real man; a good human being.

Meshugga/meshugganah: Crazy, mad; a crazy person.

Mezuzah: A passage from the Torah (q.v.) written on a small piece of parchment and placed inside a wooden or metal case that is attached to the doorpost of a Jewish home. It is customary for an Orthodox Jew to touch her/his fingers to his lips, then to the *mezuzah*, each time she/he passes the doorpost.

Mincha: Daily afternoon religious service.

Minyan: The quorum of 10 men required for holding public prayers.

Mishegass: Madness, absurdity. The abstract noun from *meshugga* (q.v.).

Mishmosh: Hodgepodge.

Mishpocheh: The entire family network of relatives by blood or marriage.

Mitzvah: Good deed.

Mohel; moil: The religious man who performs ritual circumcisions according to rabbinic regulations and customs.

Momzer: A bastard.

Naches: Pride, pleasure, good fortune.

Nu: Well, so.

Obber meer hobben for das a shiksa: But me, I have a *shiksa* for this.

Oy; Oy, Oy: Exclamation to denote pain, rapture, awe, astonishment, surprise, delight.

Oy gevalt: Exclamation to denote fear, terror, astonishment.

Oy veh; oy veh iz meer: Oh, woe is me; oh what sadness/misfortune.

Passover: Jewish festival commemorating liberation of Jews from their bondage in Egypt.

Payess; peyess: Side curls worn by ultra orthodox males.

Pesach: A Jewish festival.

Pish: To urinate.

Pisher: One who urinates; an inexperienced or insignificant person.

Polkeh: Chicken drumstick.

Potch: Smack.

Purim: A Jewish festival.

Puppik: Navel; belly button.

Putz: (vulgar) Penis.

Rebbetsin: Rabbi's wife.

Rosh Hashanah: The Jewish New Year.

Saychel: Common sense.

Schlep: To drag, carry; haul, a long journey.

Schmooze: To gossip, chat up, blarney.

Seder: The traditional evening home service and meal during Passover.

Sfirah: Short for *Sfirat Ha-Omer*, the Counting of the Omer, the seven weeks from end of Passover to *Shavuot*, the Feast of Weeks, when cutting of certain kinds is forbidden.

Shabbes: The Sabbath, which lasts from sundown on Friday to sunset on Saturday.

Shadchen: A professional marriage broker.

Shammes: Synagogue sexton or caretaker.

Shema Yisrael: A Hebrew prayer recited three or four times daily by Orthodox Jews, and the last prayer she/he utters on her/his deathbed.

Shiddach: Arranged marriage partner.

Shiksa: A non-Jewish woman.

Shivah: The seven-day period of mourning after a person's death.

Shlemazel: An unlucky person/clumsy oaf.

Shlemiel: A fool, a bungler.

Shlong: (vulgar) Male organ, penis.

Shmatta: Rag.

Shmekeleh: Little penis.

Shmo: Fool.

Shmuck: A stupid person; a penis.

Shmuckelotomy: From the word *shmuck* (penis).

Shnorrer: Cheapskate, professional beggar.

Shofar: A ram's horn blown in a synagogue during services for *Rosh Hashanah* and *Yom Kippur*.

Shochet: Ritual slaughterer of animals intended for kosher eating.

Sholom aleichem: Hebrew for 'Peace be unto you'. Used as a greeting like 'hello' or 'goodbye'.

Shprinkles: Sprinkles.

Shtetl: Jewish village community in Eastern Europe.

Shtick dreck: A piece of shit, someone cheap, shoddy, useless.

Shtup, shtupping: Vulgar Yiddish term for having sex.

Shtoom: Keep quiet.

Shtook: In trouble.

Shul: Synagogue.

Shviger: Mother-in-law.

Shyster: Unscrupulous person.

Siddur: The daily and Sabbath prayer book.

Simcha: A joyous celebration.

Smicha: Rabbinical ordination.

Tallis: A prayer shawl, usually in white silk with fringes, and worn over clothes.

Talmud: A massive compilation of writing that forms the basic body of Jewish laws and traditions.

Tefillin: Two small, black leather boxes with straps attached that contain passages of Hebrew script. The boxes are strapped on (one on the head and one on the arm) by Orthodox Jewish men each weekday morning.

Tisha B'av: A Jewish day of fasting and mourning.

Toches: The rear end, bottom, buttocks.

Torah: The Five Books of Moses, or the scroll containing them and read in the synagogue; it can also imply all sacred Jewish literature.

Trayf, treif, traf: Non-kosher foods.

Tsatskelah: Cute little girl.

Tsimmes: A side dish of carrots and fruit; a vegetable stew; big deal; fuss.

Tsitskehs: Breasts.

Tsodoka: Charity.

Tsoures; tsouris: Troubles; worries; suffering.

Tzitzits; tzitzis: Fringes or tassles found on the corner of a prayer shawl worn by observant Jews.

Vemen bares du?: Who are you kidding?

Vienna: A type of sausage eaten by Jews.

Vos is dos?: What is this; what's with this?

Weenie: Frankfurter. Also slang for *shlong*.

Yachna; yachner: A gossip, a busybody, a meddling, trouble-making female.

Yahrtzeit: The anniversary of someone's death.

Yarmulka: Skullcap; see also *kippa.*

Yenta: A gossipy woman.

Yentz: Make love. Alternatively: cheat/screw.

Yeshiva: A Jewish school theological college.

Yeshiva bucher: A yeshiva student; a gullible or inexperienced person.

Yom Kippur: Jewish festival – the Day of Atonement.

Zaydeh: Grandpa.

Zer gut: Very good.